Inside the Manson Jury

From Deliberation to Death Sentence

◆ ◆ ◆

Inside the Manson Jury

From Deliberation to Death Sentence

◆ ◆ ◆

Herman Tubick
Helen Tubick
with
Deborah Herman

Micro Publishing Media
Stockbridge, Massachusetts

Printed in the United States of America

First Edition
ISBN 978-1-944068-86-8

Micro Publishing Media, Inc
PO Box 1522
Stockbridge, MA 01262
(413)298-0077
www.micropublishingmedia.com

Original book written with Helen Tubick
Editor's Notes by Deborah Herman
Editing by Rick Ortenburger
Cover and Interior Design by Jane McWhorter, Blue Sky Multimedia
Illustrations by Anna Lachmann

DEDICATION

To our Beloved Daughters
Sister Mary Gabriella
Sister Mary Paulynne

"But from their graves......
they cry out for justice"
—Vincent Bugliosi

TABLE OF CONTENTS

Contents

ACKNOWLEDGMENTS

By Rick Ortenburger

Thanks to the following people and organizations that made this book possible and helped to enhance this manuscript.

Herman Tubick who kept copious notes while serving on the Manson Jury.

Helen Tubick who insisted she and my Uncle Herman write a manuscript in 1973 even if just for posterity. It was Aunt Helen who hand wrote the book based on my Uncle's notebooks and their discussions about the trial.

Sister Mary Paulynne for providing this unpublished 1973 manuscript.

Bruce Everett Howell, a photographer for the Los Angeles Herald Examiner for the "iconic" photograph of my uncle, the jury foreman and my aunt at the April 1, 1971 press conference at the Los Angeles Ambassador Hotel, used on the front cover of the book.

Anna Lachmann for her sketches to enhance this book.

William McBride, Tate La Bianca murder trial juror number 3, for help with identifying photographs related to the trial, for answering many questions about the trial, deliberations and some of the jurors.

Los Angeles Public Library (LAPL Photo Collection).

UCLA Film and Television Archive Media.

Jane McWhorter for her wonderful cover and interior design.

Dianne Lake for her support and cover quote.

Cielodrive.com for their support and permission to use excerpts from their digitized trial transcripts.

And thanks to my Publisher Deborah Herman at Micro publishing Media (MPM) who also served as a present-day co-author, not only polishing the book, but adding the editor's notes and expert insights.

ACKNOWLEDGMENTS 1973

This book would not have been possible if it were not for the encouragement and work of my dear wife Helen. She felt inspired to share our message with others. Originally, I had no intention of a book being published, but now, with the passing of time, both of us realize that there must be answers to the continuous queries of interested citizens and explanations for the ways and means of long-suffering, prayer, and justice.

My story is written, first, for the honor and glory of God and secondly, for the knowledge and inspiration to you, the public, a message meaningful and moving. If we can touch but a few hearts and bring them closer to the love of God and neighbor, then all our efforts will not be in vain.

It is clear to me that our good Lord not only protected me, my wife and my family but also the rest of the jurors during this fateful trial. And so, he gave us the grace to endure our personal hardships.

For me and my wife this experience was a test of strength and character, a challenge to accept and accomplish. Even our marriage, which was always good, became more closely knit and fortified.

In my daily work I meet and talk with many people. I am amazed at the number of good citizens who refuse and shirk jury duty, even those individuals that can serve. They expect "George to do it all." This attitude is wrong and unpatriotic, even unhealthy. How are we going to improve our society and system, even ourselves if our good citizens uphold and live this idea? Only by getting involved, working together as a team, giving our time and talents to better our community, our government and our country; then and only then will we see an improvement in renewal and advancement of mankind. Let us mediate upon the famous words of a wise philosopher;

"Any good that I can do, O Lord, let me do it now, for I shall not pass this way again."

Serving as a juror on this trial was an education. I learned a greater tolerance, patience, perseverance, and the fulfillment of a challenge, satisfaction in administering justice, joy in helping and guiding fellow jurors when they needed me, and the benefit of meeting some wonderful people and making new friends.

My wife and I wish to express our personal, grateful thanks to deputies Ann Orr, Elaine Slagle, William Murray, and Oden Skupen for their kind consideration and help during my wife's illness.

The jurors of the Tate La Bianca Trial, 9 ½ months endurance, did a commendable job. I applaud each one for a remarkable undertaking.

— Herman Tubick Year 1973

BY SISTER MARY PAULYNNE

"Semper Fidelis," the Marine Corps motto, describes Herman Tubick, my Dad and jury foreman of the Manson trial perfectly. As a Marine, Herman was a man of honor and integrity who served his country faithfully. He not only lived the motto "Semper Fi" in the Corps, he embodied this standard in his everyday life. He always believed that "doing the right thing was the right thing to do." This unobtrusive yet genuine philosophy dominated Herman's life as husband, father, co-worker, friend, associate and acquaintance.

And so, when he was selected to serve as a juror on the Manson trial Herman embraced the opportunity remembering, Semper Fidelis to God, family, country, state. Even though the trial lasted over nine and one-half months, Herman was undaunted and persevered to the final outcome. He said he would even serve again because it was his civic duty and justice needs to be served.

A few years ago, a movie was produced entitled "A Few Good Men." I dare to say that Herman Tubick is one of those few good men that we need to hear more about today who lived life courageously, honestly and truthfully. May his story and recollections of his jury service on the Manson trial inspire others to also embody the motto: "Semper Fidelis."

Alongside every good man is an outstanding woman of courage and fortitude. This awesome woman is Helen Tubick, wife of jury foreman Herman Tubick. Helen had the foresight to recognize that the words Herman penned about his daily experiences as a jurist on the Manson trial and the way he embraced his selection on this jury as God's will, was unique and had to be shared with the public. And so, for the next two years, 1971-1973, Helen and Herman conversed and dialogued with each other about the trial. They composed the story of the daily happenings of the Manson trial and the jurors. The manuscript contains many references to God's revelation and guidance in the decisions that had to be made regarding the fate of Charles Manson and his accomplices. Helen believed the story of the Tate La Bianca murder trial as observed through the eyes and presence of Herman Tubick was authentic and history was well served.

My dear Mom, Helen, then gifted me with this precious manuscript and for years this diamond in the rough remained dormant. Then approximately two years ago, my cousin, Rick Ortenburger, family historian and genealogist, contacted me inquiring about any family artifacts, memorabilia and history. When I mentioned the unpublished work of the Tate La Bianca murder trial authored by my parents, Rick was intrigued and requested a copy of the document.

Rick labored tirelessly to polish, refine and present the document into the form that it is today. He also contacted sketch artists to portray the persons mentioned in the book so that you, the reader, could insert yourself into this piece of history and understand more fully the ordeal of the jurors, the work of the providence of God in decision making and the courage and tenacity of the jury foreman, Herman Tubick.

I am deeply grateful to my Dad, Herman Tubick for his loyalty and trust in the judicial system and upholding the truth despite the obstacles. My admiration for my Mom is limitless. Her wisdom and her vision of encouraging her husband to tell the story of the ordeal of the Manson murder trial are profound and prophetic.

Finally, I am deeply indebted to Rick Ortenburger, who believed that this story has a message for everyone: fidelity, truth, love, loyalty and trust in God. The "diamond" that once was hidden for so many years is now revealed to you the reader to behold, savor and relish in its richness.

Sister Mary Paulynne Tubick
Sister of Notre Dame
Beloved and grateful daughter of Herman and Helen Tubick
May 5, 2019

BY RICK ORTENBURGER

I am Rick Ortenburger, a nephew of Herman Tubick. I was in the US Army and a few days away from being stationed in West Germany in August of 1969 when these tragic events happened. While in West Germany I heard nothing more on what happened. I did not know who was arrested. I didn't know of the trial and I had no idea that my Uncle Herman Tubick was selected to serve on this jury. "Stars & Stripes" told us about other events.

I found out that my uncle, Jury Foreman Herman Tubick, did in fact write a manuscript with his wife Helen on the Tate La Bianca murder trial in the year 1973, two years after it ended. I was told about this manuscript by my first cousin Sister Paulynne in August 2017, forty-four years after it was written. I don't think many knew about this manuscript before 2017. He had given a copy to his two daughters. I saw my Uncle Herman a number of times after the trial ended in 1971 until he died in 1985. He never mentioned that he had written this manuscript with his wife Helen. My Aunt Helen never told me about it either. And my Aunt Helen and I had many conversations through the years.

My uncle stated after the trial ended that he was not going to "cash in" on his experience with this murder trial. It was his "duty to serve." He was not going to make any money from it. And he was a man of his word.

I received the only remaining copy of this manuscript in April 2018 from my cousin Sister Paulynne. Once I received the manuscript and read through it I thought to myself, I have to get this into a printed book. I wanted to preserve my uncle's legacy related to this trial and tell his version of the events of the trial and the jurors' experience.

It was not to "cash in" as was his wish, but rather to preserve a piece of written history experienced by him and the other jurors and put into words with my Aunt Helen. With my cousin's blessings I added a "table of contents." I combined some chapters and I added title headings. I retyped his 206-page manuscript, "typewriter made," (no disk).

I edited the book. I added many "newspaper references." I bought a few photos that relate to this Trial for "Commercial Use." I received permission to use other photos. Some of my friends helped; they created sketch drawings from the Trial. I verified the witness names in my uncle's book and created a "witness list" in the "Prologue." I researched this trial and the people involved for many months.

My uncle did not "cash in." Any of my proceeds generated from the sale of this book, published 46 years later, will go to the Sisters of Notre Dame in Thousand Oaks, CA at the request of my cousin Sister Paulynne. This would make Herman and Helen Tubick very happy. This book is a piece of history written in Herman and Helen Tubick's words. This book provides a different take on what the jurors went through during the trial. My uncle writes from the point of view of someone who took his role as juror very seriously. He politely, but realistically explained how difficult it was for the jurors to be sequestered for such a long time and describes some of the personalities of those with whom he shared a place in history. The book reflects the times, especially with the insights of my Aunt Helen and what it was like for her to be without her husband during those trying times. There's was what we might today consider an old-fashioned relationship of interdependence with their love of family and religion at the center of their lives. I left their writing relatively untouched so today's reader could see it through the lens of what life was like in the early 1970s.

The Tate La Bianca Trial was the first to ever sequester a jury for the length of time it took to present this very complicated case. There was no way my aunt and uncle could have known that the interest in Charles Manson, the cult surrounding him, and the details of the trial would be of interest to readers 50 years later. The Manson crimes changed society as we knew it especially for those living in Los Angeles during the summer of 1969.

Coincidentally, in August of 2017 when I was made aware of the existence of this manuscript, my current publisher was finishing a manuscript she was writing with Dianne Lake, the youngest member of the Manson family who joined the cult at age 14. Dianne had not participated in the crimes but was with Manson almost from the beginning and was a key witness in the trial for which my uncle served as jury foreman.

Member of the Family: My Story of Charles Manson, Life Inside his Cult and the Darkness that Ended the Sixties, (William Morrow, 2017) by Dianne Lake and Deborah Herman came out on October 24, 2017 and Charles Manson died on November 19, 2017. I started reading the book but didn't read it from cover to cover until I started working with Deborah and Micro Publishing Media, Inc to bring this book to fruition.

I immediately saw the connection and felt even more certain that this book needed to be given to the public when I read Dianne's reason for wanting her book written after 47 years of silence. Dianne had never told her story to anyone except her husband, including her own children until she felt she had no other choice. A documentary was being made that could have revealed her identity to the public. Dianne had been widowed and felt it was time to give the glory to God for her own survival. Many times, throughout his own book, my uncle used almost those exact words.

There was another connection I felt to Dianne's book about her time with Charles Manson. For many of us, the true horror was the idea that "there but for the Grace of God go I." Like many, I lived in Los Angeles during the same times that Dianne Lake did. Much of what is written in the first part of her book leading up to her meeting Manson, I remember very well.

I went to a few of the "Love in's" at Griffith Park. It was exciting and they were exactly as she has described them in the book. I graduated high school in 1966 and remember well the evolving hippie culture at that time. I had tickets to the 1966 Dodger Stadium *Beatles* concert, but I gave them to a former classmate as I had to work that night (sigh). I remember the concerts in San Fernando Valley; I went to a few of them. 1967, the *summer of love;* I was there. I experienced it for nine months into February 1968 where I stopped. I went to Haight Ashbury in 1968; everyone had to go there. But, by the time I went it had already turned very ugly. I remember being influenced by people from that scene at the time, but somehow, I recognized the signs early on or was simply lucky.

Dianne writes, "Charlie's form of guruism was in the California air and all up and down the coast there were men leading groups like ours and espousing many of the same things he was." And it was so true. There were so many out there, I met a few in those days and hung around with many of them.

Maybe I had a more stable home life (somewhat), so I always went back home, even though this "other world" intrigued me. For me, the realization of the Vietnam War, made this type of hippie existence seem inviting.

But in early February 1968 I somehow awoke to the fact that this was not me. I had to change. Somehow, I pulled it off. I stopped "in my tracks." I was at the 1968 *Doors* concert at the Hollywood Bowl, after that night the hippie path was over for me, thank God.

I was drafted into the Army in February 1969 and somehow wound up in Germany for 18 months, which removed me forever from this scene. A different type of fairy tale evolved for me at that time. Life went on in a really good way.

Many of us who lived in Los Angeles at this time imagined ourselves being sucked into the darkness. People defined their lives as we typically do after major events as how things were before and then how they were after. I know the children were terrified too and no longer carefree. They worried the Charles Manson family would "get them."

When I brought the book to Deborah Herman to publish I didn't realize the contribution she would make to the book as a co-author. Through the writing of the book with Dianne Lake, Deborah used her background as a journalist and a lawyer to see beyond what my uncle was able to understand at the time of the trial. I am sure he would be very happy with the additions made to his book as they put the trial into a context not seen before in other places. My uncle evaluated the evidence as presented in trial without pre-judging it. He took to heart his sacred trust as part of a body of men of women tasked with determining the facts of this very complicated case. As the reader follows his notes and Deborah's additions, it is the closest thing to being in that courtroom in 1970/71, but with the benefit of hindsight.

I am thankful that I could turn this typewriter written manuscript into a printed book with photos and illustrations in memory of my aunt and uncle. This is the version of the trial and the jurors' experiences from my uncle's viewpoint. We see from his notes what he found important in the testimony of each of the witnesses which aided him in his own decision in the trial of the twentieth century. My uncle was a man of God and would not have taken lightly his duty to decide the fate of four people who were innocent until proven guilty. And I agree with my Aunt Helen Tubick who writes this sentence about her husband within this book, "A good man was certainly chosen!"

PROLOGUE

BY DEBORAH HERMAN

I was amazed that Herman Tubick's historic artifact had been collecting dust in a drawer. It holds a blueprint to understanding one of the most complicated cases of all time and provides insight into the decision-making process found only in the inner sanctum of the jury deliberation room.

There were many events in the summer of 1969 that were noteworthy. However, the seven senseless murders that took place between August 8 and August 10, 1969 ended the idealism that was changing our American way of life for the good. There was chaos and questioning. There was good and there was bad. However, Manson drew all eyes upon him and forever became the face of evil and fear. Our fascination with him allowed him to wield too much power. Even after his death, we as a society, allow his madness to continue to permeate our collective consciousness.

I had already spent two years immersed in Charles Manson and his cult through the book I co-authored with Dianne Lake, the youngest member of the Manson Family, titled: *Member of the Family: My Story of Charles Manson, Life Inside his Cult and the Darkness that Ended the Sixties,* (William Morrow, 2017). During the time I collaborated with Dianne we unpacked her memories of what it was really like to live with Charles Manson; how she witnessed his descent into madness, was rescued and ultimately testified against him and the women she had once considered sisters.

I had wanted to write a book like this since I switched from a standard law school education into a dual degree with the Graduate School of Journalism.

My obsession with this case and with cults preceded my meeting Dianne by many decades, but it was truly the culmination of a dream. Having a second chance to write about the subject was beyond my expectations.

I originally only did some polishing on this book, with every intention of keeping the narrative exactly as written by Helen and Herman Tubick. The portions of the book clearly written by them in 1973, are a time capsule. In the early seventies the roles of men and women were first starting to change. Family values were restructuring and the "regular people" were holding fast to a lifestyle fading into memory. For many in today's world of cell phones and technology, co-habitation and career priorities, the life of Herman and Helen Tubick will seem ordinary. However, for others their story will bring nostalgia for simpler times.

As this was the second "Manson" book I have researched, I spent more time reading or skimming most of the 20,000 pages of transcript representing the nine and a half months of the trial. I have been drawn into this world and see it as a way for me to use my skills and training to breathe life into the greater issues. The victims of these crimes and those of other high- profile cases are often relegated to footnotes. Although Sharon Tate was a beautiful movie star with a bright future ahead of her, she was also a human being who wanted nothing more than to be a mother. She is more than a symbol or a curiosity. Sharon Tate and the other victims had lives that were cut short by someone who was having a psychological temper tantrum against the world.

As I worked with the original manuscript and compared the trial transcript the opportunity became obvious. The juror's experience and notes from inside the courtroom, reveal a narrow vision. When combined with what Manson was doing behind the scenes and the arguments held outside the jury's presence the rest of the story emerges.

For example, Herman Tubick's notes make some references to Manson and the women defendants acting out during the trial. What he and the other jurors didn't know was Manson planned his strategy of disruption long before the jury was even empaneled and sequestered. There was an undercurrent of agenda that Manson manipulated through threats, and intimidation in addition to counting on the loyalty of some of his acolytes.

The Judge heard most of these motions and arguments outside of the purview of the jurors. This protected the jury from becoming biased and rightly was not to be public. However, this also preserved the illusion of Manson mystique that still exists to this day. People still question his guilt and see him as a victim of the system. Some think he should be deified. There is so much half-truth information and speculation leading to rabbit holes at every turn. In my opinion, this unique combination of perspective reveals facts that should diminish the Manson legend once and for all. He was simply a delusional con man who did everything in his significant power to try to avoid responsibility for heinous crimes for which he was clearly accountable.

I am grateful to the website cielodrive.com, and the project that has digitized most of the trial transcript if not all of it, because anyone can see the facts for themselves. They gave me permission to quote from the transcript.

There are innumerable self-proclaimed Manson experts who are focused upon whether or not Helter Skelter was real or whether it was a creation of the prosecution. I personally believe, and I will take the liberty of speaking for my co-author Dianne Lake, who unlike the armchair theorists, was there, that this was not a theory concocted by the prosecution. Our conclusion in *Member of the Family* was that Charles Manson believed in the idea of a revolution and a war between the races that would lead him and his followers to a "bottomless pit," in the desert. Dianne helped search for it when the family was hiding out in Death Valley after the crimes. Now that I have spent additional time with the original testimony, I believe the evidence clearly supported that conclusion as well.

To this day, Manson aficionados like to argue why Manson ordered the murders. That is if they believe he ordered them at all. What I find most interesting is that the motive didn't really matter. Fifty years of discussion has missed the point that the burden of proof for the prosecution was not to prove motive. Evidence of motive was only used circumstantially to make sense of what happened and why. To paraphrase a statement of Manson himself: "sense is no sense." His reasoning was circular. From a legal standpoint, all the prosecution had to prove was that the people charged, committed the crimes. They also needed to show Manson's influence over the people who physically committed the crimes to support a charge of conspiracy. The law of conspiracy holds a person responsible for a crime as if he too held the knife. The prosecution created the best narrative it could to explain what happened, and it was clearly supported by the testimony. However, it never mattered if it was the only motive behind the crimes.

Ironically, it was Charles Manson, himself, who provided the clearest evidence of his control over his followers through his actions during the trial. He manipulated his co-defendants, his own attorneys and tried to control everything. As I reread some of the behind-the-scenes conversations between Charles Manson, defense attorneys and the prosecutors, I was proud that Judge Older was an advocate of the law being carried out in a dignified manner. Manson did everything in his power to undermine a system for which I have great respect. When I earned my law degree it felt auspicious. No matter what lawyers do in practice or how they are mocked and perceived, the education we are universally given is based upon principles intended to provide justice for all citizens. Judge Older was threatened, cajoled and pushed to the brink. But he held the principles of the law in place and set a firm boundary against Manson's criminal intentions.

Please accept my editorializations and theories as just that. Although I am a co-author, we felt it would be confusing to integrate my work into the existing manuscript directly without showing any separation of timeframe and point of view. In some ways, I am an interloper from the future. In other ways, I am an omniscient narrator with the benefit of missing pieces of the puzzle. To make it simpler to follow, my contributions are listed as editor's notes and separated by brackets. These additions are my own and are not necessarily reflective of the opinions of Herman Tubick, Helen Tubick or Rick Ortenburger. My hope is these additions do the subject justice and put to rest some questions about what really happened.

Herman Tubick's book adds something new about Charles Manson and the trial. Herman Tubick was a very religious man with his two daughters choosing the life of nuns. He took his role very seriously and I am grateful to have the chance to provide this credible addition to the Manson literature.

Preface (1973)

By Herman Tubick

This book was created at the insistence of my wife Helen Tubick, that we pick up the pen and write the facts, culled from my two courtroom notebooks, our conversations, correspondence and in journal form the reflections and the intimate experiences of the wife at home during the many days of jury sequestration. I, myself, told news reporters that it was not my intention to write a book. However, there is still an important story to be told.

This is my true story, the inside facts, which you have the right to know. We have included the following:

Herman Tubick, Jury Foreman

What it was really like to be sequestered (isolated from society) and on jury duty for 9 ½ months on the historical Tate La Bianca murder trial.

How it happened that I was called to serve on this case, my personal feelings and experiences, the effect it had upon me, my wife and my family.

The hardships, the agony, joy, sorrow, and inspiration that touched many lives during this lengthy probe.

My life at the Ambassador Hotel and that of the jurors, how we felt and how we spent our time during the long hours of sequestration.

Clearing the statement of "promiscuous behavior," an accusation made by one male juror.

The remarkable cooperation and labors of the deputies, their patience and concern for the jurors' well-being and safety.

The power of prayer that helped to sustain me and others, especially during those endless months, and the spirit of endurance for the jury during this marathon trial.

How I was chosen Foreman to direct harmony and understanding among the panelists, the incredible guidance of the Holy Spirit.

The earthquake, February 9, 1971, as if divine providence intervening, a major factor in Honorable Judge Charles H. Older's decision for the jurors respite at home and in dispersing the peak of high tensions in the jury.

Victory over difficulties in reaching the final decision of a death verdict for Mr. Manson and his female trio.

My awareness of the manifold work of our prosecuting and defense attorneys, the outstanding performance and patience of Judge Older during this trial, and my prayerful hope that our judicial courts will strive for genuine renewal and quick justice in our criminal trials.

Witness List

The following pages show the names of the witnesses called by the Prosecution during the trial as well as the witnesses from the penalty phase at the end of the trial. This list is according to what Herman and Helen Tubick wrote and the witnesses are listed in the order of when they were initially called to testify. Their testimony takes up a good portion of this book but is a minor reflection of the thousands of pages of trial transcript. Taken from Herman Tubick's notes, the excerpts are synthesized into what was important about each witnesses' testimony as it related to the building of the case. These witnesses were under oath; the jurors listened intently to what each one had to say and would base their decision on guilt or innocence of the defendants from the evidence. In the jury instructions at the end of the trial the Judge explained how the jurors were to weigh the evidence in making their ultimate decision.

In general, the role of the jury was explained as follows by Judge Older at the end of the trial:

"It is my duty to instruct you in the law that applies to this case and you must follow the law as I state it to you.

As jurors it is your exclusive duty to decide all questions of fact submitted to you and for that purpose to determine the effect and value of the evidence. In performing this duty, you must not be influenced by pity for any defendant or by passion or prejudice against him. You must not be biased against any defendant because he has been arrested for this offense, or because a charge has been filed against him, or because he has been brought to trial. None of these facts is evidence of his guilt and you must not infer or speculate from any or all of them that he is more likely to be guilty than innocent.

In determining whether any defendant is guilty or not guilty you must be governed solely by the evidence received in this trial and the law as stated to you by the court. You must not be governed by mere sentiment, conjecture, sympathy, passion, prejudice, public opinion or public feeling. Both the people and the defendants have a right to expect that you will conscientiously consider and weigh the evidence and apply the law of the case and that you will reach a just verdict regardless of what the consequences of such a verdict may be."

For fifty years people have been studying the events of August 8 and August 9, 1969 that led to the brutal slayings of Steven Parent, Sharon Tate, Jay Sebring, Wojciech Frykowski, and Abigail Folger and then the slayings of Rosemary and Leno La Bianca. The two-year cult and ultimate reign of terror associated with Charles Manson and his "family," was very complicated. It was made more so by efforts at obfuscation and a desire to draw the attention away from Manson as having any culpability in the crimes. His acolytes claimed full responsibility to clear the man they considered the second coming of Christ.

As in any trial, the jury is the tryer of facts. The attorneys on both sides must build their case much like putting together a puzzle. They may make a narrative argument to show their theory of the case, but the jury must determine guilt or innocence by what is presented. This book provides insight into the facts as they were presented and, according to the perception of Herman Tubick, what was important in the testimony. These facts that were determined to be credible were what the jury used to derive a guilty verdict.

The Prosecution presented an extensive case with 83 witnesses, some of whom were recalled during the trial. It was the job of the Prosecution to prove their case beyond a reasonable doubt. They had the higher burden of proof.

During the prosecution the defense attorneys had the opportunity to object to evidence and to cross examine the witnesses. However, when the Prosecution rested its case the defense chose not to call any witnesses. Charles Manson had wanted to represent himself as could be found in many pre-trial motions and through the course of the trial. Tubick, as a juror, was not privy to these motions made out of the presence of the jury. However, it was likely a choice by the defense not to allow Manson to testify as according to the law, no person can be forced to testify and they likely thought it was not in his best interest.

Right until the day he died, Manson claimed he was never given his day in court. He also claimed he was not guilty of anything. Here is the list of witnesses and a synthesis of the testimony as Herman Tubick recorded it. The jurors never questioned the decisions they made with Herman Tubick as their jury foreman.

Prosecution Witnesses

1. Paul J. Tate (Father of Sharon Tate)
2. Wilfred Parent (Father of Steven Parent)
3. Winifred Chapman (Tate Polanski housekeeper)
4. William Garretson (Guesthouse occupant at 10050 Cielo Drive)
5. Frank Guerrero (House painter at 10050 Cielo Drive)
6. Tom Vargas (Gardener at 10050 Cielo Drive)
7. Dennis Hearst (Bicycle shop employee)
8. Linda Kasabian (Former "family" member, indicted for the Tate La Bianca murders, main Prosecution Witness)
9. Timothy Ireland (Lived near the Tate Estate)
10. Rudolf Weber (Retired chief steward)
11. Jim Asin (Neighbor near 10050 Cielo Drive)
12. John Harold Swartz Jr. (Spahn Ranch truck driver)
13. Jerry DeRosa (West Los Angeles Police Officer)
14. William T. Whisenhunt (West Los Angeles Police Officer)
15. Robert Burbridge (West Los Angeles Police Officer)
16. Raymond Kilgrow (Telephone repairman)
17. Michael J. McGann (Sergeant, Los Angeles Police Department lead investigator)
18. John Finken (Coroner's office investigator)
19. Dr. Thomas T. Noguchi (Los Angeles County Coroner)
20. King Baggott (KABC-TV cameraman)
21. Joe Granado (Los Angeles Police Officer)
22. Helen Tebbe (Deputy Sheriff Sybil Brand Institute)
23. Frank Struthers Jr. (Stepson of Leno La Bianca)
24. Ruth Sivick (La Bianca Dress shop co-owner)
25. John Fokianos (Newspaper vendor)
26. William C. Rodriquez (Los Angeles Police Officer)
27. Edward Cline (Sergeant LAPD Officer)
28. Danny Galindo (LAPD Homicide Sergeant)

29. Gary Broda (LAPD Sergeant)
30. Dr. David Katsuyama (Deputy Coroner)
31. Jerrome Boen (LAPD fingerprint Expert)
32. Frank Escalante (LAPD fingerprint Officer)
33. Jack Swan (LAPD fingerprint expert)
34. Harold Dolan (LAPD fingerprint expert)
35. Steven Weiss (Sixteen-year-old boy)
36. Michael Watson (Los Angeles Police Officer)
37. Robert Calkins (LAPD Sergeant Investigator)
38. Dudley D. Barney (LAPD Sergeant Robbery Div)
39. William J. Lee (LAPD Sergeant Firearms Expert)
40. Edward C. Lomax (Firearms salesman)
41. Thomas J. Walleman ("Family" member)
42. Danny DeCarlo (Gunsmith and "family" member)
43. Eleanor Lally (Beach house apartment manager)
44. Ruby Pearl (Stable Manager at Spahn Ranch)
45. David Hannum (Ranch Hand at the Spahn Ranch)
46. William Gleason (Los Angeles Deputy Sheriff)
47. Ralph Marshall (San Fernando Valley Police Officer)
48. Samuel Olmstead (Malibu Station Deputy)
49. George Grap (Former deputy / real estate salesman)
50. Barbara Hoyt ("Family" member)
51. Donald Dunlap (Deputy Sheriff)
52. Juan Flynn ("Family" member)
53. David Steuber (Fresno, CA CHP investigator)
54. Paul Whitely (Los Angeles Sheriff Detective Homicide Dept)
55. Manuel Gutierrez (LAPD Detective Homicide Dept)
56. Albert LaValle (LAPD Sergeant)
57. Jack Holt (Los Angeles County Deputy Sheriff)
58. DeWayne Wolfer (LAPD criminologist)
59. Jerrold Friedman (Friend of Steven Parent)
60. Gloria Hardaway (Clerk LAPD Sheriff Department)
61. Rachel Burgess (LA County Deputy Sheriff)
62. Virginia Graham Castro (Cellmate of Susan Atkins)
63. Ronni Howard (Cellmate of Susan Atkins)
64. Gregg Jakobson (Record Talent Scout)
65. Shahrokh Hatami (Sharon Tate's photographer)
66. Rudolph Altobelli (Cielo Drive property owner)

67. Charles Koenig (Standard gas station attendant)
68. Roseanne Walker (Inmate Sybil Brand Institute)
69. Harold True (Student)
70. Terry Melcher (Record Company Owner)
71. Stephanie Schram ("Family" Member)
72. Janet M. Owens, alias Kitt Fletcher (Former inmate Sybil Brand Institute)
73. Lila Koelker (Deputy Sheriff Sybil Brand Institute)
74. Carolyn Alley (Lieutenant Deputy Sheriff Sybil Brand Institute)
75. William McKellar (State of Alabama Detective)
76. Frank J. Patchett (LAPD Sergeant)
77. Brooks Poston (Former "Family" member)
78. Paul Watkins (Former "Family" member)
79. Frank H. Fowles III (District Attorney of Inyo County)
80. James Pursell (California Highway Patrol Officer)
81. Dianne Elizabeth Lake ("Family" member)
82. Dr. Blake Skrdla (Psychiatrist)
83. Dr. Harold C. Deering (Psychiatrist)

Penalty Phase Witnesses

Called by Prosecutor Vincent Bugliosi
1. Bernard Crowe (Musician)
2. Captain Thomas Dynan (Oregon State Trooper)

Called by the Defense Attorneys
1. Joseph Krenwinkel (Father of Patricia Krenwinkel)
2. Dorothy Krenwinkel (Mother of Patricia Krenwinkel)
3. Mrs. Jane Van Houten (Mother of Leslie Van Houten)
4. Samuel Barrett (Probation & Parole Officer)
5. Lynette (Squeaky) Fromme ("Family" member)
6. Nancy Lora Pitman (Brenda McCann) ("Family" member)
7. Sandra Good ("Family" member)
8. Catharine (Gypsy) Share ("Family" member)
9. Pete Miller (Investigator Channel 11 TV News)
10. Susan Atkins ("Family" member)
11. Patricia Krenwinkel ("Family" member)
12. Leslie Van Houten ("Family" member)

13. Vincent Bugliosi (Prosecutor)
14. Linda Kasabian (Former "family" member, indicted for the Tate La Bianca murders, main Prosecution Witness)
15. Aaron Stovitz (Deputy District Attorney)
16. Paul Caruso (Court appointed lawyer for Susan Atkins)
17. Steven Grogan ("Family" member)
18. Lawrence J. Schiller (Photographer & journalist)
19. Dr. Andre R. Tweed (Psychiatrist)
20. Dr. Keith S. Ditman (Specialist in alcoholism and drug use)
21. Dr. Joel Forte (Psychiatrist)
22. Richard Caballero (Former attorney for Susan Atkins)
23. Dr. Joel Hochman (UCLA Psychiatrist)
24. Evelle J. Younger (State Attorney General)
25. Carnella Ambrosini (Reporter and stenotype secretary)
26. Catherine Gillies ("Family" member)
27. Mary Brunner ("Family" member)

CHAPTER ONE

A JURY SUMMONS

This is in my mind an amazing but heartwarming story of jury duty performed by simple middle-class citizens. The jurors on the Tate La Bianca murder case were a mixed group, mostly secretaries, technicians and housewives. I am a funeral director.

Many people have been amazed by the steadfast endurance of the panel on this trial that lasted nine and one-half months. Much has been publicized about the sensational investigation but little, if anything is known about the personal impressions and the depths of emotions that touched the lives of the jurors and their families during the long sequestration (i.e. secluded from society and communication). The ordeal and experience will long abide in my memory and I am certain that the other persons have been impressed as deeply. We are living testimonies that in this modern 20th century era, God still works in mysterious ways, using men and women as His instruments to accomplish heroic feats.

Before going on with my story let me tell you a little about myself, my wife and family. I am 59 years old and my wife is one year younger. We are the proud parents of two daughters, ages 39 and 25 who are nuns. We feel blessed as a family. Our daughters, both high spirited, are a joy in our life, and their good humor and enthusiasm penetrate the communities where they live and work.

My wife and I live in a small suburb in North Eastern Los Angeles, California. We occupy a two-bedroom apartment in a complex of 10 buildings, 12 units in all. My wife does most of the apartment managing for the owners while I help out on my days off from my regular job at Rose Hills Memorial Park in Whittier, California.

On that memorable day, June 22, 1970 when I was summoned to appear for Jury Duty, little did I dream what lie ahead. It was my first experience in civic duty to serve on a trial, which I considered a responsibility and a privilege. I decided against driving the family car to the courthouse, since taking a bus to town was less of a hassle than trying to find a parking place. And so, in my good, neatly pressed suit and shined up shoes, I made my first appearance in Superior Court, Los Angeles. After looking around, I finally found my way to the assembly room of the courthouse, room 222. A large group of 100 or more people were sitting and waiting.

Finally, a court trial judge and bailiff entered the room. The Judge began procedures with instructions on the juror's creed, the sacred functions that entailed, the responsibility and privilege of duty rendered, the obligation for each juror to answer truthfully all questions concerning personal history and qualifications, impartiality and intelligence in issues of facts on the case presented to jurors, directives about personal attire and behavior in the courtroom, and lastly the ruling of the trial judge upon questions of law. Upon completion of instructions the Judge told everyone to stand and take the oath as prospective jurors.

Then all the waiting began again. Sitting around, "killing time," I tried to relax and kept wondering if I would be called on a civil or a criminal case. A woman court clerk eventually appeared, and the first name on her list was mine, along with about 30 others. We were ushered to room 304, where Judge Marshall was presiding on a civil case. Twelve prospective jurors were selected. I was excused along with some others, so we walked back to the assembly room. It was packed with people, a larger crowd than before.

Casually taking a seat again, I thought, "with all of these people, it'll be a long time before I will be called again." Then the court clerk returned and to my surprise called out loud and clear, "Herman C. Tubick!" I was flabbergasted! "Among all of these people" I pondered, "why should I be called first again?" The court clerk proceeded to call and select about 64 prospective jurors. A bailiff led the group down a flight of stairs and outside to a sheriff's bus. With several deputies accompanying us, we road to the back entrance of the Hall of Justice. We were instructed, "No talking, no smoking."

We were led to a small courtroom, Department 104 and told to be seated. Everyone was getting anxious and edgy, wondering why all the secrecy and precaution. The air of silence and tension was frightening and nerve rack-ing. Several deputies were keeping a watchful eye on us.

At last a male clerk entered the room. It appeared he had a box in his hands, for he pulled out a slip of paper; he read off my name. Unbelievable!

I was swallowed up by a strange feeling as I followed the clerk into the court chamber. Here was my first meeting with the Honorable Judge Charles H. Older, a gentleman of medium height and reserved distinction. Judge Older introduced himself and those present in the room; the prose-cuting attorneys Vincent T. Bugliosi and Aaron H. Stovitz; defense attorneys Irving A. Kanarek, Daye Shinn, Ira K. Reiner and Paul Fitzgerald (at the very beginning of the murder trial); and lastly Charles Milles Manson and his three female "family" members, who at that time were only referred to as co-defendants, Susan Atkins, Patricia Krenwinkel and Leslie Van Houten.

My first meeting with Mr. Manson and his girl trio had no effect on me whatsoever; to me they were just names and faces. I had no knowledge of the nature of the crime they were accused of until the Judge mentioned that they were being held for murder. I had not read about the crime in the newspapers and I pay little attention to what I hear from people about crime and killings, there is so much of this that goes on each day; my mind just doesn't dwell on it. My news interest is sports mostly so whenever I read a paper, I glanced through the sports page and the race-track section. After all the introductions, Judge Older and the attorneys proceeded with the "third degree." I was bombarded by personal questions on all sides; my per-sonal history, wife, family, occupation, if and what I heard or read about Mr. Manson and his three girls. Upon hearing that this trial would take three and one-half to five months with sequestering of the jurors, I attempted to explain to the Judge that this length of time would cause a hardship for my wife, leaving her alone to manage all the apartments. Then there was the concern about my job at Rose Hill Memorial Park, having no assurance that my employer would hold my position open until I return. I also worried if my salary would be paid if I serve jury duty this long. I honestly wanted to do my part in civic jury duty and serve as a juror, but I didn't dream that I would be stuck with anything this lengthy and with sequestration.

After more questioning for hours it seemed, it was finally all over. The bailiff ushered me back to Department 104 and told me to take a seat in the jury box, chair number 12. The people in the jury box looked up and smiled understandingly as I took my designated place. A short time later the Judge and attorneys entered the courtroom and proceeded with more questioning of the potential jurors. Several panelists were excused before the court adjourned for the day. What a hectic ordeal it was, my first day in the courtroom!

[EDITOR'S NOTE: Voir Dire is a legal term that means the preliminary examination of a witness. It is the process used to "interview" prospective jurors and as you can see from the actual transcript of Herman Tubick's voir dire it can be very tedious. This does not include the discussions and arguments held outside the presence of the jury pool as the attorneys and judge try to figure out who should serve. Here is the actual transcript of the Voir Dire Examination of Herman Tubick.

COURT: Mr. Tubick, the attorneys have estimated that this case will probably take between three and five months to try after the jury is selected. That will probably take two to three weeks. it is my intention that the jury will be sequestered after the jury is selected during the balance of the trial, which means that instead of being permitted to go home every night as you are now, you would be residing in a hotel.

TUBICK: Yes sir.

COURT: Knowing all these things and what you do know about this case, do you believe that you would be willing and able to serve as a juror in this case if you were selected?

TUBICK: Yes, sir.

COURT: Now, I mentioned to you and the rest of the prospective jurors some preliminary matters regarding murder cases in general and their opinions regarding the death penalty in particular. Now, I am going to put to you the two specific questions that I referred to while I was on the bench. To refresh your recollection, first, in a murder case, if there is a verdict of murder in the first degree, which carries with it a penalty of either life imprisonment or death, then there is a second phase during which the jury determines which of those two alternatives, life imprisonment or death, should be imposed.

Now the law provides that if you have such conscientious opinions regarding the death penalty that either you are unable to make an impartial decision as to guilt, that is, during the first phase, or you would automatically refuse to impose the death penalty, that is, during the second penalty phase, then you will neither be permitted nor compelled to serve as a juror.

So, my first question, then, is do you entertain such conscientious opinions regarding the death penalty that you would be unable to make an impartial decision as to any defendant guilt regardless of the evidence developed during the trial?

TUBICK: No sir

COURT: And the second question is, do you entertain such conscientious opinions regarding the death penalty that you would automatically refuse to impose it without regard to the evidence developed during the trial?

TUBICK: No sir.

COURT: Have you lived in Los Angeles county continuously since last August?

TUBICK: Yes sir.

COURT: Now, the killings that brought about this case occurred last August. Did you first learn about them about that time?

TUBICK: Oh, I have heard of it there, in my work. I am a mortician there, just what I hear. People saying is bout all.

COURT: What part of the County do you live in?

TUBICK: Los Angeles, Monterey Park.

COURT: Do you subscribe to a newspaper?

TUBICK: No, sir.

COURT: Do you watch TV?

TUBICK: Yes, sir.

COURT: Have you seen anything on TV about the case or any of the defendants?

TUBICK: No sir.

COURT: Do you listen to the radio?

TUBICK: Yes, sir.

COURT: Did you learn anything about the case from the radio?

TUBICK: No, sir. I have not.

COURT: Have you read any magazines or books about the case?

TUBICK: No sir, I have not, no. In my work I really am very much taken care of there, because I work mortuary work there. I am taken care of all day long there. I haven't much time for anything at all except maybe sports, football games.

COURT: What is the nature of your work?

TUBICK: Funeral director, embalming.

COURT: Well then, I take it from what you say you know very little about the case?

TUBICK: Yes sir. I don't know much, if anything, about it at all.

COURT: Do you know the names of any of the people that were killed?

TUBICK: No sir.

COURT: Have you read anything about any of the defendants?

TUBICK: No, sir, I have not.

COURT: Did you know any of their names before you came in here today?

TUBICK: No sir, just what I heard, some relations at services there. I heard people mention Mr. Manson or something like that. That is about all.

COURT: Where was this that you heard that?

TUBICK: When I conduct the funeral services at the mortuary, at the chapel in Rose Hills.

COURT: Was this just conversation?

TUBICK: Just bystanders, standing around during the service.

COURT: But did you hear anything in particular being said, or just the name mentioned?

TUBICK: No, sir, just the name mentioned.

COURT: Aside from that you cannot remember anything else that you might have learned about the case.

TUBICK: No, sir, not a thing.

COURT: Have you formed any opinions about the guilt or innocence of any of the defendants in the case?

TUBICK: No, sir, I have not.

Voir Dire By Defense Attorney Fitzgerald:

FITZGERALD: Are you familiar with the name Sharon Tate?

TUBICK: No, sir, I am not.

FITZGERALD: You never heard of Sharon Tate?

TUBICK: No, sir.

FITZGERALD: You have never seen the name in print either?

TUBICK: No.

FITZGERALD: You have heard the name Charles Manson?

TUBICK: I have heard the name Charles Manson.

FITZGERALD: And that was in discussion with some other people.

TUBICK: Yes, sir.

FITZGERALD: Did those people purport to know personally Mr. Manson?

TUBICK: No, sir.

FITZGERALD: What can you recall anybody saying about Mr. Manson?

TUBICK: Oh, they just related if I heard anything about the Manson case, and about when the trial was going to take place. It was just heard from the outside there, the people going in and out of the chapel.

FITZGERALD:When you heard the name or the title, the Charles Manson trial, what did you think Mr. Manson was charged with?

TUBICK: I did not know at that time, sir.

FITZGERALD: And when did you first learn if you ever did?

TUBICK: Well, all I heard about it was just when I came into the court today.

FITZGERALD: I have nothing further.

Voir Dire by Defense Attorney Reiner:

REINER: Mr. Tubick, prior to coming to court today you had, of course, heard of Mr. Manson:

TUBICK: Yes, sir.

REINER: And you had heard of him in connection with the killing of Sharon Tate or other persons, is that correct?

TUBICK: I just heard the name Manson I did not know what he was connected with.

REINER: Were you in the Greater Los Angeles area last August?

TUBICK: Yes, sir.

REINER: Did you recall the public attention that was given to certain killings that occurred in the Benedict Canyon area, that is the home of Sharon Tate?

TUBICK: I just heard about it, that was all.

REINER: And did you hear the next evening of certain other killings at the La Bianca residence?

TUBICK: Just what I heard from the other people, yes, sir.

REINER: What did you hear at that time from other people of those killings that occurred on those two evenings?

TUBICK: Well, just that it was a terrible killing and so on, like that there. People did not understand why this thing went on.

REINER: At the time from conversations that you had with other persons, or any newspaper accounts that you may have read, or from any other source you were aware, were you not, that those people had been stabbed?

TUBICK: No, sir.

REINER: Were you aware at all of how they met their death?

TUBICK: No, sir.

REINER: But you were aware that there had been a large number of killings?

TUBICK: Yes, sir.

REINER: And sometime later it came to your attention that Mr. Manson had been arrested and charged with these killings, is that true?

TUBICK: Yes, sir.

REINER: And also, that certain other persons, certain girls had been arrested and charged with these killings with him, is that true?

TUBICK: Yes, sir.

REINER: And all of this was prior to coming to court?

TUBICK: Yes, sir.

REINER: And the conversation that you had with other persons and newspaper accounts that you may have had and from any other source, you had heard the girls referred to Mr. Manson's Family, had you not?

TUBICK: Yes, sir.

REINER: And in conversations or from any other source had you heard of or learned of a certain purported confession by one of the girls that was published in the newspaper?

TUBICK: No, sir, I have not.

REINER: Had you heard of any books that had been written about this case?

TUBICK: No, sir.

REINER: Had you had occasion to look at any magazines dealing with this case or any of the persons in it?

TUBICK: No, sir.

REINER: Do you ever watch television?

TUBICK: Yes, sir.

REINER: Do you watch television in the evening?

TUBICK: Yes, sir,

REINER: Is there any particular newscaster that you watch more than the other casters?

TUBICK: No, sir, I don't.

REINER: Do you watch the news on television from m time to time?

TUBICK: No sir.

REINER: Did you ever watch the news on television?

TUBICK: No, sir.

REINER: Did you ever listen to the news on radio?

TUBICK: No, sir.

REINER: Do you subscribe to a newspaper?

TUBICK: No, sir.

REINER: Do you ever read the newspaper?

TUBICK: Yes, sir.

REINER: From reading the newspaper you have read from time to time accounts of this case and persons in it, have you not?

TUBICK: No sir, as far as I go with the news, I go as far as the sports page and the obituary columns.

REINER: Well, since last August, these last ten months, have you read a single account of this case, the victims or any persona connected with this case in any newspaper?

TUBICK: No, sir, I have not.

REINER: Have you ever seen even a headline connected with this case or the persons in it since last August?

TUBICK: I have seen a headline, yes.

REINER: What sort of headlines have you seen, to the best of your recollection?

TUBICK: I remember seeing Mr. Manson's name on the headlines.

REINER: And in what context do you recall seeing his name in the headline?

TUBICK: Well, just Mr. Manson was arrested.

REINER: And these conversations that you had with other persons, were you referring to co-workers?

TUBICK: No, the public.

REINER: Oh, I see. Then would it be a fair statement to say that the persons whom you overheard speak, or the person with whom you directly had conversations would be a cross-section of the clientele that would come to your particular establishment?

TUBICK: Yes, sir.

REINER: And would it be a fair statement to say that most of the people who had come to your establishment in the course of business evidenced at least some familiarity on their part if not on your part with the facts of the case.

TUBICK: Well, they wouldn't state any facts or anything like that sir, just the conversation I heard among the other people there.

REINER: Well, did this conversation generally take the form of indicating that Mr. Manson and the certain other girls who have been charged as defendants had committed these killings, would that be a fair statement of the conversation?

TUBICK: Yes.

REINER: And did this sort of conversation occur with any regularity over these last few months with the cross-section of customers that had come to your establishment?

TUBICK: No, sir.

REINER: How frequently did you overhear persons discuss the facts of this case or at least their impression of the facts of this case?

TUBICK: Oh, I have heard about, oh, once or twice a day there, because I have five services every day and some of the people would bring up this Manson case. I would not get in on the conversation because I don't get in with the clientele that much to speak to them personally.

REINER: Then would it be a fair statement to say that at least once or twice a day of the five services per day that you hold, you would overhear other people discussing this case?

TUBICK: Yes, sir.

REINER: And that wouldd be on a daily basis since the killings occurred?

TUBICK: Yes, sir.

REINER: And the general tenor of the discussions that you would overhear related to Mr. Manson's involvement in these particular killings?

TUBICK: Yes.

REINER: And the involvement of the other defendants as well.

TUBICK: Yes.

REINER: And the general tenor of these discussions, these other persons had among themselves, was it to the effect that Mr. Manson in all probability was guilty of these killings.

TUBICK: Well, they would be pro and con on it. Some would say yes, and some would say no.

REINER: It would be a fair statement to say that the overwhelming majority of persons who had discussed this, that you had overheard, indicated that their belief was Mr. Manson was guilty.

TUBICK: Yes.

REINER: And that related also as well to the other defendants in this case, the girls?

TUBICK: Yes.

REINER: No further questions.

Kanarek had no questions.

Voir Dire by Prosecuting Attorney Stovitz:

STOVITZ: Is Rose Hills-is that the name of the company you work for?

TUBICK: Yes, sir, Rose Hills.

STOVITZ: Do you know whether a young boy by the name of Steven Parent was buried there?

TUBICK: I cannot recall offhand, sir, as I say, we have five services every day, we average 12 to 14 services every day now.

STOVITZ: If it were to come to pass, now I'm not saying that he was, because as far as I know his folks were from El Monte, and there is another funeral burial ground north of El Monte, is that right?

TUBICK: Yes, sir, Forest Lawn.

STOVITZ: Is there a Forest Lawn in El Monte?

TUBICK: Yes, sir.

STOVITZ: Have you ever heard of a magazine or publication known as *The Rolling Stone*?

TUBICK: No, sir.

STOVITZ: Are you married, sir?

TUBICK: Yes, sir.

STOVITZ: Have you ever discussed the facts of this case with your wife?

TUBICK: No, sir.

STOVITZ: Do you have any children, sir?

TUBICK: Yes, sir.

STOVITZ: How old are they?

TUBICK: One is 37 and the youngest is 23.

STOVITZ: Did you ever discuss the facts of this case with your children?

TUBICK: No, sir, they are both in the convent and they are away from home.

STOVITZ: I take it they are girls.

TUBICK: Yes, sir.

STOVITZ: I have no further questions.

COURT: Mr. Tubick, I don't understand some of the answers that you gave. You say that these conversations occurred between people who were attending the services, is that right?

TUBICK: Yes, sir.

COURT: Now, were you actually participating in the conversations?

TUBICK: No sir.

COURT: Or were you standing next to these people for some period of time?

TUBICK: Oh, yes, sir. Because I have to pass out these memorial cards.

COURT: Were you actually following the conversation between the groups?

TUBICK: No, sir.

COURT: Just fragments?

TUBICK: Just fragments here and there.

COURT: Do you mean to say you could tell from these fragments that these people who were saying that Mr. Manson, or any of the other defendants, were probably guilty, or more likely to be guilty than innocent?

TUBICK: Yes, sir.

COURT: You could tell that from fragments of the conversation?

TUBICK: Well, they would come out and say they were guilty, yes, sir.

COURT: You definitely recall that?

TUBICK: Yes, sir.

COURT: Did this happen on more than one occasion?

TUBICK: Yes.

COURT: Do you remember exactly what was said?

TUBICK: Not exactly, no sir.

COURT: Did any of these people indicate the basis for their opinions?

TUBICK: No, sir.

COURT: Did you, on the basis of these fragments of conversations form any opinions of your own as to the guilt or innocence of any of the defendants?

TUBICK: No, sir.

COURT: Now, if you were selected as a juror in this case, Mr. Tubick, do you believe that you could put aside whatever you have heard or earned about this case and decide the case solely on the basis of the evidence that comes in during the course of the trial?

TUBICK: Yes, sir.

COURT: And would you promise the Court to do so?

TUBICK: Yes, sir.

COURT: Would you follow the Court's instructions on the law even though those instructions might differ from your own opinion as to what the law is or should be?

TUBICK: Yes, sir.

COURT: Do you promise the Court that you will do that?

TUBICK: Yes, sir.

Additional questions by Defense Attorney Kanarek:

KANAREK: Mr. Tubick, during this period of time that the Court has indicated that you might be sequestered, kept away from your family, is Rolling Hills going to pay you?

TUBICK: I really don't know, sir.

KANAREK: You don't know whether they will or will not pay?

TUBICK: Yes.

KANAREK: You haven't discussed it with the people at the mortuary?

TUBICK: I have not discussed it, no, sir. I don't know what setup they have there about jury duty.

KANAREK: Do you have any income, Mr. Tubick, other than in your work at Rose hills?

TUBICK: Yes, sir.

KANAREK: What is that income?

TUBICK: My wife is a manager of apartments.

KANAREK Does she get more than room and board?

TUBICK: Yes, sir.

KANAREK: Do you mind stating what that income is?

THE COURT: That is an imposition.

KANAREK: Very well, your honor.

COURT: Mr. Tubick, I am going to ask you to refrain from discussing with anybody else, including the prospective jurors, you wife or anybody what has been said back and forth in here today. Will you do that?

TUBICK: Oh, yes.

COURT: All right. Thank you.

This was said in chambers after Herman Tubick left. It is the discussion of whether he should be empaneled:

REINER: Your Honor, there will be a challenge for cause, actual bias.

BUGLIOSI: We oppose the challenge.

KANAREK: I join in the challenge, your Honor.

SHINN: I join in the challenge.

FITZGERALD: I join in the challenge, your Honor.

COURT: Do you wish to argue?

FITZGERALD: We will join and submit it.

COURT: the challenge will be disallowed.

KANAREK: Your honor, I believe the gentleman may not be aware of the hardship aspect. He does not know, your Honor, whether or not Rose Hills will pay him.

STOVITZ: I submit anybody who works for a mortuary sees hardship every day your Honor.

FITZGERALD: Well, he is willing to serve.

COURT: Well, he was advised, Mr. Kanarek, of the length of the trial, the fact he would be sequestered, it is apparent from that he does not want to be at work. He said he doesn't know whether he will be paid or not, so we are not aware of a contingency here.]

❖   ❖   ❖

The next three and one-half weeks, every day, five days a week, I made my daily appearance at the courtroom, department 104, and took my familiar place in the jury box, seat 12. Superior Court, Department 104 was a windowless mahogany walled courtroom. During this time more than 100 jurors were questioned and challenged by Judge Older and the defense and prosecuting attorneys. This slow jury selection procedure reminded me of the musical chairs game; someone gets up and leaves; another one walks in and takes his place. The selection process was laborious and nerve racking not only to the participants but to the Judge, attorneys and anxious news starved reporters. I have always mused why crime is so greatly publicized and glorified in our country by the news media, while good things are usually hidden on the last page of the newspaper. Unfortunately, the general public gloats over sensational news, so even the conscientious reporter feels bound to oblige.

During these few weeks I too was questioned and challenged by the Judge and attorneys. I mentioned the hardship for my wife if I were to be sequestered for a long period of time; but this excuse was not valid, as I learned later. I honestly had a feeling that any day now I would be excused, but it was not meant to be.

I had plenty of time to meditate upon Judge Older's discussion on sequestration and judgment of two trials; the first phase to decide innocence or guilt of murder in the first or second degree. The second phase; if the guilt is murder in the first degree, to decide on a penalty of life imprisonment or death. I become more and more aware of the ordeal facing the selected jurors; the responsibility, the stamina, the hardship, and even the danger that would face each one.

Then there was the concern about safety for wives and families and adjustments at home. Yes, I was worried. If I remained on this drawn out trial, would my wife be safe, could she manage the care and the work of the apartments by herself, what would she do all alone? But I kept reassuring myself that, come what may, with God's help things would work out all right.

When I reported to my employer at Rose Hills Memorial Park, I was assured of my job remaining open during my jury duty with the continuance of my salary. At least on these points my mind was at rest.

We, the potential jurors were admonished by Judge Older not to discuss court procedures at home, with relatives or with friends, nor to listen to news relating to the Manson case. This was no problem for me; I abided by the rule. My wife, having her high hopes that I would be excused from the hearing, didn't want to discuss it at all.

With each passing day the reporters and spectators were increasing in the corridors and the courtroom. I was aware of the impact of publicity surrounding the bizarre murder case, creating a headache to Judge Older, the attorneys and some of the potential jurors. A good part of the questioning related to how influenced we were by media reports. But to the spectators and reporters the hubbub provided an exciting, spectacular field day. I've never seen so many newsman and cameras at one time for any one occasion.

I will always remember Tuesday July 14, 1970. Right after lunch all the attorneys walked into the courtroom, looked up and gazed at us. I knew they were sizing us up, but I couldn't read their expressions. They seemed to be grinning or amused but that must not have had anything to do with us. In a few moments Judge Older stepped in from his chamber. He made us feel comfortable by smiling pleasantly. I still felt nervous. The Judge said something to the effect of, "Ladies and Gentlemen, you have been selected, with the agreement of the defense and prosecution attorneys, to serve and pass judgment at this trial as jurors; you will now take the oath and be sworn in."

"This is it." My heart kept pounding. I visualized the long stretch of tedious, laboring days in the courtroom and total isolation from normal life. I didn't really think about what it would mean when I was being questioned. At first it was an abstraction. I felt numb! I didn't really want to serve on a prolonged, sequestered murder trial such as this. I don't care less for publicity. This extended sequestration would create exposure to danger for jurors and their families. But now I was called and chosen; as a citizen I would have a duty and obligation to meet the challenge. So, with leathered determination I vowed to do my best.

Consequently, on the afternoon of July 14 we were sworn in; seven men and five women in this order; Mrs. Thelma S. McKenzie, Mrs. Shirley B. Evans, Mr. William T. McBride II, Mr. Alva K. Dawson, Mrs. Jean K. Roseland, Mr. Anlee Sisto, Mr. William M. Zamora, Miss Marie M. Mesmer, Mr. John M. Baer, Mrs. Evelyn J. Hines, Mr. Walter A. Vitzelio and myself.

The Jurors

Mrs. Thelma S. McKenzie, juror number one, was a housewife and social worker, generally liked by everyone, and was very friendly and sociable. She has a way of speaking in a slow and relaxed manner. During the long confinement, Mrs. McKenzie added some color and jest to our hotel environment with her display of numerous wigs, colorful jewelry and fashionable wardrobe. Many of her clothes were sewn in her room on a portable sewing machine. Some of the members in the group called her Madam Butterfly.

Mrs. Shirley B. Evans, juror number two, a secretary for the board of education, was a very quiet and reserved person, she kept secluded in her room, when she mingled with fellow jurors, which was seldom, she had little to say, and when she did speak, it was a comment on some grievance. However, when her spouse and teenage son would come and visit her at the Ambassador and we were dining together, she would be talkative, exuberant and glowing with happiness.

Mr. William McBride, juror number three on the panel, was a young bachelor, very likeable and friendly chap, he possessed a modest and warm personality and got on very well with jurors. As the Trial would grind on,

Mr. McBride, an engineer by trade, would express his dismay by uttering his favorite quotation; "Unbelievable" he would say time and time again.

The next man in the jury section was Mr. Alva Dawson, juror number four, a retired deputy sheriff and the oldest in the group. Dawson, congenial and sociable was not only pleasant to have around, but he was an inspiration and a good example for the others. Dawson, jolly and good natured, young in spirit, took the long ordeal in stride. He kept fit by riding an exercise bicycle in his room; sometimes he passed the long hours working cross-word puzzles, playing cards and dancing with the ladies. Whenever dining out and there was music and a dance floor in sight, Dawson was on his feet asking the ladies in our group if they would care to dance.

Juror number five was Mrs. Jean Roseland. A youthful mother of three teenage children, a housewife and secretary for T.W.A Airlines; Mrs. Roseland was very friendly and vivacious, she had a sense of humor and a great zest for the many pranks and jokes invented by fellow jurors to lighten the long ordeal. In a press interview, Jean Roseland talked about some of the experiences on the Manson trial; she came about as close as any of the women could, to being the jury's sweetheart.

In jury section number six was Mr. Anlee Sisto, a former Navy man and a repair technician for the school district. Sisto was a very friendly and compatible man, he was liked by everyone. A patient and happy family man, he enjoyed music. Sisto passed the long hours by playing his guitar and having songfests and duets in his room. He enjoyed doing jigsaw puzzles, playing cards and even started knitting a shawl.

Mr. William Zamora, in jury seat seven, a state employee for the highway department, was a bachelor with a temperamental disposition. Zamora was very friendly and talkative and tried to make an impression with flattery and compliments. If something displeased him or upset him, he flared up in anger. On the other hand, he could be quite charming in the Latin American way, with a flashing smile, he was well-groomed and neatly dressed to the norms of youthful and colorful fashion. Looking lean and physically fit, he liked to perform on the dance floor with graceful agility in the latest dance steps. Like Mr. Dawson, our fellow juror Zamora enjoyed dancing. The ladies in the group never lacked a dance partner when dining out. During those long and tedious "locked-up" days at the Ambassador Hotel, Zamora had a difficult and unhappy time; lacking patience, a sense of humor and fair play, he could not establish a communicating friendship with the other jurors. His resentment grew, and he frequently commented, "You're all against me!"

Miss Marie Mesmer was juror number eight, a retired free-lance writer and drama critic. Miss Mesmer was very friendly, sociable and outspoken. If she had anything to say, she said it, regardless of anyone's feelings. Generally liked by everyone, Miss Mesmer self-assuredly, accepted the ordeal with resignation; and in her leisure hours she enjoyed a swim in the pool, reading and writing.

Juror John Baer, number nine was an electrical tester for the Los Angeles Department of Water and Power, a dignified and religious man, Mr. Baer, respected by all, was quiet and reserved. He remained mostly secluded in his room, spending the time reading the Bible, making Macramé belts and writing. A proud and happy family man, whenever his sociable wife and teenage son and daughter came to visit, he emerged and beamed with pleasure. Mr. Baer, a very conscientious citizen, withstood the long sequestration with amazing tolerance.

Panelist Evelyn Hines, number ten, was a Dictaphone operator and housewife, a kind and friendly person; she would chit chat about anything and everything. Mrs. Hines enjoyed a good laugh; she was delighted with the many pranks and jokes invented by the jurors during our extended incarceration. The boys nicknamed her "Gigglebottem." Mrs. Hines indulged in playing cards, working jigsaw puzzles and swimming to pass the time.

Mr. Larry Sheely, juror number 11, was a telephone repairman, a young father of two small boys, and was friendly and high-spirited. Sheely got along well with everyone. He kept fellow jurors and deputies on their toes with his enthusiastic gags and jokes. He came up with various pranks and capers to release the strain and stress of the long trial. Sheely enjoyed a good workout with the boys on the panel, a fast game of paddle ball, table tennis and swimming in the pool.

Mr. Herman Tubick, juror number 12, was 59 years old; his wife Helen was one year younger. He had two daughters, age 39 and 25 who were Nuns. Tubick wrote, "I feel blessed as a family. My daughters, both high spirited are a joy in my life, and their good humor and enthusiasm penetrate the communities where they live and work.

I live with my wife in a small suburb in North Eastern Los Angeles, California. We occupy a two-bedroom apartment in a complex of ten buildings, 12 units in all. My wife does most of the apartment managing for the owners while I help out on my days off from my regular job at Rose Hills Memorial Park in Whittier, California."

On Friday January 15, 1971 Herman Tubick was elected the Jury Foreman

Judge Older

and led the guilt / penalty phase portions of the trial. "It was not so much the extraordinary achievement of the Tate La Bianca jury, but rather, through the grace of God, the extraordinary endurance and harmony of the 12 selected panelists prevailed into the very end."

Later in the day Judge Older gave instructions to the newly selected panel to come prepared for tomorrow's court session, with suitcases ready and packed.

After court adjourned for the day the new jurors expressed their personal views and feelings except about the details of the case. We had been told several times to discuss that with no one. Some were complaining; some were indifferent, some seemed completely enchanted to serve as jurors on what would be the dramatic Tate La Bianca murder case.

CHAPTER TWO

BREAKING THE NEWS

Riding the bus back home, many troubled thoughts raced through my mind. The one that bugged me the most was how to break the news to my wife. My heart felt heavy. "My poor darling, oblivious to any foreboding, would probably be working in the gardens," I imagined as the bus neared our street corner.

The bus stop was a short distance from our home, but I didn't see her as I approached the front yard. I opened the back door and in my best *father knows best* voice, I called out, "Hello, honey, I'm home." There was no answer. "She must be outside at the far end of the grounds," I surmised. I quickly changed clothes, washed up, and walked outdoors to look for her.

Halfway towards the last apartment I saw her coming toward me. My throat tightened as I approached and embraced her. She knew just by looking at me what I could only sputter. "This is it, darling, I've been sworn in today on the Manson trial." My wife, of quiet serene temperament, never one for outbursts, replied resignedly, "Somehow I knew it was coming."

I must have been be a worried sight, for she kept reassuring me that things will work out.

Later my wife mentioned wanting safety latches to put on our doors before I left in the morning. I hadn't thought of that kind of risk. Perhaps my wife knew something about this case that I did not. I complied without question. While she prepared dinner, I scouted around to find a hardware store still open at that late hour. After trying about a half dozen places, I finally found one that hadn't closed for the night. When I returned home, dinner was ready and waiting.

I couldn't help thinking that this would be our last dinner at home. I knew that it would not be forever, but we hadn't been separated for any length of time before. I kept wondering how many days would pass before we would dine at our table again. We tried to be cheerful, making small talk; but try as we might, we couldn't shake off our melancholy. I studied her face. We had been through so many things together; good things mostly. Ours was a simple life that worked.

After dinner, late as it was, I banged away installing safety latches on our front and back doors. I felt like a fool disturbing our next-door tenant with all the commotion but welcomed the distraction of the task at hand. Now I had an even more unpleasant task to face; packing my suitcase in preparation for tomorrow's departure. My wife, bless her, tried to help, folding my shirts in a neat stack and checking the condition of my supply of socks. We were both very tired and weary when we finally retired, but our sleep was troubled and choppy. As we finally fell asleep the alarm exploded as if to herald the arduous journey ahead.

My wife, the first one up, was preparing breakfast. By the time I washed, shaved, dressed and finished last minute packing, she beckoned me to the kitchen. We sat down to what was now truly our last meal together at home and I could see it was made with extra loving care.

I dreaded my departure but didn't want to show her my concern. We walked out through the back door together to say goodbye. Tears were welling up as we warmly embraced and kissed. "Pray for me, darling," I whispered; "and I'll be praying for you."

I lingered for a moment, picked up my suitcase, then turned away quickly, not daring to look back. The walk to the bus stop and seeing other people helped me to get a grip upon myself and gain composure, but the empty feeling was still there.

Upon arrival at the courthouse I noticed all the jurors standing with their suitcases milling around, anxious and waiting. Everyone appeared to be wondering the same thing, "Where do we go from here?" When the sheriffs' bus arrived, we boarded it with five deputies accompanying us. After a ride to the Hall of Justice, everyone was once again escorted to the courtroom in department 104. Judge Older entered the courtroom, and the court clerk was instructed to proceed with the first agenda of the day.

That morning, July 15, 1970 Sergeant William Maupin, Elaine Slagle, Ann Orr, William Murray and Odin Skupen were the five deputies sworn in to guard and protect the 12 jurors and then the six alternates, yet to be selected and sworn in at a later date.

The court was adjourned for the day. We, the twelve jurors, were to leave soon for our sequestered residence. Everyone seemed to know where we were going except the jurors themselves; we were kept in the dark. Once again, we boarded the sheriffs' bus, this time with four deputies, and started out for our destination. The bus driver weaved into several side streets, even a few alleyways, no doubt for safety precautions and to escape news media. Not until we drove to Wilshire Boulevard did some of the panelists predict that we must be going to the Ambassador Hotel.

It was a warm, bright, sunny mid-day that brought us to the famous Ambassador Hotel. Who could ever dream that this would be our "lock-up" home for the next seven months!

As we approached the front entrance, we saw the news and TV reporters, laden with cameras and swarming the area. Our bus stopped, but we were told to remain seated. We noticed Captain Alley, head of the Security Division, out in front talking to the news reporters. The Captain arrived earlier trying to disperse them, but it was obvious that he had no success; a fact that had to be reconciled.

Captain Alley approached and boarded our bus, instructing the driver to proceed to the back area, the delivery entrance. Even there several reporters managed to scale the back fence and snap a few pictures as we jurors came out of the vehicle. The deputies escorted us through the back-tunnel passageway to the elevators up to the sixth floor. We assembled in a small recreation room off the hallway, where we sat down, trying to relax a bit, while Captain Alley gave us brief instructions on privileges and restrictions for panelists. "There will be no TV or telephones in your bedrooms," he said. However, in the evenings, after dinner, each juror was allowed a three-minute phone call, which could be intercepted by a deputy, to a spouse or family member.

In case of emergency a spouse or family member could phone the Ambassador switchboard and contact a deputy to relay the message to the panelist. No private telephone calls were allowed. For each juror's safety and welfare, no one was permitted to wander about solitarily away from the sixth floor; this rule was always strictly enforced. Deputies would be posted on 24-hour guard on the sixth floor at the entrance of both hallways and the staircase. During mealtime, assembled as a group in a secluded area, the panel would dine together in the company of one or two deputies.

Having completed the instructions, Captain Alley gathered all the room keys into a hat for a drawing selection of the rooms. It was understood that the choice rooms would be given to the ladies; and the Captain mentioned that one penthouse room was available on the seventh floor. One of the juror's spoke out that he would like that penthouse, if the women had no objections. No one objected being fully aware of that particular juror's temperament and being sincerely desirous of a congenial and peaceful commencement. The very first day I met this man, William Zamora, I knew that if he remained on the jury panel, we would have trouble and we all would have to employ diplomacy for the sake of harmony.

One of the deputies accompanied the man to inspect the seventh-floor room, but after a quick look the panelist came down and announced the room as unsuitable. Desiring to please everyone, Captain Alley conceded that the juror could have another choice; but the second selection didn't please him either. By this time the captain threw up his hands in desperation and told the man to go ahead and have his pick. And so, it was no surprise that the best sixth floor room was taken as personalities began to take shape.

After the others selected their room keys, I picked up the last remaining one to room 639. The deputies searched and inspected each room before the occupant entered and unpacked. After these harrowing preliminaries, the jurors began to settle down in their new quarters, seemingly content and carefree, many commenting on the attractive decor and pleasant environment.

A deputy announced that it was time for lunch, so all of us gathered around the elevator descending to the main floor and spacious dining room. Sitting around, getting better acquainted, we were all animated with happy chatter and optimistic spirits that mixed well with our first meal together at the elegant Ambassador.

That evening we hotel newcomers had time to relax, finish unpacking, hanging up and straightening our clothes in roomy closets and ample drawer space, and we even exchanged mattresses for firmness or softness, making ourselves feel right at home. I doubt any of us understood what we would be facing in the days, weeks and months ahead. We certainly had no inkling that we were becoming a part of one of the longest and most visible trials of the century.

Chapter Three

Six Alternate Jurors

The juror's returned to the courtroom on July 17, 1970; and Judge Older granted a request for a change of Leslie Van Houten's defense attorney from Ira Reiner to Ronald Hughes. Miss Van Houten had submitted a written petition for Mr. Reiner to be relieved and replaced by Mr. Hughes, who was Mr. Manson's attorney for a brief time. She was briefed by the Judge on Mr. Hughes's inexperience in any type of case, not to mention murder cases, but this information did not alter her decision.

[EDITOR'S NOTE: This was the juror's first introducton to the behind the scenes manipulations of the case, but they would have been completely unaware of the implications. The substitution of Attorney Ronald Hughes for Attorney Reiner was only one of the first indications of Manson's effort to control the court, his attorneys and his co-defendants. During Voir Dire, out of the presence of prospective jurors, Charles Manson wanted to ask questions directly of the jurors.

His attorney, Irving Kanarek, made a motion for Manson to be his co-counsel indicating that he should be permitted to directly speak to the jury. In pretrial motions Manson has already been denied several times the motion to represent himself. Here is the transcript of that interaction.

KANAREK: I say this because it is a very critical state of the proceedings, he has a right to effective counsel, your Honor.

COURT: Don't you think you are effective, Mr. Kanarek?

KANAREK: Yes, your honor, but he has a right. The motion is that Mr. Manson be allowed to interrogate the prospective jurors. Mr. Manson, it is his life which is at stake your Honor.

MANSON: All I would like to do, your Honor, is maybe ask two questions;

COURT: To Whom?

MANSON: To the prospective jurors, if they are going to sit in judgment on me, I should be allowed to ask a couple of questions.

COURT: As I explained to you, Mr. Manson, under our rules, when a person, a defendant, is represented by counsel, all of the matters during the trial must be handled by that counsel, except when the person takes the stand, if in fact he does take the stand, and of course no defendant can be compelled to testify. So, the answer to your question is simply the same answer that I have to give to any defendant who wants to speak when he is represented by counsel. He has to speak through his counsel.

If you have some question that you think should be asked the prospective jurors, then I suggest that you discuss these with your attorney and he can then consider those and if he feels that they should be asked then he may ask them.

MANSON: Your honor, it is a simple thing for me. If you were to talk with this man through me, it would be almost impossible to talk to that man through me.

It is like proving yesterday happened today. It would take you all day, and by then it would be tomorrow.

Now I am sure that you are wise, or you wouldn't be in this position that you are in. I don't want to lose sight of the father image. I don't wish to do this. I look at you and I am trying to accept the father image and obey, like a good child should, but there are times in a man's life when he must stand up and be a man.

Now, if I could explain to you with a motion and put in the papers and the words that you use from your books, I would, but I can't because my logic is childlike, and my vocabulary is simple.

I have many degrees of the picture that I see up IN front of me, the subliminal pictures, the picture of the father-son relationship, the picture of the people in the street, the Press, the picture of the juror's minds knowing that it is practically impossible for a juror to react tO common questions that I would put forth that wouldn't be as confusing as perhaps these gentlemen, who have esoteric teachings, and they understand things, they understand things that the layman doesn't seem to grasp.

COURT: I understand from what you say that you want to ask these questions directly, but what I am telling you, Mr. Manson, is that you are not able to do so.

MANSON: I am not able to do so?

COURT: That's right. You are not permitted.

MANSON: I am not permitted; that is better.

COURT: And your counsel will have to do the examination for you. So, if you have some questions that you feel in your own mind should be asked, then so inform Mr. Kanarek.

MANSON: Those questions come up just like the conversation here. If I had to say what I said to you through him, it would be impossible. You know that and so do I.

COURT: You have a pencil and a pad, and you can go along and make notes.

MANSON: That presents another problem. I don't write that well, and especially that fast and good. Then by the time that I tell this man something to explain to this man, the moment is lost, the thought is gone.

In order to get on top of the thought and understand the thought and to look into it and see if it is true or not true, you do it as you speak and as you judge people every day, you look into the thought, you look into the person, and you see if there is any truth there, or you see if there isn't any truth there, and you can bring that out at the second, the moment you speak with each other, and be truthful with each other, and then I can see when you are not honest with me .

This is what I wish to do, to talk to the jurors in this respect.

COURT: I am sorry, but the answer to your question is no, that the questions must be asked by your counsel.

MANSON: Then I have two alternatives. I have one alternative. No defense to employ in that direction or to be a disobedient child.

I don't wish to be a disobedient child. I am willing to accept your authority, as I have done all my life, and I am willing to if you will let me accept your authority. But allow me to stand up and be a man for once. I am not a eunuch.

COURT: I am sorry. Those are the rules. They are not special rules for you, they apply to every defendant in every case.

MANSON: The rules are that if you went to 74 and you read that book, it would send you to 103 and if you read 103, you would have to go to 99. You could travel in those books for millions of years in circles. You could travel in circles for millions of years.

It amounts to your discretion, your opinion. It amounts to what you wish to do. You could say Manson vs. so and so or you could say Robles vs. such and such. You can say the Constitution allows me to stand in the entrance to the courtroom.

Maybe, in a simple, child-like way and in a layman's sort of form of English, I wouldn't be able to speak with big words, but I could speak to be understood. I don't wish to dab in the law and try to confuse anyone with any dilatory tactics or do anything but ask a few simple tiny child-like questions that are real to me in my reality.

Now, if the meaning is leaning in these gentlemen's minds and they think on a certain level, a certain reality, I can see that and I can understand that is where their minds are and that is why they are placed as they are and why your Honor is on another level looking up above the rest of the children that are down there. I see why there is 12 seats there and I see why there is one there. I see with my awareness what is going on in the courtroom, and I see that my motion in the courtroom could bring the truth forward.

If I don't have the motion in the courtroom, then the truth is going to be distorted, it is not going to be brought forward.

Innocence or guilt, I think, is relative, as the Judge knows, as well as I know, and we all know. Guilt is not for you to decide; it is For the Man to decide himself.

You can kill me, but you can't judge me. You can bring witnesses in that dislike me and they can bear witness against me. But what it amounts to is that it doesn't amount to anything in my mind except what you let me enter into and let it amount to me. If you don't let it amount to me, then there is nothing I can do but act like a fool.

COURT: Well I hope you won't do that, Mr. Manson, because I think you would only be hurting your own case.

MANSON: My own case, sir? Your Honor, please let me say this.

This is a case I have had all my life.

There is actually nothing you can do to me.

You know, you are in a position where you can send me home, because I have lived in the penitentiary for 22 years. The penitentiary is mine just as this free world is yours.

The penitentiary belongs to me, as much as I wish it to belong to me. I understand the penitentiary. I understand the men that run the penitentiary and the people in the penitentiary far better than I do the people in your world. I don't understand your world. Your world is confusing to me. I understand your logic and I am trying to look into your justice. If you will let me. Now if you don't let me, let me say this to your Honor. My word doesn't mean much on the outside, but in the inside, it rings a long way. It rings all the way across the country in every penitentiary that you have got.

Now, I am not asking anything unreasonable. The constitution allows this. The Constitution says that I have a right to confront the witnesses and cross examine the witnesses not in an angry sort of way, because I am not mad at anyone. I am not disturbed at the jury. I am not disturbed at the court or this Judge or the district attorney. I am not mad at anyone. I am just pleading.

COURT: Well I understand what you are saying, Mr. Manson, at least some of it.

MANSON: Some of it?

COURT: The answer, unfortunately, has to be the same, the same for you and for every other defendant. Where you are represented by counsel, then you must permit counsel to conduct the trial in your behalf.

MANSON: Well, then is there any possibility that I could be dis-represented by counsel.

COURT: That you could what?

MANSON: Be unrepresented by counsel.

COURT: Well, no. That has been taken up a number of times before and the court has ruled against your request to represent yourself.

MANSON: All right. Now, I have two alternatives. I will try the first one, and I will ask my lawyer.

MANSON To Mr. Kanarek: You will not say another word in court. Let the Court do what it does. Because if you do, I will either have to direct…

After Manson lost the plea to act as his own attorney all the defendants tried to silence their attorneys. Patricia Krenwinkel tried to move attorney Fitzgerald as counsel when he refused to comply with her order for him not to question prospective jurors. They explained they don't think they should participate in the hypocrisy of an Establishment trial in which the outcome has been determined.

On Friday, July 17 in the Judge's chambers out of the hearing of the jury Leslie Van Houten made a Motion to Substitute Counsel of Record from Attorney Reiner to Ronald Hughes. Ronald Hughes had represented Charles Manson early in the case before he substituted Irving Kanarek. The Court questioned Leslie Van Houten if she was aware of a possible conflict of interest. Attorney Hughes claimed he was prepared to proceed and indicated that his understanding of the primary claim for the reason for substitution was irreconcilable differences between Leslie Van Houten between herself and Attorney Reiner in the course and tactics which he proposed and which she proposesd in the course of the trial.

The court asked attorney Hughes the following: (taken from the transcript)

THE COURT: "If you are substituted in, Mr. Hughes, are you prepared to come in and act as an attorney and not simply -the reason I am raising this question is because of your last statement.

The mere fact that an attorney, for example, if such is the fact, and I don't know if it is or not, disagrees with his client as to the conduct of the trial does not constitute an irreconcilable difference which would warrant a substitution in the middle of the trial.

The attorney is in charge of the case. It is not uncommon for attorneys and their clients to disagree as to the way a trial is handled. The function of the attorney is to provide a professional representation for the client with skill, knowledge and ability to defend a client in his own best interest. Sometimes the client is the most incapable of judging what is best for him or her.

The Court then explained to Leslie Van Houten that the implications of the fact Ronald Hughes had represented Charles Manson in the past meant that his interests in the case and hers might not exactly coincide. He was trying to show her what a conflict of interest could mean to her case. She said she understood and that she did not see any conflict of interest. Attorney Kanarek confirmed that Manson had no objection to the substitution of counsel and didn't see any conflict.

The Court explained to Charles Manson that when Ronald Hughes would become Leslie Van Houten's attorney he would owe 100 per cent allegiance to her and has no allegiance to Manson or his interests whatsoever.

The prosecution pointed out Attorney Hughes' lack of experience, which is what many people think was the concern about him. However, Van Houten insisted he become her attorney.

After further discussion but before the court ruling on the motion for substitution Attorney Reiner spoke to the court. Here is the transcript of what he said:

REINER: Mr. Hughes stated that there appeared to be certain irreconcilable differences between my self and Miss Van Houten, and I suppose that that is true. Miss Van Houten has indicated in open court that it is her desire that I remain mute, that I not ask questions on Voir Dire, that I not exercise preemptory challenges, and presumably continue to remain mute. It is my view of competent and ethical practice that I cannot accept such instruction I indicated to her that I cannot and would not accept such instruction. She feels very strongly that that is what she wants and for that reason there is a difference between Miss Van Houten and myself, and it is an irreconcilable difference.

Ira Reiner was a young defense attorney at the time of the Manson trial trying to help Leslie Van Houten, but she chose to follow Manson's directives to her ultimate downfall. It is interesting to note that Ira Reiner went on to have an illustrious career ultimately becoming District Attorney from 1984-1992. He prosecuted high profile cases such as that of murderer Richard Ramirez, the police arrest against Rodney King and the McMartin pre-school trial.

After Reiner made his statement about why he was dismissed, the Court asked Ronald Hughes if he planned putting on a defense and he said he was. Then Leslie Van Houten revealed what was likely the motive behind her desire to change counsel.

VAN HOUTEN: I was just going to say that Mr. Reiner is in one way, he is dividing the defense up, and that is the difference.
THE COURT: I don't understand what you mean? What do you mean, dividing the defense up?
VAN HOUTEN: Well, he says the difference was because I asked him to be quiet, you know. That is just one part of it. He is like dividing up the defense.

Then Manson revealed the agenda of the substitute of counsel for the defendants by telling the court: "If all the attorneys are happy together, then they can offer a better defense in front of the Judge in the court, that is the primary reason."

It appears with the benefit of hindsight that this is how Manson was trying to take charge of the case to assure none of the co-defendants would implicate him in any way. He was indeed, as many suspected, guiding them from behind the scenes.]

❖   ❖   ❖

Our daily routine as panelists began at about 6 a.m. when the deputy sounded reveille by knocking at our Ambassador Hotel room doors. An hour later all jurors, assembled in the hallway ready to go down to breakfast, accompanied by at least two deputies. By 8:30 a.m. all of us were to be in the courtroom as court was in session at 9 a.m. A 15-minute rest time was at 10:30 am. At noon, the lunch hour, the panel and at minimum, two deputies boarded the sheriff's bus that took us to a downtown restaurant. The deputies arranged a variety of dining places, most frequently the Hilton Hotel coffee shop.

The Court session resumed at 1:30 p.m. until a 4:30 p.m. adjournment, with a 15-minute rest. Dinner for the panel at the Ambassador varied from 7 p.m. to later, depending upon each day's number of hotel guests and outside patrons. The table space and waitress service were available for the jurors after the rush time. Recreation after dinner was limited. There was TV watching in the hallway or recreation room (a nearby deputy always switching off the news), playing cards, and reading (with a bailiff carefully removing Manson trial stories and pictures from the daily newspaper in the recreation room). Some panelists played scrabble, knit, painted, sewed, and strummed guitar or banjo. Later as sequestration dragged on, bowling enthusiasts organized a team for a weekly practice game in an off-the-beaten-path bowling alley, chaperoned by deputies.

During the long warm summer months, I and other jurors shared the refreshment and exercise of swimming in the enclosed Ambassador courtyard. Another outlet to release tension was paddle ball tennis, played mostly by the male jurors. Occasional treats were escorted evening walks on Wilshire Boulevard or side streets. Saturday evening an old movie film was usually shown in the recreation room.

As the trial proceeded, panelists with their spouses and family members enjoyed weekend visits. What a consolation and joy for my wife and me to see each other, even for that short time. Together, we attended Wilshire Boulevard's St. Basil Church Sunday worship and received Communion. The deputies were so willing to accompany jurors to church services. Weekend outings for the panelists were planned and arranged by the sheriff's deputies who were trying to ease the monotony of lengthy sequestration.

I can't help mentioning the stupendous work of the deputies. There were times when one must have the patience of a saint and the wisdom of Solomon in endeavoring to please everyone.

Daily courtroom attendance continued for the jurors, patiently awaiting the final selection of the six alternates. While Judge Older and the attorneys conducted business as usual in the chambers with appointment of prospective alternates, a young lady (named Linda if I remember correctly) was selected for the panel and was seated next to me in the jury box. Linda was enthralled with the honor of being an alternate juror. She promptly earmarked me to be her fatherly guide. Of an amiable, generous spirit, she quickly made friends with everyone. Linda offered her help to shop for the sequestered. So, we made our list of needed toilet articles and submitted our money for the purchases to be negotiated by Linda. However, one morning Judge Older and the attorneys stepped into the courtroom and informed Linda that she was excused.

On the spot she emptied her purse and handed over money and shopping lists to me. Embarrassed, I raised a protesting hand, as if an embargo signal for self-defense, to halt the avalanche; but she kept dumping everything into my lap. I must have looked like some sort of lottery collector! The Judge and attorneys eyed me quizzically for little did they suspect that Linda was already the juror's self-appointed purchasing agent!

Finally, on July 21, after approximately five and one-half weeks of jury selection the six alternate jurors were sworn in; Mr. Robert R. Douglass 34, of Arcadia, a civilian employee for the U.S. Army Corps of Engineers, Mr. John N. Ellis 25, a General Telephone Company employee, Miss Frances Chasen, a retired Civil Service employee, Mrs. Victoria Kampman, a housewife, Mr. Larry D. Sheely, who worked for Pacific Telephone Co, and Mr. Kenneth Daut Jr. of West Los Angeles, a State Division of Highway employee. Before court adjourned for the day, Judge Older set 9:45 a.m. on July 24 to hear the first of the opening statements; 38 days after the trial began.

CHAPTER FOUR

EMOTIONS OF A JUROR'S WIFE

The following words came from my wife Helen:

Before continuing the jurors' secluded life and experiences, I wish to tell a little of what it was like behind the scenes, for the wife at home. My life and feelings were affected, as I'm sure were those of the other wives, husbands, and family members, by making unexpected adjustments and facing personal problems.

That unpredictable and painful July 15 dawned upon me again as I reminisced about that awful departure of my husband from our home. I tried to be brave, not wishing to upset him; holding back my emotions. But as soon as he walked away, I recoiled into our apartment in grief. In my solitude, feelings spilled over. Weeping didn't do much; just bequeathed red eyes, a headache, and one big heavy heart. So, I vigorously plunged into household chores, dish washing, and apartment tidying. Then I tackled the outdoor work, garden sprinkling, yard weeding, and carport cleaning. Work was a blessing, good for the body and soul, helping to release tension and emotions.

But the nights were unbearable. Once inside with the doors and windows locked, I felt safe enough, somehow right from the start. God spared me fearful anxiety. But loneliness was my greatest ordeal, accustomed as I was to my husband's presence giving me a sense of happiness and security.

For the first time, I realized how empty an apartment can be. Everything loses its glow. I found eating alone distressing. My appetite faded; soon I almost had to force myself to bother preparing balanced meals. To help create a happier atmosphere, I tuned in soft radio music. Listening to the news was not good company. Manson trial reports were dismal; court procedures moved at a snail's pace; the whole affair was predicted to stretch into months. Although at times I felt uneasy because of the nature of these bizarre crimes, luckily, I never reached the point of distress.

During the daytime whenever I met tenants, conversation invariably focused upon the Manson case. Well intentioned, everyone had some comment; how can I manage alone? Aren't I afraid? Why did my husband get "roped in" for a trial to be sequestered for months? Isn't he smart enough not to be in such a predicament?

They really didn't intend any harm in airing their thoughts and didn't reflect anything that would upset me. I tried to be cheerful, but worries began to gnaw at me; perhaps my husband could have avoided this hearing if he really tried. Maybe he was overlooking me, letting me down, taking me for granted. This attitude was my downfall. I didn't immediately squelch this egotism, and so it grew. The old devil was at play; he had his victim. But whenever I grew too depressed, I picked up my prayer beads, sat in my rocker, and prayed the 15 rosary decades.

Several months passed before I conquered my mental stress, caused right from the beginning because I did not wholeheartedly accept God's will. What a mistake that was! It was incredible how my eyes finally opened to the truth. I forgot myself and the crisis passed!

Knowing so well my husband and his character, I knew a good man was chosen for the jury panel. He is a man of tolerance and conscientiousness, amiable and unassuming, with a warm personality and a charm for quickly acquiring friends and setting them at ease. Women especially found an attraction in his chivalrous gallantry.

He was a devoted husband and father, resulting in a happy well-knit understanding family. With sorrow and pity, I reflected upon families torn apart because of lacking love, respect, interest and discipline. Good homes are the heart of a good society and it's the parents who must set examples of Christian attitudes to enrich family life.

CHAPTER FIVE

OPENING STATEMENTS

That eventful July 24, 1970 day finally dawned under a warm, sunny yet overcast, smoggy Los Angeles sky, when 12 jurors and 6 alternate jurors with anticipation and suspense filed into the jury box in department 104.

Deputy district attorney Vincent Bugliosi delivered his opening statement in the murder trial of Charles Manson and his three female "family" accomplices. The prosecutor explained how the 35-year old hippie type leader of the cult "family" derived his scriptural views about a black versus white uprising from the "Book of Revelation," the *Bible's* last book, and from songs from the Beatles, a famous English singing group; basing his beliefs on the Bible and the Beatles. Charlie thought that the murders of actress Sharon Tate, Steven Parent, Jay Sebring, Abigail Folger, Wojciech Frykowski, Leno and Rosemary La Bianca and an unborn child would trigger a

Prosecutor Vincent Bugliosi

race war. Mr. Bugliosi alleged that the motives behind the August 8 and 9, 1969 slaughter rampages were Mr. Manson's passion for violent death and anti-establishment ideas.

The prosecutor was confident that evidence would show the accused fanatical obsession with "Helter Skelter," a term borrowed from the Beatles, of whom Charlie was an avid fan convinced that the singers spoke to him through their lyrics; and the leader informed his followers that he found complete support for his philosophies in the Beatles sung words.

Consequently, Mr. Manson hated black people as well as the white establishment, members of which he labeled "pigs." "Pig" was printed in blood on the outside front door of the Tate estate; "Death to Pigs," "Helter Skelter" and "Rise" was emblazoned in blood inside the La Bianca home.

Prosecuting attorney Vincent Bugliosi was our first introduction to the case when he addressed us with his lengthy opening statement. He explained what the evidence would show and how each witness represented the "bricks" that would build their case. He further explained that the only task for the prosecution was to prove beyond a reasonable doubt that those accused committed the crimes for which they are charged. There is no requirement that they show motive. However, he said "Where we have evidence of motive, we naturally offer it, since if one has a motive for a murder, it is very powerful circumstantial evidence that it was he who committed the murder."

At the end of his opening statement, Mr. Bugliosi urged us to take notes during the trial. This was something I had already started. He said without notes it would be an impossible task to recollect even the highlights of each witness's testimony much less the details.

I took his suggestion to heart and with each witness and observation I took notes on what I thought was important to remember. This was what I would bring with me into the jury room at the time we were tasked with deliberation.

I took note of the following from Mr. Bugliosi's opening remarks.

Mr. Bugliosi alleged that one of Mr. Manson's principal murder motives was to ignite "Helter Skelter," in other words, to start the black-white revolution, by making it appear that Negroes killed the five Tate residence victims and Mr. and Mrs. Leno La Bianca, then the white community would turn against the black populace, ultimately leading to civil war.

[EDITOR'S NOTE: Negro was an archaic reference of the times. African American people were referred to as black, negro or colored interchangeably without necessarily any racist intent.]

◆ ◆ ◆

The prosecutor continued, that the accused envisioned the victorious colored group murdering and destroying the entire white race, with the exception of Charlie and his followers, who would escape from "Helter Skelter" by living in the desert's "bottomless pit," a place culled from the "Book of Revelation."

Attorney Bugliosi then claimed that Charlie pictured the blacks, unable to handle the reins to the surviving whites, would surrender power to the cult leader and his "family." The prosecutor finished with a description of the accused; "He is a man with a satanic mind, who at times, had the infinite humility to call himself Jesus Christ."

Charles Manson appeared in court with an inch high X cut into his forehead with a razor blade, his way of speaking for himself, as we jurors learned later, his method of alleging, "No man or lawyer is speaking for me; I speak for myself; I am not allowed to speak with words, so I have spoken with the mark that I will be wearing on my forehead."

[EDITOR'S NOTE: In Bugliosi's closing remarks he adds a possible motive for the X cut into Charles Manson's forehead which supports a theory we espouse in the book I co-authored with Dianne Lake, *Member of the Family: My Story of Charles Manson, Life Inside his Cult, and the Darkness that Ended the Sixties* (William Morrow, 2017) Bugliosi stated, "Incidentally, Revelation 9, you will be reading it back in the jury room, speaks of locusts going out into the world and destroying everything, including men who do not have a mark on their foreheads. So maybe Charlie put that X on his forehead to save himself from the locusts."

After examining Dianne Lake's time with Manson, his constant espousal of his philosophy and the need for his family to hide in the bottomless pit in the desert, we surmised that his mark was because he believed in his own distorted view of the meaning of "Revelations." We believe he was marking himself to survive a coming revolution. There are many people who firmly believe Manson was just conning people and never really bought into the concept of the race war and coming apocalypse. However, Dianne Lake lived with Manson and the family almost from the beginning. Although she was not present for the murders, she was present at the Gresham Street house when Manson insisted everyone listen to the Beatle's White Album over and over, backwards and frontwards. It was just a theory we surmised so I was grateful to have found this statement by Bugliosi in the transcripts digitized by cielodrive.com.]

❖   ❖   ❖

The first witness called by the prosecutor was Paul J. Tate (Witness number one) the father of the slain actress who identified himself as a retired Army Intelligence Lt. Colonel and stated he was the father of Sharon Tate. The goateed, mustachioed father identified for the prosecutor, photographs of his daughter Sharon Tate, Jay Sebring, Wojciech Frykowski, Abigail Folger and the Tate residence. Defense attorney Shinn asked about Mr. Tate's relationships with Jay Sebring, Wojciech Frykowski and Abigail Folger. Shinn asked if he had ever seen them under the influence of drugs or alcohol. Mr. Tate answered, "Never." The answer was "stricken" per an objection by Mr.

Paul Tate

Stovitz. Mr. Kanarek did make a motion at the very beginning to exclude witnesses which was denied. Paul Tate was excused, subject to recall.

Following Mr. Tate to the witness stand was Wilfred Parent, father of Steven Parent, one of the Tate home victims (Witness number two). He said he was a construction superintendent and identified his son in a photo with his girlfriend (where he broke down and cried). He also identified the car that his son drove the day he was murdered. He testified his son was employed at Jonas-Miller Stereo on Wilshire Boulevard near Beverly Hills and had been interested in hi fi and stereos since he was four or five years old.

The next witness was Winifred Chapman, the housekeeper who discovered the bodies at the 10050 Cielo drive residence (Witness number three).

Winifred Chapman

She stated that when she arrived at the gate of the Tate residence, she noticed the wires (that were cut).

She stated she went into the house from the back door and found the bodies, blood and everything else. She said she ran out of the house screaming "Murder, death, bodies, blood" to a neighbor's house, Jim Asin; the neighbor made the phone call to the Police and they waited for their arrival.

She also identified the house and the front door (with the words "Pig") from photographs. The prosecutor also questioned her about the washing of the two doors before the murders took place.

Irving Kanarek asked the witness if she had ever seen Charles Manson before this court appearance. She answered, "I have not."

The last witness of the day was William Garretson (Witness number four), a 19-year -old caretaker for the Tate estate who lived in the Guesthouse at 10050 Cielo Drive and was taken into custody the morning after the murders and released three days later. Garretson received a visitor about 11:45 p.m. on August 8. Steven Parent came by to see if William wanted to buy a radio, he had brought with him. William didn't buy it. Steven Parent then left the guesthouse. Garretson said later he tried to make a phone call around dawn, but the line was dead. He stated that in the morning two policeman showed up at his guesthouse at the Tate residence. "They had guns drawn and they kicked in my door."

One policeman dragged him onto the patio on his stomach. He asked, "What's wrong?" Then he was shown the two bodies on the front lawn and the one in the car.

Mr. Garretson identified from photo exhibits presented by the prosecution; the guesthouse, Abigail Folger's car, Jay Sebring, Steven Parent, the clock radio on the passenger side of Steven Parent's car and the living room inside the guesthouse and a few photos of the residence.

He stated he was employed by Rudi Altobelli, explained his duties there and described what he did the day and night of the murders. He said he heard nothing the night of the murders, no screams, no gunshots and stated he was writing letters and playing his stereo.

Defense attorney, Mr. Fitzgerald cross-examined the witness and asked him about his arrest and the police officers. Mr. Fitzgerald asked about any of the dogs barking that night. The witness said it was not unusual for the dogs to bark. He again stated that he heard nothing that night. He only awoke to one of the dogs barking and saw a police officer pointing a rifle at him in the patio. Mr. Fitzgerald also asked who lived at the main residence, were there frequent visitors and frequent parties held there.

The witness stated who lived there, said there weren't many visitors and there was one party in June that he remembered. Mr. Garretson was looking very pale and was excused but would be recalled.

Court adjourned and the July 25 weekend began, affording the first family reunion for jurors since sequestration. Spouses and family members, upon arrival at the Ambassador, were admonished and signed statements not to mention the Manson trial to the jurors.

My wife arrived Saturday afternoon and departed the following day. For us it was a joyous occasion attending Sunday morning services at St. Basil Church, walking distance away on Wilshire Boulevard, and once again eating breakfast and lunch together.

Parking and food at the hotel were paid individually by each of our allowed visitors. Saturday evening some of us viewed an old-time movie on a small screen in the recreation room; some tried their hand at playing cards, some just relaxed and chatted. Departure deadline for all our guests was Sunday at 9 p.m.

CHAPTER SIX

THE HORROR OF THOSE NIGHTS

Court reopened Monday, July 27, the jurors refreshed and alert after a relaxing weekend at the Ambassador.

The first witness recalled to the stand for cross examination was William Garretson, Tate caretaker, who declared how he met Mr. and Mrs. Polanski (Roman Polanski & Sharon Tate) at a June 1969 party in their home. Living in the guest house, he testified that he neither saw nor heard anything indicating murders occurring that fatal night, even though at 10 P.M. he walked past the Tate residence at a distance of about 25 to 30 yards away. Screams and gunshots probably were engulfed by stereo music that he played, the distance being about 35 yards from his guest house to the swimming pool (the scene of Miss Folger's death).

The second witness was Frank Guerrero (Witness number five), a house painter, who testified that he worked at the Tate lodging, by painting the nursery, from Wednesday August 7, 1969, until the following afternoon, at which time all was in order at the home with window screens secure and intact.

He told of who was at the residence when he finished the job for the day August 8. He identified the Tate residence dining room window and screen in a photo exhibit. He stated that when he left that day the screen was on the window with no slit in it. In the photo exhibit he was asked to identify the nursery room.

Mr. Fitzgerald cross examined the witness. He asked the witness about the screen, the days that he worked at the Tate residence, and asked about the visitors at the Tate residence and asked if he had been introduced to them.

Mr. Shinn also cross examined. He asked, "you stated there was a cut in the screen?" The answer was, "no sir."

Mr. Shinn also asked about his employer, if he worked alone those days at the Tate residence (the witness stated he worked alone) and if he had any conversations with the guests on those days. His answer was "no."

The third witness for the day was Tom Vargas (Witness number six), a gardener, a five-year employee (employed by Rudolph Altobelli) at the Tate residence, who testified that on August 8 (after arriving there between 4:30 and 5:30 p.m.) he signed for a delivery (of a trunk) at the back gate, the delivery was deposited at the front door. He identified the trunk (actually two) in a photo exhibit. He stated he saw Abigail Folger in a yellow car coming down the driveway when he was driving up. He also saw Wojciech Frykowski leaving in his car. He was asked about the telephone wires and stated there was nothing unusual. He stated he also saw Mrs. Tate, Bill Garretson, his brother Dave Martinez (also employed there) and Mrs. Chapman that day. He left the premises at 6:30 p.m. with everything in order.

The fourth witness was Dennis Hearst (Witness number seven), a Bank of America employee, a UCLA student and former bicycle shop employee (at his father's shop Hans Ohrt Bicycles). He said that he made a bicycle delivery (exchanged one bicycle for the other in the garage) for Miss Folger at the Tate homestead on August 8 about 7:00 p.m. He said he conversed with Jay Sebring about putting the bicycle in the garage but did not see Abigail Folger. He identified a photo exhibit of the garage.

Defense attorney Shinn cross-examined the witness. He asked about the conversation with Jay Sebring. Shinn asked if he had anything in his hands. The witness replied it was a green bottle but couldn't say what was in it. Shinn asked if he could smell Jay Sebring's breath and if he appeared to be under the influence of alcohol or narcotics.

"No" the witness answered to both questions. The witness stated he did not notice anything unusual when he left. Shinn asked about the telephone wires.

The witness stated that he drove over a pressure plate when leaving but didn't look for any overhead wires and that everything looked okay from what he could see.

Shinn said that there could have been wires above you that were perhaps cut, which maybe you did not see, might that not be correct?

The witness answered, "It is possible." The witness left the Tate residence at 7:20 p.m. on that evening before the murders.

In the afternoon court session at 2 p.m. the Prosecution main witness, Mrs. Linda Kasabian, 21-year-old wife and mother of two children, one aged two and one-half years and the other four months, took the stand and began her tale of two nights of terror when actress Sharon Tate and six others were slain. (Witness number 8)

But before she was able to testify many disruptions took place.

Mr. Bugliosi called Linda Kasabian to the stand.

Mr. Kanarek's words were; "Object, your Honor, on the grounds this witness is incompetent, and she is insane."

Mr. Bugliosi asked to strike that, and he asked the Court to find Mr. Kanarek in contempt of court for gross misconduct stating that this is unbelievable on his part.

Mr. Fitzgerald chimed in with, "This witness is incompetent to testify as the result of unsoundness, and we are willing to make an offer of proof in that respect."

Kanarek also made a motion for a mistrial. Mr. Shinn chimed in. We were beginning to see disruptions that would become the norm during the trial. I had nothing from which to compare it. For all I knew, all trials were filled with the theatrics that would become common for our experience.

[EDITOR'S NOTE: Right from the start there was controversy regarding the testimony of Linda Kasabian. She had been named as a defendant and was said to be a prosecution witness. Apparently, the defense wanted her to be named as either a defendant or a witness so they could question her as part of discovery. The defense also wanted to have her appear along with the other defendants during all aspects of the trial which would have put her with Manson. Up until the day of her appearance she had been held in Sybil Brand prison.

According to the transcript, before her arrival into the courtroom she had been sent from the prison in what Bugliosi described as a large old maternity outfit as she had given birth while in prison. Out of the hearing of the jury, he asked the court to wait until they could bring over a proper dress for her. He wanted her to "look halfway decent when she walks into the courtroom to testify." The court allowed it.

After Kanarek's many objections the lawyers approached the bench and the prosecution said that Kanarek should not have made the statement about Linda Kasabian's insanity in front of the jury in open court. The defense was claiming it wanted a hearing on Kasabian's competency and that it would bring witnesses such as Catherine Share, and others to show Kasabian used LSD over an extensive period of time and "this would make her of unsound mind, mentally ill, insane and unable to differentiate between "truth and falsity, right and wrong, good or bad, fantasy and reality, and incapable of expressing herself concerning the matter so as to be understood." The Judge told Kanarek, "Your conduct is outrageous." The Judge agreed the matter should not have been brought up in front of the jury.]

◆   ◆   ◆

Finally, with a lot commotion put aside, Judge Older allowed the witness to testify.

The State's main witness has been charged with seven counts of murder and one count of conspiracy to commit murder. District Attorney Bugliosi established that Mrs. Kasabian would be granted immunity for testifying if she told the truth, the whole truth, and nothing but the truth about the murders and motives.

Linda Kasabian

Mrs. Kasabian during May of 1969, in Los Angeles returned to her husband Robert, who rejected her, resulting in a separation. Living in a truck with friends, she met Catherine Share, a Manson family member called "Gypsy," who invited Linda to come to the Spahn Movie Ranch in Chatsworth, California, to see a man who would change her life. Linda Kasabian testified that July 4, 1969, she went to live on the Ranch, the next day she met Charles Manson and other "family" members, numbering about 20 and being mostly females. The Head of the "family" was Charlie, who dictated to everyone what to do.

Court was in session the following day, Tuesday, July 28. During the opening statement and testimony of the main witness Mrs. Kasabian, Mr. Manson's defense attorney Mr. Kanarek bombarded court procedure with incessant objections and interruptions. I was amazed by Judge Older's patience and composure during these continuing disturbances and delaying tactics. We jurors had to grit our teeth at times to restrain our uneasiness and disapproval.

Linda resumed her testimony describing the lifestyle of cultist Mr. Manson and his "family." He made love to her. He impressed Linda with his diagnosis of her father hang-up; she admitted hating her stepfather.

Mrs. Kasabian declared that Mr. Manson planned a remote, camouflaged camp site behind the Spahn Ranch. Fearing that the "clan family" had been spotted, he ordered a walkie-talkie system set-up from the camp to the road's end, the wiring being camouflaged.

A second camping site was two or three miles down the road with equipment and dune buggy parts. All the "family" took turns guarding the camp sites. Charlie instructed the girls to hang on trees little "witchy" objects, like weeds, wires, branches and rocks, markings that would help in the dark to show the way from one camp to the other. The cultist called his men and women followers witches. He indoctrinated the girls to make love to male visitors at the Ranch, enticing them to join the "family"; if they refused, enticers were to cease wooing and begin ignoring them.

The vegetarian "family" members diet depended on garbage runs to the back of supermarkets and restaurants for discarded food, cleaned and cooked by the girls. The men worked on dune buggies, rugged jeep type vehicles.

Mrs. Kasabian testified to sexual orgies at the main camp site by Manson "family" members, and visitors at the Ranch on a night in mid-July 1969. Believing and feeling called by the Beatles, Charlie, during his conversations with Linda would ask, "Don't you know who I am?" Returning from a trip on August 8, he mentioned that it was time for "Helter Skelter," for the cult leader gloated that the white and colored races were not in harmony. The night of August 8, Mr. Manson told Mrs. Kasabian to equip herself with a change of clothing, a knife, and her driver's license and accompany Charles (Tex) Watson, Susan Atkins and Patricia Krenwinkel. Before departing with changes of clothes, one license, three knives, and one gun, the foursome was instructed by the ringleader to dress in black, "to do what he told them to do," and to leave a sign, "something witchy."]

[EDITOR'S NOTE: There are persistent questions remaining until this day whether attorney Bugliosi created the theory of Helter Skelter. Here is an excerpt of the transcript which corroborates other testimony regarding Manson's mindset at the time, which supports the idea that he believed the Beatles were giving him coded messages through their music.

Linda Kasabian's testimony was very influential in the ultimate decision made by the jury. Although Mr. Tubick's notes were comprehensive we decided to include some additional explanation and direct excerpts from Kasabian's testimony taken from the transcript. For example, as Linda Kasabian resumed testimony about the first time she met Charles Manson, Kanarek objected when Kasabian stated Manson made love to her. He then moved for a mistrial claiming her statement that they made love impugned the integrity, the moral integrity, of Mr. Manson by this allegation of conduct. The Court denied the motion. Kanarek tried continuously to disrupt and prevent Kasabian from telling her story in any consistent manner that could make sense to a jury. From the transcript:

KASABIAN: She told me that there was a beautiful man that we had all been waiting for, and that he had been in jail for quite a number of years, that the establishment..."

The court, after argument at the bench from Kanarek that Manson's name should not be sullied by referring to jail, told the jury to disregard Kasabian's comment about anyone spending any time in jail.

BUGLIOSI: Would you please relate your first meeting with Mr. Manson.
KASABIAN: Actually, it was the next day, it was not at night, it was the afternoon.
BUGLIOSI: That would be July 5th then?
KASABIAN: Right, and he was up and back at the Ranch, in a cluster of trees, and he was working on a dune buggy, and there was a group of girls with him, Brenda and Snake, and Gypsy and Barry and Tapia, who were with me...

Here is a sampling of how Kanarek kept interrupting Kasabian's testimony particularly when there was anything considered potentially damaging. (Transcripts Page 4835)

BUGLIOSI: You mentioned earlier, Linda, about a family. Is that what the people were called out at the Spahn Ranch?
KASABIAN: Yes.
KANAREK: Objection on the grounds it is assuming facts not in evidence. There is

no evidence of any family. What they are called is hearsay, your Honor.

COURT: Mr. Kanarek, I told you before I just want the motion or the objection and grounds without the argument.

KANAREK: And I respectfully ask the Court to ask the witness—

COURT: Sit down, sir.

KANAREK: --not to respond.

COURT: Sit down, sir. Delay your answer, Mrs. Kasabian, to permit counsel to object.

BUGLIOSI: So, the group is called the Family, is that correct?

KANAREK: I object, your Honor, leading and suggestive, hearsay and a conclusion.

BUGLIOSI: She already testified to it, your Honor.

COURT: Overruled.

BUGLIOSI: The group was called the Family, Linda?

KANAREK: I object, leading and suggestive, calling for hearsay.

COURT: Overruled.

KASABIAN: Yes.

BUGLIOSI: Did you become a member of the Family?

KASABIAN: Yes.

After further questions and objections Kasabian answered:

KASABIAN: We lived together as one Family, as a Family who lives together, a mother and a father and children but we were just all one, and Charlie was the head. There were maybe 20 that stayed there all the time and there were few coming in and out.

Kanarek objected vehemently to Kasabian's testimony about a particular group sex event and was told by the court not to interrupt the answer. It is not surprising Herman Tubick did not include further details of this testimony in his narrative description in the book. 1970 was a time when there was a clear distinction between segments of society that had strict moral standards and those who were exploring free love and the sexual revolution. The birth control pill had been introduced in the 1960s, but it was just the beginning of sexual exploration outside the strict boundaries of heterosexual marriage. This was before the movie "Deep Throat," with a voluntary X rating, became the topic of late-night television. Mr. Tubick was a devout Catholic with two daughters who had chosen the Convent. It might have been unseemly at the time for him to have taken notes of this testimony. It was likely difficult to hear. However, the scene she described is an indication of the control and intimidation Charles Manson used. It is also an example of Manson requiring his followers to act in a way that could be considered criminal, in this case an act of rape.

KASABIAN: "She was fairly young, I'd say maybe 16, and she was very shy and very withdrawn, and I remember she was laying in the middle of the room, and Charlie took her clothes off and started making love to her and kissing her and, you know, and she was really rejecting him and, you know, trying to push him off, and he just sort of pushed her back down and kissed her. And at one point she bit him on the shoulder, and he hit her in the face, and then she just sort of let go and got behind it, or whatever.

Then he told Bobby Beausoleil to make love to her and he told everybody to touch her and to kiss her and to make love to her. And everybody did." Transcript page 4929

Here is some additional testimony from the transcript to expand upon Mr. Tubick's notes that was relevant to the ultimate determination of guilt:

BUGLIOSI: Did Charles Manson ever talk to you about the Beatles?
KASABIAN: Yes.
KANAREK: Immaterial, your Honor.
COURT: Overruled.
BUGLIOSI: What did he say to you?
KANAREK: Object on the grounds of hearsay, conclusion, foundation—improper foundation as to who was present, the time when it occurred.
COURT: Place?
KANAREK: Place, right. Thank you, your Honor.
COURT: Overruled.
KASABIAN: Yes. There was a certain passage in one song where he said that he thought he heard or he did hear, I am not sure if it was thought or whatever-that the Beatles were calling, saying, "Charlie, Charlie, send us a telegram" or "put out a song," or something. I can't exactly remember what it was. But yes, he felt that the Beatles were calling him.
BUGLIOSI: Did he say anything about the government?
KASABIAN: Yes, he did. He was referring to a certain song. (Kanarek raised the same objection and was overruled)He was referring to a certain song that John Lennon sings about Christ, you know, *it ain't easy, how hard it is going to be, they are going to crucify me.*

And he said, Charlie said, that they are not going to crucify him this time like they did last time. That he is going to go and hide in the hole. And that John Lennon, through this song, is programming the people, the establishment people, to crucify him.

Although there has never been a clear diagnosis of Charles Manson's pathology, it is arguable he had a "Messiah Complex," in addition to an assumption that he might have been a psychopath, although the term was not part of the common diagnosis at the time. Manson was likely a type of cognitive psychopath. He could assess anyone's need, make them believe he was the solution, but he did not have the empathy to really care. As is apparent by his attempt at control during the trial, he professed to love his "girls," but it was clear he used them to exonerate himself. He had no real concern about what would happen to them. As with most psychopaths he used his charm and manipulation of others emotions to suit his needs.

Linda Kasabian's testimony as found in the transcript page 4943, seems to support the messiah complex and the theory that he truly believed what he told his followers, thus lending credence to the motive behind the crimes. A messiah complex is not a clinical term, or a diagnosis listed in Manual of recognized mental illnesses. However, it is associated with such things as delusions of grandeur, the extreme manic side of bi-polar disorder and schizophrenia. If it is combined with such things as narcissism and the traits of a psychopath, it leads to disaster. Hitler was said to have had a messiah complex. Manson was highly charismatic and if you assume, he believed in the delusion, it would have been more likely for his followers to believe in it as well.

Bugliosi questioned Linda Kasabian about Manson's concern about the Black Panthers.

BUGLIOSI: Did Mr. Manson ever say anything about protecting the children from anyone?

Kanarek objected, was overruled and for some reason Manson asked the Judge if he could object to his lawyer's objections.

KASABIAN: Yes. He wanted us to keep the children out of sight. In other words, not to let them walk around in front of the ranch.
BUGLIOSI: Why did he say that?

KASABIAN: We were being watched. He told us we were being watched by the Black Panthers.

Kanarek continued to object and was told not to interrupt.

BUGLIOSI: Did he say what the Black Panthers might do with the children?

KASABIAN: Well, the Black Panthers hate white people, and these were our children, from us, and that they probably would kidnap them or kill them or whatever.

BUGLIOSI: Did Mr. Manson ever have a conversation with you in which he said that the Panthers might have some designs on the adult members of the Family?

(Numerous objections by Kanarek, overruled).

KASABIAN: Yes. He said that we were being watched and that back people would come to the Ranch at the weekends and take the horses out and go up into the hills behind the Ranch, and they probably-he thought-may have the setup of the Ranch and that we were supposed to keep out of sight during the night, that is why we had to wear black clothing and we had guards.

(Kanarek objects).

KASABIAN: At nighttime there would be one or two men with guns walking around the Ranch.

BUGLIOSI: Did Mr. Manson indicate to you why he thought Black Panthers were coming out there to rent horses?

KASABIAN: Well, they knew that we were super-aware, much more than other white people, and they knew we knew about them and that they were eventually going to take over, his whole philosophy on the black people; that they wanted to do away with us because apparently they knew that we were going to save the white race or go out to the hole in the desert. (4961)

As a typical cult leader, Manson convinced his followers that they were-somehow "chosen" or superior and meant for a higher purpose. In this case, the reference was they were "more aware." Bugliosi asked Linda Kasabian what Manson had said to her about Helter Skelter and she defined it. He then asked

:

BUGLIOSI: Did he say who was going to start Helter Skelter?

KASABIAN: Blackie. He was telling us about his trip up in Big Sur and that the people were really not together, they were just off on their little trips, and they just were not getting together. So, he came out and said, "Now is the time for Helter Skelter."]

Chapter Seven

Linda Kasabian's Testimony About the Crimes

Not told the destination, Linda, driver of the car, owned by ranch-hand John Schwarz Jr., thought the drive would be a creepy-crawl mission, entering people's houses and taking things, as though actually belonging to the invaders since everything originally belongs to everyone. Tex gave Linda driving directions, resulting in about an hour's ride from the Ranch and reaching a hill-top house at around midnight. Tex told her to stop the car. He got out, climbed the telephone pole, and cut the electric wires. Then the wanderers drove to the bottom of the hill and climbed over a fence. Auto headlights approached. Tex cautioned the girls to move back down into the bushes.

At this point of the testimony, Mrs. Kasabian's composure began to shatter, words escaping in a rush. With tears and anguish, the witness continued her account.

The auto stopped in front of the prowlers. Tex jumped forward grasping the gun, which he thrust at the driver's head. The man shrieked, "Please don't hurt me; I won't do anything." But unhesitatingly the culprit shot his prey four times. The driver slumped over the seat, and Tex turned off the engine. Then the foursome walked towards the ranch-style house. Tex told Linda to search the back of the home for open windows or doors. Returning from her futile investigation, she saw him cutting a screen and was directed to remain outside as a look-out. A few minutes elapsed when Linda heard a man scream, "No, no, please!"

The witness sobbed, attempting to speak; "It was horrible, terrible!" She was at a loss for words to express the agony in the piercing screams of men and women pleading for their lives.

Linda said she felt that the bedlam would never end. She ran back towards the dwelling, hoping that the terror would stop. She knew people were being slaughtered. A man, Wojciech Frykowski, staggered out the front door, blood streaming down his face, his eyes meeting hers for a split moment. Linda cried, "Oh God! I am so sorry; please make it stop!"

Then the man slumped over and fell to the ground. Susan (Sadie) Atkins dashed out of the house and Linda shouted, "Sadie, please make it stop!"

"It's too late" blurted Sadie, who added "I lost my knife." Then Sadie asked for Linda's knife and disappeared back into the edifice. Now wounded, Frykowski was up, trying desperately to escape, but Tex sprung upon him and they struggled. Again, and again the doomed man's head was battered by a pistol butt and his body slashed by the knife blade. Shrieks filled the night air. Amid the rampage Linda glimpsed a running girl, Abigail Folger, chased by Patricia (Katie) Krenwinkel with an upraised knife. Linda also ran, away to the car at the bottom of the hill.

The entire court was silent as time stood still. Impressions of horror permeated the room. Seconds later, press reporters jumped to their feet and dashed outside. Jurors, heaved a sigh and stirred to reality, jotted down final notations. Court was adjourned.

The succeeding day, Wednesday July 29th, Mrs. Kasabian resumed her testimony.

In a state of shock, Linda sought refuge in the parked car, where she waited for the trio. Soon the aggressors, blotched in blood and carrying two knives and one gun, entered the auto. Tex started the engine and drove off. Sadie and Katie complained about their heads and hands hurting; in the death struggles hair had been pulled by the victims; in the brutal stabbings, hands ached from striking bones. During their drive in the search of a place to wash off the blood, the murderers changed their clothes. They stopped at a house to wash themselves with a garden hose, when a woman came out of the lodging and asked what they were doing. Tex replied that they were getting a drink of water. Then the woman's husband appeared and followed the four walking back to the car. As the husband approached the driver's side and began to reach for the ignition key, Tex blocked him, grabbed his hand, and then stepped on the accelerator.

Later, according to her testimony, Linda was directed to throw the stained clothes and knives from the car. At a gasoline station restroom, the murderers finished washing themselves. Then, with Linda driving, they returned to the Spahn Ranch, where Charlie awaited them. He commissioned the girls to clean all the blood from the vehicle, and then wait in the bunkroom, where Clem and Brenda McCann were when they entered. Charlie and Tex strolled in afterwards, the latter boasting, that he said, "I am the devil here to do the devil's work," and narrating that the slaying site had been filled with plenty of panic and messy, bloody bodies, all dead. Charlie interrogated if they had any remorse.

Mrs. Kasabian's testimony was interrupted time and time again by Mr. Kanarek. The court was then recessed for lunch.

In the afternoon session, Linda alleged that she and Tex, Sadie, and Katie, answered "No" when questioned by Mr. Manson about remorse. She (Linda) felt remorse but was afraid to admit it. Then the foursome was directed to go to sleep; the next day they watched TV and heard the news report about the massacre announcement and the victims' names.

That evening, August 9, Charlie instructed Linda to obtain a change of clothing and her driver's license. He ordered her, Sadie, Katie, Tex, Clem Tufts (also known as Steve Grogan), and Leslie Van Houten into their car for another night out; since yesterday's escapade was too messy, he would demonstrate his technique. The leader planned two different house raids in two groups; he would deposit one group and accompany the other. Linda did not want to be among the raiders but was afraid to refuse. Charlie wore a leather thong around his neck and gave another to Linda, which she put in her pocket. Two knives were taken as weapons. Linda stated that Charlie, as the mastermind, drove the same vehicle used for the Tate slaughters and gave directions when Linda was driving. They stopped at a house; Charlie got out and told her to drive around the block. When she reappeared, she saw him standing in front of the residence and a man and woman sitting in a nearby car. Explaining that the man was too big, Charlie got back into the car with Linda and instructed her to drive away. He mentioned seeing children's pictures at the homestead but later stated that they could not let children deter them for the sake of future offspring.

They journeyed to another house in a modern, upper class section, but Charlie decided the buildings were too close together. They reached a church, where he tried opening the doors, but they were locked. Charlie drove to Sunset Boulevard, and then switched the wheel over to Linda again. They continued their wanderings up a dirt road to stop at yet another house before heading down to the ocean by Will Rogers State Beach. Along Sunset toward the city, they followed a white sports car through a residential area. Linda was instructed to pull beside it at the next red stop-light signal so Charlie could jump out and shoot the driver. Charlie proceeded to get out of the car, but the light changed, and the sports car pulled away.

Changing his mind, he decided to cease the chase. Then specific directions were given for Linda to drive to the home of Harold True, the neighbor of Leno and Rosemary La Bianca. Linda recognized the buildings and mentioned that she and her husband stopping in Los Angeles en route to New Mexico attended a party there. She asked Charlie if he intended raiding this house. He answered, "No," he was going next door. She watched Charlie go up the driveway leading to Mr. True's home until he disappeared from view.

For several moments the car group waited. Then Charlie reappeared, calling Leslie, Katie and Tex out of the car. Clem jumped into the back seat with Linda and Sadie. Charlie explained that he tied the hands of the man and woman in the La Bianca house, exhorting the couple not to be afraid since he was not going to hurt them. Charlie then warned Tex, Katie and Leslie "not to let the people know that you are going to kill them and not to cause fear and panic in these people."

Final instructions were for Tex and Leslie to hitchhike back to the Spahn Ranch and for Katie to go to the waterfall, the camp site near the Ranch. When Charlie reentered the car, he handed a woman's wallet to Linda, telling her to take out the change and wipe off the fingerprints. As they drove to a gas station, he directed her to hide the wallet in the women's restroom, where it would not be discovered for a long time as belonging to Mrs. La Bianca.

Prosecutor Bugliosi introduced into court a picture of a dune buggy and a sword for identification by Mrs. Kasabian. Finally, court adjourned for the day.

[EDITOR'S NOTE: During Linda Kasabian's testimony she was asked if she heard a conversation between Charlie, Mary Brunner, Bruce Davis, Bobby Beausoleil about getting the girls certain types of clothing. She answered yes and continued that "One night at suppertime he (Manson) told Mary Brunner (and the others) to go out with some credit cards and buy all kinds of clothing for us and the children, and to buy certain parts for dune buggies." This seems to confirm the preparation that was being made. She also testified "He (Manson) wanted each one of us girls to have two sets of clothing, like straight dress to wear during the day and maybe on the weekends if we were in front of the Ranch when the riders would come by. We each should have a pair of moccasins, and then a pair of Levi pants, and a shirt or a blouse or whatever. And some straight clothes for Tanya or Bear, diapers, things like that." She then said Mary Brunner, Bruce Davis and Bobby Beausoleil returned with the items. Although we don't know the timing of this, it is an indication that there was indeed planning involved. Manson was clearly getting ready.]

◆　◆　◆

The jurors continued to make daily notations of all testimony and exhibits in the courtroom, since notes provided the best means for future reference and consideration in such a lengthy trial.

Thursday, July 30, major witness Linda Kasabian continued with her testimony.

After leaving Tex, Katie and Leslie at the La Bianca residence Charlie drove to the ocean front with Linda, Clem and Sadie. Linda alleged that while walking along the beach with Charlie, she noticed that his neck thong was gone, and she told him that she was pregnant. The twosome turned into a side street, and at the corner a police car approached and stopped; they were asked what they were doing, and Charlie answered they were taking a walk. After a short conversation, the police drove away. The couple returned to their auto, where Clem and Sadie were left waiting. The quartet reentered the vehicle, Linda behind the steering wheel. Charlie inquired if someone knew any people at the Oceanside; all replied "no."

Charlie then questioned Linda about an actor met by her and Sandra Good, a "family" member. Linda admitted meeting him and described him as an Arab or Israeli; she had been picked up hitch-hiking and went to his apartment. So, according to her testimony, Charlie instructed her to kill that man, giving Linda a small pocket-knife and showing her how to slit the actors' throat. Clem was then ordered to shoot the man. At this point Linda protested, telling Charlie, "I am not you. I cannot kill anybody." But, at the time, she was afraid to refuse. They headed to the man's apartment. Charlie gave Clem a gun and instructed the trio, if anything happened, to hitchhike back to the Spahn Ranch, Sadie going to the waterfall. Then the witness described Sadie and Clem hiding around the corner as she intentionally knocked on the wrong door, to prevent another killing and to stifle the Manson murder mission.

Because the right man was not found, the trio retreated to the Oceanside, searching for a hiding place for Clem's gun. They stopped near Malibu Feed

Bin at a house where Linda's acquaintances, a man and girlfriend lived and where they all smoked some pot before they hitchhiked back to the Ranch.

Mrs. Kasabian was questioned by the prosecutor about drugs. She admitted taking LSD approximately 50 times over a period of four years, off and on.

Linda Kasabian then related her desire, after the two nights of murder, to leave the Ranch. She packed a sleeping bag with some clothes belonging to her child Tanya and hid it in the bushes by the road. Afraid of Mr. Manson, Mrs. Kasabian resorted to escape, even though temporarily leaving Tanya in the dependable care of Brenda, a "family" member, until she could return for the baby. David Hannum loaned Linda Kasabian a car and Bruce Davis gave her a Shell Oil credit card. Linda picked up two hitchhikers bound for New Mexico. Outside of Albuquerque the auto broke down. Unable to finance repairs, Mrs. Kasabian hitch-hiked in search of her husband, Robert, until she found him in Ojo Sarco, a commune near Taos, New Mexico. She confessed to him the facts of the multiple murders and her concern to retrieve Tanya. Robert Kasabian, living with another woman, had no means of offering help. So, Mrs. Kasabian hitch-hiked back to Taos to talk to a friend, Joe Sage, who operated a Zen Buddhist macrobiotic retreat in that city, and who questioned her until she surrendered the facts of the murders and the desire to obtain Tanya. Mr. Sage checked her story by having Linda telephone the Spahn Ranch; Linda gave Mr. Sage the phone who talked first to an unidentified female and then to Mr. Manson who said that Linda had flipped out and that her ego was not ready to die and so she had to run away. Joe Sage gave her money for the airplane flight to Los Angeles.

Three weeks of legal complications and Mr. Sage's money for attorney fees retrieved Tanya. Then Linda visited her father in Miami, Florida, for about a month and eventually went to live with her mother in Concord, New Hampshire. Fearing police, being pregnant, and supporting Tanya, Linda waited until November to surrender to police, after learning she was wanted in connection with the Tate La Bianca slayings. She was brought to Los Angeles by the authorities in early December 1969, and while in custody gave birth to her second child, "Angel."

In the afternoon session, Mrs. Kasabian, calm and composed, took the witness stand to be cross examined by defense attorney Fitzgerald. Linda testified taking LSD about 50 times, the first time in Boston, on Christmas Eve, 1965. Linda Kasabian admitted using other drugs, peyote, mescaline, methedrine hydrochloride or "speed"; however, she did not know the exact dosage of these drugs, which were obtained illegally. Linda described the LSD experience as a realization and explained the LSD and peyote results as hallucinations and delusions. She thought she could see God through Acid but realized that He can be discovered without LSD. The witness stated that "family" members at the Ranch called themselves witches. Gypsy informed her that they all assumed different names; Linda was known as Yana the witch. Mrs. Kasabian admitted frankly and unemotionally to love making and sex orgies in group participation by "family" members on the Ranch and to her voluntarily submitted participation.

Court was adjourned.

The following day, Friday, July 31, the State's 21-year-old key witness in the Tate La Bianca slayings faced her fifth day of testimony. Defense attorney Fitzgerald commenced with cross examination.

Linda Kasabian appeared relaxed and composed as she narrated leaving home at age 16, marrying in Boston for a short-term union, contracting a second marriage with Robert Kasabian and having a child.

The Kasabian family drifted from one "drug oriented" commune to another from Florida to Boston, New York, Venice, San Francisco, Washington, then New Mexico, and finally returning to California. After separating from her husband in July 1969, Linda with infant Tanya, sojourned at the Spahn Ranch in Chatsworth.

The witness alleged to Ranch life catering to love-making and sexual freedom by all male and female members in groups or singularly; and encountering Tex Watson and having sexual relations with him. In conversation with Tex, the sum of $5,000 was mentioned, that Linda reportedly obtained from her husband and his roommate, Charles Melton, before she arrived at the Ranch. But this money was not brought into evidence.

Mrs. Kasabian was then questioned about Mr. Manson and his philosophies. She explained that he made love to her and told her about his philosophy. Linda did not always agree with the cult leader but was afraid to question him; she was told by the other girls never to disagree with Charlie. Mrs. Kasabian admitted that she loved him, whom she felt was the Messiah, a second Jesus Christ but not believing that Manson was God.

She said she felt like she was a blind little girl in the forest, and she took the first path that came to her.

Fitzgerald asked how many times she was at the Tate residence.

She answered, "twice, the night of the murders and then with Prosecutor Bugliosi." She cried about the second visit, saying the dogs came running to the gate, she thought "why weren't the dogs here (on the first night)."

Fitzgerald also asked why she didn't go to the police in August, September, October or November; it was only when you were charged with murder that you went? She stated that she had to delay going to the police until her baby was born.

The witness alleged that she was testifying because from the time everything happened, she knew that she would be the one to tell the truth. Immunity did not enter her mind. Linda felt she had to reveal what occurred, regardless of gaining immunity or not. The prosecuting attorney Bugliosi then explained to the witness the immunity agreement; that if she testified truthfully to everything, she knows about the Tate La Bianca murders, the district attorney's office will petition the court to grant prosecution freedom and to dismiss charges.

Chapter Eight

The Juror's Life Outside of the Courtroom

Panelists were approaching the 18th day of sequestration and becoming well accustomed to daily life at the Ambassador Hotel and the routine of court sessions. Weekends afforded leisure time to enjoy a few extra hours of sleep to unwind and relax from tension. There was the option of having breakfast in the recreation room or going downstairs in a group with deputies to the dining area.

Saturday was dedicated to "home chores," personal laundry and grooming. During warm months and on sunny days the enclosed swimming pool and courtyard were put into ample use for paddle ball, overall exercise and lounging for sun soaking. That was a good way to relax. Jurors were admonished not to talk with hotel guests, a rule by which we abided.

Monday was drugstore day. Jurors wanting to make purchases were taken to Thrifty Drugs immediately following dinner. Drugstore purchases on other days were made by the bailiff when convenient.

Tuesday featured occasional specially planned activities, personal laundry, TV, and other activities during free time.

Wednesday offered night bowling. Ten pin enthusiasts brought sweaters to dinner at the hotel coffee shop and departed directly afterwards. Panelists not attending bowling sessions spent the evening on the jury floor.

After Thursday dinner we were brought to the drugstore or beauty parlor for those lady jurors desiring professional hair care. Hair care appointments needed to be made no later than Monday of the same week and had a choice of the Magic Mirror Salon or Ambassador Salon and had to agree to attend the same parlor on the same night.

Friday highlights were dinner out at a different restaurant.

Any panelist not participating in a planned activity was taken to the sixth floor only, since no other activities could be handled due to personnel limitations. Any juror with a request or idea for entertainment of the jury advised Deputies Murray or Skupen, who considered the matter for feasibility and approval; other deputies should not be and were not asked for approval or recommendation.

Panelists were allowed a designated amount for weekly laundry expense, but were required to pay for their own haircuts, salon appointments, pharmacy or other purchases, and bowling entertainment.

Sunday catered to varied excursion trips to sites of interest and entertainment for the jurors and families desiring to attend. Deputy Ann Orr, whom we sometimes called our "social director," arranged most of these outings and performed a magnificent feat trying to please everyone. Each excursion was an all-day event, including dinner out, family members paying for their own meals.

This particular Sunday a beach party was on the schedule. But I remained at the hotel expecting a visit from my wife and daughter Sister Mary Paulynne. (Sisters in the convent were permitted visitations usually once a month). Since I was "locked up" our daughter had permission to come and visit me. My wife drove to Santa Monica to pick her up at the parochial school where she taught. When they arrived, I acted like a typical, proud father, going around and introducing Sister Mary Paulynne to jurors. Later we three retired to the privacy of my room and, like the happy, lively family that we were, chatted about past events.

Our daughter brought her accordion, which she played as a hobby, and entertained us with some of her favorite melodies. It was a joyful family reunion. But our oldest daughter, Sister Mary Gabriella was unable to join us. She was just ending a two-and one-half year stint in West Pakistan and flying to her next destination in Australia. By some strange coincidence she had a change of scenery and address about the same time as my transfer to a "new home" address at the Ambassador Hotel. But only in miles, were we separated, because in our family, the spirit of love and communication kept us always close. We corresponded regularly to keep "tabs" on each other.

Now to you the public, I disclose a glimpse of the wonderful inspiring correspondence and prayers from my loved ones and the members of our daughters' congregations. Many of the letters, read to the jurors, were a great moral booster, not only to me but to all the others. Words fail me in expressing my gratitude to my understanding family and all the dear Sisters for their loving support and magnitude of prayers.

Here is a treasured letter from my daughter. It helped keep my spirits up during the long sequestration to know she was thinking of me. It is followed by a sampling of the letters, greetings and notes from the other Sisters in solidarity and prayer for the father of one of their own.

Dear Dad,

Since I can't call you up to say hello to my favorite Dad, this little note is chuck full of greetings and prayers from me and all the Sisters. The Novitiate heard about your long stay at the Ambassador Hotel, and so they were inspired to write to you to let you know that they are thinking and praying for you. You and the other jurors will be feeling a downpour of prayer because the second year Novices all began their 10-day Retreat today. The first year Novices begin on Tuesday. Hope you enjoy the creative cards and notes; they were told not to mention anything about the proceedings.

Dad, it was indeed a wonderful pleasure and delight to see you last week! Thank you for the tour and introducing Mom and me to other jurors. Hope to surprise you again sometime. Mom will be just fine, don't worry, I told her to call me if she gets lonely around the apartments.

Only two weeks left of summer school, time seems to fly by. With only two classes: Linear Algebra and Cultural and Historical Geography, one has few moments to catch up on reading, preparing for school and extra visits to the Lord. .

Retreat begins on August 8th in the evening and ends after Mass on August 15th.

We even had a baseball game here Dad! The Junior Professed played against the Senior Professed. We had a lot of fun, even though we lost 5-2. But it was rather humorous. Like the New York Mets in both the infield and the outfield, butterfingers a plenty, and that wasn't the candy bar either! We had rooters for both teams; even the neighbors and passing cars stopped for a while to look. At the end of our game both the winning team and the losing team divided the purse. There was taffy for everyone!

Well Popsi, I will close for now but will write you again very soon. You are in my daily prayers as well as the other jurors. If you ever want to tell your friends a mortuary joke maybe you can say; "What did one casket say to another casket?" "Is that your coffin coughin'?"

Love and prayers always, Sister Paulynne.

August 31, 1970

Dear Mr. Tubick.

It is time again to visit you with a short letter and a few timely thoughts. We thought these cards would give you a few thoughts for your daily meditation.

We pray for all of you daily, please tell your juror friends, and all those you come in contact daily.

Keep your chin up; keep smiling and most of all praying.

The Sisters saw Sister Paulynne over at your former parish yesterday. From all reports, it was a fine gathering of Sisters who taught there and came from the parish.

In just a few more days classes will open here for the young Sisters. We have only one more postulant entering in September and we do so much want many more; this is another item to add to your daily prayer list.

God love you and bless you and guide you each day.

Many hearty and prayerful greetings from all the Sisters.

24 July 1970

Dear Mr. Tubick.

Cheery greetings. How are you? Our summer here is flying by very quickly. Today was the last day of our summer class. We took a course in teaching art to grade school children. We learned much but at the same time had a lot of fun working on our projects and trying out techniques.

Now the big event is our upcoming investment on August 4th. This Sunday night the Postulants go on retreat. I will pray for you and share with you the blessings of the retreat. Please say a prayer for us. May the Lord be with you?

Dear Mr. Tubick,

This is just a little note but it's full of greetings and prayers. Along with our cards we're sending a couple of prayer cards which we designed, and silk screened in art class this summer. We thought you'd like them. We really enjoyed making them.

May the Lord keep you ever in His care.

Dear Mr. Tubick,

Greetings. It looks like we are going to miss your smiling face on junior visiting days now that Sister Paulynne is teaching. You will be in our prayers, however as all the families of the Sisters are.

Pray for us and keep up your beautiful rosary devotion.

Dear Mr. Tubick,

Greetings, you must be very happy to have all that special extra time to give to God. He will bless you and take care of you. We Postulants are getting ready for our big day. Investment! It is August 4th, so please keep us in your prayers!

Dear Mr. Tubick,

Many greetings from the warm hills! How are you doing? The old homestead is here, safe and sound yet, although we do miss Sister Mary Paulynne and the other Juniors! Summer is coming to a close. It seems as though we just started. I guess it was all so busy, it sped by. Too bad we can't slow time down sometimes. God bless you; we are praying every day for you!

Dear Mr. Tubick,

Many special greetings to you from all of us here at the Novitiate. As usual we are all very busy with many things. Sunday, we begin our retreat and on August 4th we eight Postulants will be invested in the Habit. I know we can count on your prayers in our behalf.

Our thoughts and prayers are with you. God love you and Mary keep you.

Dear "Sister Mary Paulynne's Dad,"

Just a little note to tell you that another one of your daughter's Sisters is thinking and praying for you. I remember meeting you a couple of times on visiting day. Pretty soon we will have a whole new group of Novices, in exactly 11 days. They are all getting excited and anxious and all that goes with getting ready for a big day! I'll be anxious to hear from Sister Mary Paulynne, we all love her, especially her accordion, it keeps the Novitiate in good spirits. Please keep us in your prayers. God bless you.

Dear Mr. Tubick

Greetings! How are you? We saw Sister Paulynne last week, she is looking wonderful.

We told her to give you our greetings. Bye take care of yourself. You are in our prayers.

Dear Mr. Tubick,

Greetings! We saw Sister Paulynne on Saturday when we went in to celebrate one of our Sisters' Golden Jubilee. She looks very well. It was so nice to hear her laugh again.

God bless you Mr. Tubick! Please pray for us all!

Dear Dad of a Nun,

Loving and prayerful greetings to you. Just five months from today is Christmas! The hunting season for deer opens the first week in August, so there will be plenty of shooting in the Valley. The enclosed cards are products of our art class this summer. Please keep us in your prayers. God love you and bless you.

Here is a letter from my other daughter, Sister Mary Gabriella who is serving in Australia.

August 5, 1970
Dear Mom and Dad,

Thanks for your July 25th aerogramme.

Now we've all changed addresses; you Dad to the Ambassador Hotel, Sister May Paulynne, and me. What about you Mom? With all the work at the apartments, it doesn't seem like much of a holiday or change of environment. Hope you get some of the tenants to keep you good company.

I pray for you, especially now Dad, that God guides you so that you will not be intimidated; that you perform a good apostolate with the case and among the jurors, deputies, etc.; that seemingly long days are grace-filled.

Australia is prosperous and modern enough. We are able to meet our expenses, whereas in Pakistan we are always in the "red" when it comes to the USA $$$.

How peaceful and clean is everything compared to Pakistan, where things are so intriguing. The miniskirts in Sydney are outrageous. Communism is evident but illegal. Dope has not yet become a major problem. Food and clothing are priced similar to those in the U.S, but wages are proportionately lower. Australians seem happy and healthy and like to go shopping. (Just like you and I used to, Mom).

Tomorrow I will attend a parish exhibit, my first one in Australia. Usually I remained in the convent, "chaperoning" our pre-novice, whom I teach weekly classes to; handling book orders and bills; typing our article for the Pauline newsletter; doing household chores. Every Tuesday evening our Maltese Sister and I eat supper early at 6:30 p.m., right after the Benediction, in order to attend the counseling course held at the St. John of God Brothers Monastery, from 7:30 to 10 p.m. About 45 people are present; a few Sisters among laity, priests and several Brothers. The purpose is to know ourselves, understand others, dialog in groups, and develop leadership. Challenging, isn't it?

Keep up your good spirits, Dad. I pray for you often. May God fortify and protect you both in this time of trial.

I sit alone, reminiscing, "drinking" in a moment of serene solitude, communing with both of you. How golden are thoughts of love, pure gold that is indescribable but made more precious when offered, tried, tempered at the foot of God, at his Throne, at the tabernacle in our flower-bedecked chapel. I feel your prayers also.

Lovingly, Sister Mary Gabriella

And finally, a letter of support from my daughter Sister Mary Gabriella's order.

August 10, 1970

Dear Mr. and Mrs. Tubick,

Thank you for your lovely letter and birthday offering for Sister Gabriella. May God reward you a hundredfold for your generosity.

We just received another of Sister Gabriella's bubbling, humorous, fact filled letters in which she told us of her countless blessings and experiences of missionary life. Thank God for her sense of humor; it is a great asset for one in the missions, especially among people of a totally different cultural background. You have reason to be proud of having such a daughter as we are to have her as one of us.

You may be assured of our prayers. May God guide Mr. Tubick in this ordeal and the rest of the jurors. May God's Holy Will be accomplished.

Our grateful remembrance in our daily prayers and in those of all the Sisters

Chapter Nine

"Manson Guilty, Nixon Declares"

On Monday, August 3, court convened with defense attorney Fitzgerald's cross examination of Prosecution star witness Linda Kasabian. Questioning related to previous testimony. Mrs. Kasabian alleged that she did not report the murders sooner because of fear for herself and her child, Tanya, and again, described planning an escape and hiding a sleeping bag in the bushes outside the camp site. When publication of Linda's life was brought to light, she stated that the main purpose of her story was not solely for financial gain but for telling young people to seek a different path and to learn from the mistakes which she made and a possible 25% share of profits did not influence her testimony.

Attorney Fitzgerald asked Linda if she attempted to hide, run away or call police the night of the five murders. He also asked the same question about the La Bianca murders, and if she said anything at the Malibu Sheriff's station when she talked about her daughter Tanya or when she went to court weeks later to get Tanya back. Her answers were "no."

Linda also stated when asked by Fitzgerald that she did not suggest that they go to the house of Harold True and kill him. Linda stated she had to leave her child Tanya behind because something told her that she would be okay.

Defense attorney Shinn commenced with further cross examination of Mrs. Kasabian about her previous conversations with police officers and deputy district attorneys Bugliosi and Stovitz concerning immunity at the time of custody, additional questions regarding the publication of her life story, reiterations of her drug usage and hallucinations, and reasons for hiding the truth during the three months before her arrest.

On August 4, 1970, U. S. President Richard Nixon's comment that hippie cult leader Charles Manson is guilty directly or indirectly of seven murders without reason, hit the news headlines. As the jurors were seated in the jury box, Charlie held up a newspaper banner headline: "Manson Guilty, Nixon Declares." In split seconds, the paper was snatched from Charlie by Bailiff Murray. The headline was glimpsed by a few jurors, but I myself did not see it. Then each juror was brought into open court before Judge Older and once again took the juror's oath, "to tell the truth and nothing but the truth, so help me God." Each one declared that the headline would in no way affect ability to judge the case on its own merits. (I can vouch that everyone based the verdict solely on the evidence presented in the trial and in accordance with the court's instructions).

Before court adjourned for the day, defense attorney Kanarek began his cross examination which lasted eight days. Questions related to the previous testimony.

Mr. Kanarek's relentless interrogation was geared to rattle Mrs. Kasabian, whose composure weakened, and she was visibly shaken, yet there was no change in her story. Mr. Kanarek's performance was time consuming and tedious, to say the least, and offered no concrete evidence to the murders.

From August 4 to August 7 Attorney Kanarek dwelled on Linda Kasabian's use of LSD "about 50 times," her use of the borrowed car to drive to New Mexico after the seven murders and the use of a stolen credit card. Attorney Kanarek went over the same things; Linda's use of drugs in 1969 while with Manson for a month at the Ranch.

He questioned her about what she did at the Tate residence on the night of the murders. Linda Kasabian admitted being in a state of shock after seeing Steven Parent killed, but she stated that she followed Tex Watson's orders to look for open doors and windows in the back of the house.

Attorney Kanarek asked Linda about Wojciech Frykowski and if she spoke with him, she said "no." Kanarek asked if she felt responsible for the two nights of murder and she responded, "I don't know if I felt responsible then, but I do now."

Linda stated that she didn't know there were two other people in the house and didn't know that the woman was pregnant. She said, "Wow they killed them for $70," because Tex took money.

Kanarek asked if she had remorse for having participated in the killings and her answer was that she had extreme remorse. Kanarek reminded her about the second night of murders and asked about her state of mind. The witness stated her intent was to do what Manson told her to do.

Kanarek asked her about hiding the wallet of Rosemary La Bianca in the gas station restroom and if her intent was to return later for it and use the credit cards on her way to New Mexico, she replied that it was not her intent to do that.

Kanarek asked her to define "pig" and "piggy." Linda stated that a pig is a cop and a piggy is a person who is part of the establishment. Kanarek asked her if she thought the people at the Tate residence were "piggies." The witness answered that before she thought they were piggies but during the murders she thought these people are human beings.

Kanarek asked the witness "How you know you didn't help with the murders if you were in a state of shock."

Linda answered "I know I didn't do that. I don't have it in me to do such an animalistic thing." She also said that she did not go into the house.

Kanarek showed the witness a photo of the body of Wojciech Frykowski and Linda replied: "Oh God" and started to cry.

Kanarek also asked her why she didn't report the killings to the police and Linda replied that she was pregnant, had a baby with her and was afraid.

Attorney Kanarek showed Mrs. Kasabian the horrible photo of the body of actress Sharon Tate, the witness gasped and then sobbed and cried. Judge Older called for a recess and she did not return to the stand.

The week came slowly to a close. Friday, August 7, Larry Sheely, chosen from the six alternates, replaced one of the regular jurors, number 11, Walter Vitzelio, who was excused because of stomach trouble requiring doctor's care for medication and special diet.

The warm sultry days of summer, August 8th and 9th, were upon us, though none of us acknowledged the correspondence with the anniversary of the crimes. We, the jurors welcomed a weekend break from the court hearings, a chance to relax with family members, visiting and dining together at the Ambassador Hotel.

Saturday, after a light lunch, I sauntered down to the courtyard pool with a group of panelists (and our close companions, the deputies). Soon we were joined by our spouses and families; we all enjoyed a pleasant serene afternoon and were chatting, swimming and sunning. These precious weekend hours were a great consolation to my wife and me. They sparked both of us

to realize more and more how deep our ever-growing love was being tenderly rekindled and fortified in the face of this ordeal. This helped shorten
the dragging weeks of separation and made bearable the pressure during
the time of sequestration. In our jovial moments, my wife and I joked about
these weekends being our second honeymoon on the installment plan.

This Sunday, Marine land was the site of an excursion. My wife Helen
didn't attend these all-day weekly events. Some of the reasons included her
decision not to drive back home at a late hour and Sunday afternoons were
some of her busiest times to interview clients for apartment vacancies.

While I was isolated from my life at home, I received sad news. My wife
was reluctant to relate it to me but knew I would need to know. We received
a letter from my younger brother Joseph, who lived in Detroit, Michigan
with his family. We learned about his lung cancer, which doctors predicted
would leave him only a short time to live. During the month of August, I
frequently corresponded with my brother, trying in whatever way I could to
bolster his morale and reassure him of our prayers. On August 25, he died.
The burial was in Michigan, and I was unable to attend the funeral. Perhaps
if I'd insisted, I could have been excused from the jury panel. But I felt at this
stage my presence couldn't help my brother, while I could do more here by
completing my civic duty.

CHAPTER TEN

IMMUNITY FOR LINDA KASABIAN

While Court was in session Monday, August 10, the State's key witness, Linda Kasabian, was granted immunity from prosecution on seven counts of murder and one count of conspiracy. The Petition was approved by Superior Court Judge Charles H. Older.

Charles Manson's defense attorney Kanarek commenced cross examining Mrs. Kasabian. Questions related to previous testimony and photograph exhibits were shown to the jurors.

Attorney Kanarek asked to go to the Tate residence in Benedict Canyon and Judge Older denied the motion. Kanarek was directed to use the large diagram of the estate displayed in the courtroom. Mr. Kanarek moved Mrs. Kasabian off the witness stand while he asked questions near the diagram. The witness stated that she had seen Tex Watson leap on the back of Wojciech Frykowski and stab him repeatedly. Attorney Kanarek asked why she didn't try to help Frykowski or Miss Folger while they were being attacked. Linda said she didn't know why but said also there was nothing that she could do.

On August 11, Kanarek asked Mrs. Kasabian why she had taken LSD. She answered, "For self-realization and God-realization." Kanarek asked her what she came to realize about God. The witness replied that "He is the Supreme Being and the Creator of the Universe." She said that she had forgotten God during the weeks that she lived at the Spahn Ranch with Manson and the "family."

Kanarek asked if during the time at the Spahn ranch, she thought Manson was Jesus Christ. She answered "yes." The witness, when asked if she thought she was in a trance at the Spahn Ranch, answered "Yes, it was because of the way Manson spoke, walked, sang and danced and the way he made love." Kanarek asked the witness if she fell in love easily and her response was, "Yes, I was in love with everybody."

On Wednesday August 12, attorney Kanarek, at the very end of his questioning just before noon, got Mrs. Kasabian to admit that after she left her husband in July 1969, she returned to a truck in which they had lived and stole $5000 from a friend, Charles Melton. She said she gave the money to Tex Watson. Finally, before noon Wednesday, Mr. Kanarek completed his cross examination.

After lunch Mr. Hughes, Leslie Van Houten's defense attorney began his cross examination of Mrs. Kasabian. His questioning, having little bearing on the trial at hand.

Attorney Hughes had many typed questions, but most were not allowed, objections coming from the prosecution attorneys. One question Hughes asked was, "what is love?" Mrs. Kasabian said there were two kinds of love, earthly for humans and universal and that reality is actually happening. Hughes asked the witness about the nature of the power that Mr. Manson had over her. The witness replied that she wanted to do anything for him because she loved him, he made her feel good and he was just beautiful.

Hughes asked "Is Mr. Manson the Devil? The witness described Manson as a devil-like man the whole time, but she once thought that he was the Messiah.

Hughes asked what Mrs. Kasabian now thinks about the defendants. Linda said she felt compassion for them but wished they could get up on the witness stand and tell the truth as she was doing.

Attorney Hughes questioned Mrs. Kasabian at length about her drug use and asked her about the many different types of drugs. The witness said that she had taken LSD, speed and other chemical drugs about 50 times and had smoked marijuana many times.

On Thursday August 13, Attorney Hughes once again questioned Mrs. Kasabian about her experiences with the drugs LSD, speed, peyote marijuana and others. Mr. Hughes asked Linda if she was controlled by Mr. Manson, through vibrations. She said possibly and said that Manson put out a lot of good vibes; he's even doing it now. Attorney Hughes asked her if she knew that charges against her have been dismissed and what that means to her. She said, "Everyone says that I am a free woman," but that she didn't feel any different. The attorney read off a list of drugs that she had used and asked her if it wasn't true that a major delusion that she had while living at the Spahn Ranch with Manson and family was that Manson was Jesus Christ and she was a witch. The witness answered "yes" to the question. With that answer Mr. Hughes concluded his examination of the main witness.

Mr. Stovitz began the prosecution's redirect examination of Mrs. Kasabian. Photographs, relating to the witness's previous testimony, were exhibited to the jury.

The next day Friday, August 14, Mr. Stovitz continued redirect examination. He revisited her testimony asking her about some of her answers which the prosecution said were unclear. One question was "did she benefit from the $5,000 that she had stolen from her husband's friend Charles Melton and given to a family member?" Her answer was "Not that I know of." Attorney Stovitz asked if she had smoked marijuana during the time she lived at the Spahn Ranch with Manson and "family." She said "yes" and that it had come from a plant named "Elmer" which belonged to everyone but was "cared for" by Danny DeCarlo.

At last court adjourned for the day, ushering in another sultry, sun-bright weekend. A welcome relief.

Saturday, August 15, was the feast of the Assumption, a holy day of obligation when Catholics are exhorted to attend church services. So that evening my wife and I were accompanied by a small group of jurors and a deputy to St. Basil Church. The short walk on Wilshire Boulevard in the balmy air proved exhilarating. There was a sensation of freedom. How good it felt just walking in the open air! Then I was filled with a pang of melancholy, a mood of unrest, forfeiting freedom; something we don't ponder or appreciate until we are deprived of it. That longing for freedom from being "shut-in" haunted me time and time again. Contemplating our long sequestration at the Ambassador, I often wondered how we all managed to endure. Honestly speaking, God's grace sustained us, and in time of stress, even strengthened me to encourage others.

Sunday provided ample diversion for most of the panelists and a few spouses with a tour of the Los Angeles Harbor and Ports-O-Call and then dinner at a select restaurant.

Chapter Eleven

The Juror's Wife at Home

Once again word came from my wife Helen to you, the reader, regarding an incident that occurred in the middle of August, the 35th day of Tate La Bianca trial.

"It was difficult for me, the wife at home, to try to reveal and describe intimate emotions and experiences that left a profound impact upon my memory and life.

In a previous chapter I wrote about the mental strain that I battled against since the day my husband stepped away from our home. I continued to worry, wondering if I could cope with all the rental work, especially those 42 trash cans! Since there was no provision for trash storage bins on the premises, the manager arranged them along the street curb each Sunday for early Monday collection. With my husband around, this weekly chore seemed easy enough, for together we would wheel the 30-and 40-gallon cans to the curb. But now I was by myself, and week after week, this job was becoming a nightmare, adding fuel to my mental attitude. Here my husband went off leaving me with all of this!

The thought gnawed at me, was my husband, "letting me down." Hiring a part time worker could solve the problem, but who thinks of that with a mind shadowed in resentment. I was unhappy and listless, not at all like my usual optimistic, peppy self. Then the symptom developed; a slight tightness and pain in the chest around the heart, but I shirked off the discomfort with the diagnosis that I must get more rest.

I awakened one morning feeling really sick, nauseated, perspired and shaky. Unable to dress myself, I became panic stricken. I couldn't even remember where I put my nerve pills! My thoughts rushed to my husband; he will come and help me! I edged downstairs to the kitchen; dialed the Ambassador Hotel emergency telephone number, and the switchboard operator for the sixth-floor deputy.

It was a bit after 8 a.m., when the jurors would be having breakfast. When the deputy answered, I blurted out; this is an emergency, I must speak to my husband! My voice must have sound alarming, for the deputy replied: "Hang on I'll get him right away!" Hearing my husband's "Hello" I began to cry, sputtering "I'm sick, you have to come home and take me to the doctor!" My husband asked what was wrong with me, and I retorted "I don't know, but I am sick, and I need a doctor!"

He started explaining that he can't come home, that I should call my sister (living nearby) and have her take me to a physician. I wailed that my sister was on her way to work. My husband continued trying to reason with me, stating that he was unable to return home and suggested I ask a neighbor to help. His voice was so cool and calm that panic ebbed away from me to be replaced by anger. A sinister thought flashed through my mind; "He doesn't believe that I am as sick as I am; he thinks I'm putting on an act!" Belligerently, I asserted; if you can't come to help me, I'll get someone else who can! And with that I banged down the phone receiver.

After the panic I could again think rationally; both of my sisters would be on their way to work and most of the tenants would be gone also. Then I remembered the apartment owners, they would be home. I hesitated for a second, because I disliked bothering them at this early hour; but this was an emergency, so I phoned and explained my predicament. Both of them, husband and wife, were wonderful, and they reassured me not to worry and promised to come over promptly. I began to feel better, knowing help was on the way. I gained enough strength to get dressed and even called the doctor's office, making the earliest morning appointment.

My family physician administered an injection to calm my nerves and prescribed medication. After discussing the chest pains with the doctor, I was scheduled to return the next day for a cardiograph examination.

The apartment owners were most kind; God bless them. During the drive home they stopped at a restaurant insisting that I have lunch with them. While dining we had a chance to talk, discussing plans for a change in trash disposal. For the time being my nephew would be hired to handle the bins. Later each tenant received a letter requesting that they put out their own trash cans. After taking me home, the owners urged me to stay inside and rest and offered to chauffer me to the doctor's office the following day. How grateful I was for their consideration!

But as I rested at home, feelings of guilt haunted me. Imagine, banging the phone receiver in the ear of my husband, who must have felt despondent and helpless wondering what was happening! Anxiously I awaited his telephone call, which rang promptly at the dinner hour, and he concernedly inquired about me. I apologized for my temper fit. Also, I related the day's event, assured him of my feeling better, and mentioned tomorrow's cardiograph exam. Then my husband related what a miserable, frustrating day that he had, venting his anxiety by smoking a whole pack of cigarettes (a habit which he broke and conquered a year ago).

He explained that if I had given him the chance, he could have told me that a deputy sheriff would come to the assistance of a spouse in the case of an emergency. Finally, he and I agreed that this coming weekend, it would be best that I continue to relax and not attempt driving to the Ambassador.

For the heart test, I felt well enough to drive myself to the doctor's office. The electro-cardiograph disclosed that a cardiac problem was developing. The doctor gave me fatherly advice, warning me to lesson activity, and take daytime rest, and above all avoid tension and frustration.

Driving home I did some serious reflecting; this was it; I must get a hold of myself and change my way of thinking. Yes, even my body was telling me that I must alter my attitude if I am to be of any help to my husband, especially at this time and continue my duties. And I made up my mind that there was One from whom I can seek assistance. The next evening, I retired early and set the alarm clock so that I could attend the first Sunday church service.

I allowed plenty of time before arrival of the people of the church, to perform a private visit and the Stations of the Cross, and indulgenced devotion commemorating Christ's walk of agony. Arriving at such an early hour was serene solitude; I found no difficulty in meditating.

Kneeling at the altar, I read devotional prayers in my missal and reflected upon Christ's passion. In my own words I plead for strength in carrying my cross. Rising, I walked slowly from station to station, pausing at each one as I prayed with deep emotion.

A wave of fatigue and weariness engulfed me. Suddenly I felt a weight on my shoulders as I approached the seventh station, where vividly I became aware of God's message. I clearly realized that my "cross" was slight compared *to the cross Jesus carried for us on Mount Calvary! With emotion spilling over, I continued praying but now I was beseeching God for mercy and forgiveness. When I finally completed the prayers of the fourteenth station, I sat in a pew completely exhausted and drenched in perspiration.*

Now people began to enter the church, and the Priest commenced celebration of Mass. I gained my composure but had difficulty concentrating and following the Holy Mass prayers. After receiving Holy Communion and giving thanks, I waited for everyone to disperse. Rising and approaching the altar again, I experienced a very buoyant sensation, the weight on my shoulders seemingly gone. Kneeling I recited final prayers and again requested mercy and forgiveness.

When I walked outside, everything seemed unusually bright and the sun's rays felt penetrating and warm. I gazed up and out at an open field, the grass looked radiantly green and beautiful, as though I had never seen it before. As I commenced walking, I felt a strange elevated sensation. Startled, I peered down at my feet to see if I was still touching the ground. It felt more like standing on a fleecy cloud. In amazement and exuberance, I slowly and haltingly walked back to my car. As I started the motor and backed out, the auto sensitively moved at the slightest touch on the steering wheel, as though someone else was driving it for me.

The trip home was short, and when I steered into the carport, with one light touch, the car was parked perfectly, another phenomenon. I wished Herman had seen this because I usually have to maneuver in and out before parking properly. As I entered the apartment, the sensation of elevation vanished. I prepared breakfast and for the first time in weeks ate with gusto. I spent the day quietly reading and meditating. I experienced the happy feeling of internal peace.

From this day, my mental outlook changed; no longer did my thoughts dwell upon myself. I was now concerned about my husband and the others. I beseeched God for the safety and welfare of all the jurors and successful completion of the Manson trial. Throughout the rest of the protracted case, I experienced no fear for myself."

Chapter Twelve

"Oh no, no! God no!"

On the morning of August 17, the 21-year-old star witness for the prosecution, Linda Kasabian, commenced testifying under redirect examination by Mr. Stovitz. Questions related to the meaning and understanding of the penalty phase and perjury penalty and if the witness realized that the penalty for perjury in a capital case is the death sentence.

Attorneys Fitzgerald, Shinn, Kanarek and Hughes conducted brief re-cross examination concerning drugs, religion and yoga.

Prosecutor Bugliosi asked again about what kept Mrs. Kasabian from going to the police. She answered that she was afraid and that she thought policeman were pigs. She said she was afraid that everyone would think she was crazy, and that Charlie would kill her and her little girl. She said something inside her had convinced her that her daughter Tanya would be safe when she fled the Spahn Ranch and the Manson "family" after the seven murders

Defense attorney Hughes asked Mrs. Kasabian if she felt God had sent her to tell who Charles Manson really was. The witness replied she no longer feared Manson and thinks she has a God-sent message to tell who Manson is, a false prophet and not Jesus Christ and said that's what she felt in her heart.

Hughes asked if it was her mission to tell the world that Manson is the devil. She replied that he is a false prophet and that she stopped believing that Manson was Jesus Christ when she looked into the eyes of Wojciech

Frykowski at the Tate residence. The witness said she had a vision that Manson was leading her into self-destruction and that she felt he was the devil. She at one time believed he was Jesus Christ, but he never actually told her that. Hughes asked her if she thought of herself as an angel who came here to bring a storm of God's wrath on Charles Manson. The witness replied that she didn't think she was an angel and that she had a lot of imperfections.

The ensuing morning, attorneys Bugliosi and Fitzgerald continued redirect examination, with questions relating to the sexual activity at the Spahn Ranch with Charles Manson and other "family" members; Tex, Clem and Snake (Dianne Lake). Mr. Bugliosi asked Mrs. Kasabian to clarify her statement that she was an emissary from God. Linda believed that she was doing God's will in testifying on the witness stand as well as proving her repentance for the slayings which she knows are wrong. Mr. Bugliosi referred back to the scene of the two murder nights, asking her to relate her previous testimony to the change of clothing, driver's license and Mr. Manson's leather thong. (That leather thong was missing when he retreated from the La Bianca home). Linda was also questioned about her second pregnancy by her husband.

The Jury was shown photographs of the murder scenes at the Tate residence. And the witness remained steadfast in her story, unchanged from previous testimony.

Prosecutor Bugliosi asked whether Manson had made motions to her in court since she started to testify. She replied that he had, once he passed a finger across his throat in a cutting motion and another time, he put a finger over his mouth as if to suggest lip sealing.

Attorney Fitzgerald got the witness to admit that she told lies to authorities in California to save her child and he asked her if she would lie to save herself. She replied that she thinks more of her children than herself. Fitzgerald named several men who lived at the Spahn ranch and asked if any one of them might be the father of her son, Angel. She replied that it was possible but that she saw her husband in her child's face when he was born.

Defense attorney Shinn got Mrs. Kasabian to admit that she tried to communicate with the three women defendants by vibrations so that they would stop using the game of faces that they wore in the courtroom.

On Wednesday August 19, attorney Kanarek commenced with a few questions in redirect examination regarding the witness's lifestyle and how she regained custody of Tanya through the court.

Attorney Hughes concluded the re-cross examination by asking Mrs. Kasabian if she was willing to be examined by a psychiatrist.

Finally, Mrs. Kasabian was excused, after testifying for 18 days on the witness stand. She was subject for recall as a defense witness at a later date. (After her testimony was concluded Linda Kasabian appeared with her attorneys at a limited press conference to discuss her thoughts).

Witness number nine, Timothy Ireland, instructor at the Westlake School for Girls, and who worked near the Tate estate (at a girls sleep-out about a half to 3/4 of a mile away) and on August 9, 1969, at about 12:40 a.m. for approximately ten seconds, heard a male voice screaming "Oh God no please don't. Oh God no please don't, don't, don't." The witness identified, in a hand drawn exhibit, the Tate residence and the Westlake School for Girls locations. He stated that he took a drive around the area after talking with his Supervisor to perhaps see something, but he did not find anything.

Defense attorney Fitzgerald asked the witness about his conversation with Sergeant Henderson and what time he heard the screams. Defense attorney Shinn asked Mr. Ireland if he had contacted the Police. The witness said after sleeping all day and then hearing the news about the murders, he called the police. Shinn asked him if he had those "words" memorized. Defense attorney Kanarek also asked him about the words that he heard and if he had written them down for the testimony. The witness said: "No sir, you don't forget things like that." Kanarek asked the witness about the length of time of the screams and whether it was a man or woman or child.

The tenth witness, Rudolf Weber, Brentwood Country Club's retired chief steward, related his story, which corresponded with Mrs. Kasabian's previous testimony of the August 8 and 9 occurrences. Mr. Weber, (Witness number ten) on August 8, went to bed about 9 p.m.; but much later about 1:00 a.m., hearing water running, later realizing it was coming from out-doors, got up and confronted the people outside (who were in fact Tex, Susan and Patricia), who were using the garden hose to wash blood off their bodies and clothes (Linda was present also as the driver). Mr. Weber spoke only to the male and said: "What the hell do you think you're doing?" The male responded "Hi, we are just getting a drink of water."

After more confrontation (from Rudolf's wife also) the four people walked away towards the car parked on the street and got in. The witness stated that he followed them and tried to put his hand through the window to grab the keys, although he stated that was not his intention. The man drove off very fast.

The witness said he jotted down the car's license plate number, GYY-435, the same number frequently used on a 1959 Ford owned by John Harold Swartz Jr., ranch hand at the Spahn Ranch. The car was borrowed without his permission the night before the Tate slayings. The witness also identified his Portola Drive address in an exhibit drawing and said it was about 100 yards from Benedict Canyon Drive. The witness also stated he did not report this to the Police until December 1969 (questioned by Fitzgerald).

The eleventh witness, Jim Asin, a student, age 16, testified that he called police at 8:33 a.m. (he noted the time,) August 9, after Mrs. Winifred Chapman, the Tate maid who discovered the bodies at the Tate residence, ran into his house to report the murders. Police arrived in approximately 15 to 20 minutes. (Witness number 11)

The police department narcotics officer narrated finding a small amount of marijuana and other drugs at the Tate habitation. Urine analysis disclosed some percentage of drugs in two bodies.

During the August 20 court session, attorney Bugliosi questioned Witness number 12, John Harold Swartz Jr., a truck driver who worked at the Spahn Ranch. Mr. Swartz traded his truck for a 1959 Ford from which he removed the back seat for the Ranch girls to make garbage collections. The witness testified buying from Mr. Townsend for $50, a 1962 Ford, its license plate being used on the 1959 auto on the slaying nights. Attorney Fitzgerald cross examined Mr. Swartz Jr., regarding the cars, which were not registered. The witness was arrested for grand theft auto on August 16, 1969.

Witness number 13, Jerry Joe DeRosa, a Los Angeles police department officer, was questioned by attorney Stovitz regarding the residence murder scenes. He was the first officer to arrive at the murder scene. The witness was shown photographic exhibits including those of the victims which he identified. Officer DeRosa stated he placed William Garretson under arrest for suspicion of murder when the latter, upon officers' arrival was found sitting on a sofa in the Tate Guest house after the officers' heard dogs barking. A photo exhibit of Mr. Garretson was shown.

Witness 14, William Whisenhunt, a Los Angeles police department officer, testified to arrival time at the murder scene. He was the second officer to arrive at the murder scene.

Witness number 15, a Los Angeles police department officer Robert Burbridge, testified to the arrival time at the murder scene. He was the third officer to arrive at the murder scene.

More photographic exhibits were displayed to the jury. All three of the officers described the grisly scene in detail.

Witness number 16, Raymond Kilgrow, a telephone company repairman, explained that he found four cut phone wires leading to the Tate estate between 10 and 11 a.m. at 10050 Cielo Drive.

[EDITOR'S NOTE: Prior to the next witness at 8:35 a.m. and unbeknownst to the jury, Attorney Kanarek filed a motion on behalf of Charles Manson to allow him to interview potential witnesses without a screen partition. The Judge examined the environment at the jail and Kanarek argued on Manson's behalf.

KANAREK: Well, as I understand it, the reason that we are not being—that we are forced to the screen is that half of it is the letters. The other half is one little pill.

The jail claimed this extra security was the passing of contraband such as an LSD pill they had discovered and the possibility of passing LSD through the letters. They were concerned about other kinds of contraband as well.

COURT: The sheriff would be slightly stupid if he did not anticipate security measures and take those measures rather than waiting until something had happened. You have failed to indicate to me in any manner, Mr. Kanarek, through the testimony of Mr. Manson or anything else, how Mr. Manson is being deprived of any substantial right.

Throughout the trial and out of the presence of the jury Kanarek continued to file motions indicating that Manson's rights were being violated. It appeared Manson wanted as much direct access to his followers as possible, which was being thwarted by the rules of the jail and the security that was being put into place.]

❖   ❖   ❖

The Friday, August 21st court session commenced with Witness number 17, Sergeant Michael J. McGann, a Los Angeles police department investigating officer, testifying to his arrival at the murder site. He identified photographs portraying the number and position of the victims. The witness continued that he recorded all articles of value and the amount of drugs (marijuana, hashish, cocaine and MDA) on the premises and in the car of Jay Sebring. Attorneys Fitzgerald, Shinn and Kanarek cross examined

Sergeant McGann; and attorney Bugliosi asked additional questions on redirect examination.

[EDITOR'S NOTE: MDA is methylenedioxyemphetamine called "Sally" on the street. It is closely related to the currently more common "Molly" also known as "Ecstasy." It is considered more of a psychedelic or hallucinogen than a stimulant.]

❖   ❖   ❖

Witness number 18, John Finken, a coroner's office investigator, told of his arrival time at the murder scene and severing the rope from the bodies of Sharon Tate and Jay Sebring.

Witness number 19, Dr. Thomas T. Noguchi, county of Los Angeles Coroner, provided a complete account of the stab wounds inflicted upon all the victims at the Tate residence. Autopsy reports on Sharon Tate indicated an 8-month pregnancy, 16 stab injuries, neck rope abrasions, He stated "it is quite consistent that the decedent was hanged." The fetus lived 15 to 20 minutes.

Dr. Thomas Noguchi, coroner

Abigail Folger had 28 stab wounds. Photograph exhibits and drawings of the slain were displayed to the panel.

Court was adjourned for the week.

Although none of us discussed it, I could see the serious expressions of each of the jurors as we left the court-room for the Ambassador.

To say that the jurors welcomed the warm, shiny weekend of August 22 and 23 to relax was an understatement. I tried through prayer to temporarily remove the images of the victims from my mind and my sleep. This was a very full, engrossing five days of court testimony. I knew I needed the rest.

This was the weekend my wife would not be making her usual trip up to see me. Saturday evening, we exchanged short telephone greetings and agreed that after the short illness a rest at home was best. Since our phone calls were always limited, our conversations were usually "Hi sweetheart, how are you, how's everything, I'm doing fine." Talking on the phone while the deputy sat at the desk didn't give me much privacy; there was so much I yearned to say and explain to my wife after the upset and anguish because of last week's emergency phone call. It would be so much easier if I could tell her about the trial and how important it was for the jurors to listen to the testimony in detail. I was so torn that I could not be with her. We had always been there for one another. And now another week must go by before I can see her again, such a long time to wait! But at least my mind was at peace knowing that nothing was seriously wrong with my wife.

This Sunday our social director, Deputy Ann Orr, arranged a trip to Exposition Park. The panelists were grateful for a chance to stretch their legs and imbibe the open air.

Trial proceedings recommenced Monday, August 24, with prosecution attorney Bugliosi further examining Dr. Thomas T. Noguchi about additional autopsy accounts of the murder victims. The witness testified to the types of knives that inflicted a total of 103 stab wounds on the five victims. Two kinds of knives were used, sharp instruments, blades measuring not less than five inches long, one to one and one-half inches wide, one eighth to one fourth of an inch thick.

Concerning Abigail Folger, examination revealed 28 stab injuries, five at fatal points, and tests disclosed in the blood stream .055 of alcohol and traces of a stimulant drug (MDA).

Regarding Jay Sebring, the autopsy disclosed seven knife injuries and one gunshot wound. Dr. Noguchi testified that Sebring bled to death, the fatal wounds being three knifings and one shooting.

Concerning Wojciech Frykowski, testimony described 51 stab wounds, seven being fatal, two gun injuries, 23 head, face and hand lacerations; .05% of alcohol and traces of the drug MDA.

Regarding Stephen Parent, examination showed five gunshot wounds from four bullets, two of those injuries proving fatal; chest wounds, one knife injury and .02% blood alcohol reading.

Displayed were photographic exhibits and diagram drawings of knife and gun wounds on the five corpses and all the slaying weapons.

Tuesday, August 25, the jurors reviewed and re-examined photos of the deceased and markings of the stab wounds. Attorney Fitzgerald cross examined Dr. Noguchi in relation to dates and times of autopsies on the five bodies. Attorney Shinn interrogated the coroner about tests given and taken at the slaying scenes and calculations estimating the time of death and type of knife.

Attorney Kanarek asked about blood types of the five slain, tests at the coroner's office and the time estimation on each of Abigail Folger's 28 stab wounds.

Charles Manson was perturbed at his lawyer Kanarek's questioning and said: "This man is not doing what I want" and wanted to fire Kanarek.

[EDITOR'S NOTE: Dr. Noguchi testified for several days. After Court adjourned on Monday, August 24 attorney Hughes requested a meeting with all defendants and their attorneys. The next day, after Fitzgerald and Shinn cross-examined the coroner Kanarek examined him and asked questions about Abigail Folger and was questioning him about how long a person with her injuries could survive is she had received medical help. It is difficult to follow the reasoning behind it but evidently it was not according to whatever plan Manson had in mind. After Fitzgerald objected to the questioning by Kanarek, Manson shouted to the judge.

MANSON: Your Honor, this lawyer is not doing what I am asking him to do; not even by a small margin is he doing what I asked him to do,
COURT: Mr. Manson, you are not permitted to speak out. You may confer with your attorney.
MANSON: He is not my attorney he is your attorney. I would like to dismiss this man and get another attorney. (8986)

It remains unclear what Kanarek was trying to prove. Kanarek also asked Dr. Noguchi "is it a fact that it is not outside the realm of probability that fatal injuries could have been inflicted where you see Miss Folger." This meant outside. There is speculation that Manson went back to the house that night and moved the bodies. This, of course, would show conspiracy. He may have wanted to preempt Kanarek from raising the blood types of the victims as they could implicate him if they were found in places not consistent with the description of the events.

It is also possible that Manson wanted Kanarek to raise the possibility that Linda Kasabian might have stabbed Abigail Folger outside the Tate house. However, this is just a theory and only supports testimony raised in the penalty phase against Linda Kasabian. For whatever reason, Manson was not happy with this line of questioning.

During the recess Manson once again asked the Judge to represent himself.

MANSON: I asked Mr. Kanarek not to do certain things, and it doesn't have any effect on him. Anything I ask him he does anyway, and I have asked him to do other things that he won't do.

But then, on the other hand, he does a lot of things that are good, you know, but I have no control over him. I have no control over what he asked.

If I ask him not to ask certain questions, he asked the questions anyway. I have asked that I may be allowed to ask my own questions. I cannot see having an attorney, and then I cannot see changing attorneys. He is a good man. He is a sincere and honest and truthful human being and I like him very much as a person, but as an attorney he doesn't represent me. He cannot represent me.

In the eyes of the Court I am inadequate, and I don't know how to overcome this obstacle, so I am forced to remain silent, having been told to do so on several occasions.

COURT: that is true of any defendant represented by counsel, Mr. Manson. There is nothing unusual about that and you are not being singled out because of that…

MANSON: But speaking through a counsel on something that the Court is not versed in and understanding another awareness that may be child like in one sense, but then confusing in another sense to explain it to a man who has had maybe 20 years of schooling.

He only understands what he understands, and I cannot transfer my thought, I cannot bring him to my thought. He has his thought. I have no control over his thought, and he has no control over my thought and for me to express my words through this man is impossible. I cannot express my words through him; I can only express my words through me. I would like to, as I have said many times, I would like to represent myself. It would be much faster; it would be less confusing, and it would be not very many questions asked.

COURT: I have seen nothing during this trial to make me change my opinion that you are not competent to represent yourself in a case of this complexity.

The next surprise was Attorney Hughes wanting to join in Manson's motion to represent himself. He thought it would be critical to the defense of his client Leslie Van Houten. Then Manson requested that all of the defense attorneys be allowed to work together. He wanted to hook all of the attorneys up and make one of the attorneys the lead counsel. The court said it was not allowed and that each attorney operates independently and is not subject to any other attorney's direction or control. Manson interjected: "And he is certainly not subject to my direction or control."

The Judge tried to explain that we have attorneys because they have the expertise and the knowledge and skill to handle the case. He said the client doesn't always understand why things are done a certain way.

Before the case resumed in front of the jury after the recess Manson commented:

"Since the recess, Mr. Kanarek said he would do what I asked him to do. How long this will last, I don't know He did pretty good at the first of it, then we kind of lost control when the testimony started."

This is relating to his order that Kanarek remain mute after the Judge did not agree to allow Manson to directly question the jurors. When the Judge asked what Manson wanted he specifically asked what "relief" he sought. That is a legal term.

MANSON: The only relief that I can possibly see is that the Court would relief itself and help itself by letting me help myself.

COURT: I don't follow you. What does that mean?

MANSON: it means that the confusion hasn't started. That possibly I have a little more understanding in line with some of the things that we may get into in the defense that could be explained easier from someone who is standing on a certain street that you have never been on, to bring you to their thought.

COURT: I am still not sure I understand you.

MANSON: Well, each person has their own reality, and that ranch was a different reality from what you people think as reality. What you people live and think and breathe and walk around in is your reality, and it is no less real than my reality, but it is already beginning to lean, to be slanted, and the words that are used in my reality aren't even close to what you may use in your reality. You are going to have to have someone in the middle to interpret the confusion because it is certainly going to be confusion to you.

Manson asked again to be his own counsel and the Court denied his motion. The Judge said he had already disposed of that question. Manson said he didn't think the court will ever be able to dispose of that question and the court would have to live with it. Manson would continue to do everything in his power to control the case to hide the truth. T The jury and those observing the trial only saw the courtroom behavior that showed Manson's disobedience and occasional fits of temper. What they did not see was the clear calculation that was happening behind- the- scenes.]

❖   ❖   ❖

Dr. Noguchi remained on the stand for at least two days. After a recess he resumed testimony and was finally dismissed subject to being recalled.

The next witness called that afternoon was witness number 20, King Baggott, a camera man. Attorney Stovitz questioned him about finding blood-stained clothing in Benedict Canyon. Photos of the clothing were displayed.

Witness number 21; Joe Granado, a Los Angeles police department officer and blood type expert, testified to the blood type samples that he took from the areas at the Tate residence and some areas that he did not take samples from, assuming they were all the same. The witness also testified to finding a buck knife in a chair in the living room. He also testified to the blood type of each murdered person.

On Wednesday August 26, witness number 22, Helen Tebbe, a Los Angeles police department deputy sheriff, verified the identity of Sadie Atkins, alias Sadie Glutz, whose hair sample, gathered from a beauty salon hairbrush, was exhibited. Cross examination was held by attorneys Shinn and Kanarek, whose questions had little bearing on the previous testimony. Under cross-examination the witness did state that she gathered the hair sample without permission from the defendant.

Now followed the testimony on the La Bianca deaths, beginning with Witness number 23, Frank Struthers Jr., 16-year-old student, son of Mrs. Rosemary La Bianca from a previous marriage and stepson of Leno La Bianca. The witness testified that on August 10 he returned home, finding the residence closed and the shades drawn. Having no door key, he telephoned the La Bianca residence; receiving no answer, he called his sister at work.

Investigation ensued and the bodies were discovered; the police were notified. Also Mrs. La Bianca's wallet and wristwatch were discovered missing. Photo exhibits of the La Bianca dwelling were presented.

Witness number 24, Ruth Sivick, dress shop owner, testified being in partnership with Mrs. La Bianca and seeing her for the last time on August 8 about 4:30 p.m. The witness stated that Mrs. La Bianca called her on the morning of August 9th and asked her if she would watch her dogs while she was away on a short trip. The witness said "yes," and she did that, she went to the residence on August 9 at 3301 Waverly Drive about 6 to 6:15 p.m. She fed the dogs, getting food from the refrigerator. She stayed about 30 minutes. Prosecutor Bugliosi showed the witness a photo exhibit of the refrigerator with the words "Helter Skelter" written in blood on the door and asked if she had seen this at about 6.p.m. "No" was the reply. The witness stated everything appeared to be in order when she left.

On Thursday, witness number 25 was John Fokianos, a newspaper vendor who knew the La Bianca family for approximately two years. He last saw the La Biancas when they bought a newspaper from him between 1 and 2 a.m., Sunday August 10.

Witness number 26, William Rodriquez, a Los Angeles police department officer, arrived at the La Bianca residence at 10:45 p.m., August 10, and found Mr. La Bianca in the living room and his wife in the bedroom.

Witness number 27, Sergeant Edward Cline, Los Angeles police department officer, reached the crime area also at 10:45 p.m., August 10, discovered "Death to Pigs" and "Rise" written on the wall. He also found the lower window in the living room, open.

Witness number 28, Sergeant Danny Galindo, police officer and homicide investigator, appeared at the La Bianca scene at 1 a.m., August 11. Sergeant Galindo testified to the removed, blood-soaked pillowcase from Mr. La Bianca's head revealing an electric cord around his neck, carving fork in the abdominal area, knife in the throat, and leather thong that tied his hands behind his back. An electric cord tied Mrs. La Bianca's hands and wound around her neck, and a pillowcase covered her head. He told of no signs of ransacking and found many items of value there at 3301 Waverly Drive.

Witness number 29; Sergeant Gary Broda, Los Angeles police department officer, told of seeing a knife embedded in Mr. La Bianca's throat.

Witness number 30, Dr. David Katsuyama, deputy coroner and Los Angeles medical examiner, related a complete autopsy account of Mr. La Bianca. There were 26 wounds, about six being fatal; 12 with a knife in the neck, chest, abdomen, back and face; 14 with a fork. A blunt instrument carved "War" on the abdominal area. There was no defense attorney cross-examination for this witness.

Friday, August 28 brought Dr. David Katsuyama's testimony on the autopsy findings on Mrs. La Bianca. There were 41 stab wounds, eight being fatal. A leather thong tied her hands.

Sergeant Granado, a criminologist, was recalled to the witness stand, where he testified to the blood stains found on clothing worn by the defendants and discarded after the crimes.

Court was adjourned at noon. And defendant Susan Atkins complained of not feeling well.

THE JURORS (see page 33)

Chapter Thirteen

A Stream of Witnesses

By the August 29 and 30 weekend the jury seemed confident that the Tate La Bianca murder probe was midway through its important prosecution testimony. At this point panelists anticipated that the case would reach its conclusion in the next three or four months as predicted. It was still a long time but seemed manageable.

Some of the jurors toured Knott's Berry Farm, but I remained at the Ambassador and anxiously looked forward to seeing my wife once again after her two-week absence because of sickness. Coincidently this was also the first time for another visit from our daughter Sister Paulynne. When both finally arrived mid-Sunday afternoon, it was a joyous, lively get together, each one of us trying to outdo the other in chattering and joking in the seclusion of my hotel room. Seeing my family helped me find my center.

On Monday the court was still in session but only for a short time; the jury was excused for the day because Susan Atkins was still ill.

The panel did not reassemble in the courtroom until Wednesday September 2. Testimony commenced with Sergeant Granado, a Los Angeles police department criminologist. He provided details about blood tests, blood samples of the slain and human hair samples from the discarded bloody clothing worn by the girl defendants during the time of the murders. A hair sample from some of the discarded clothing matched almost identically to a hair sample from Susan Atkins.

The panel viewed photo exhibits and a diagram of the La Bianca building and blood spot samples from the interior of the residence. Also, there were exhibits of eyeglasses and leather thongs. Cross examination followed by attorneys Fitzgerald, Shinn and Kanarek.

At Thursday's court session, Sergeant Granado was once again called to the witness stand, questioned by Mr. Kanarek about leather thongs found at the crime location, and cross examined by attorney Hughes about human hair samples.

Witness number 31, Officer Jerrome Boen, a Los Angeles police department fingerprint expert, testified to fingerprints noted on the doors of the Tate premises. The jury examined diagrams and photograph exhibits of prints of Charles Watson and Patricia Krenwinkel.

Witness number 32, Frank Escalante, fingerprint department police officer, testified to obtaining fingerprints of Charles Watson at the time of imprisonment on April 23, 1969. These prints matched those found at the crime scene.

Witness number 33, Officer Jack Swan, Los Angeles police department fingerprint expert, obtained at the time of her imprisonment, Patricia Krenwinkel's prints, which matched those at the scene of the crime.

Witness number 34, Harold Dolan, a Los Angeles police department fingerprint expert, introduced identification and comparison of all five victims at the Tate quarters and made test comparisons of Charles Watson's and Patricia Krenwinkel's prints. He found eighteen points of identity between the print lifted from the front door of the Tate residence and the right ring finger on the Tex Watson exemplar and seventeen points of identity between the print lifted on the door of the master bedroom and the left little finger on the Krenwinkel exemplar.

Attorney Fitzgerald asked the witness about him going to the scene of 8,000 crimes. The witness eventually stated that he for two or three years had gone to between fifteen and twenty crime scenes per day. Kanarek cross-examined the witness and stated that by Sergeant Granado using benzidine to test for blood he could have destroyed some of the prints at the La Bianca residence. The witness stated that he had arrived at the La Bianca residence before Sergeant Granado did.

Mr. Hughes asked if the witness had compared a fingerprint exemplar from Leslie Van Houten with the latents found at the La Bianca residence, knowing that none of those prints matched the prints of Miss Van Houten. The answer was "yes" meaning there was no match.

Then Witness number 35, Steven Weiss, an 11-year-old boy, testified to finding a revolver on a hillside in Sherman Oaks, California, on September 1, 1969. Mr. Fitzgerald asked the witness how he had picked up the gun when he found it. The young witness stated that he had picked it up by the tip of the barrel. Fitzgerald asked why. The witness responded "For the use of the fingerprints."

Steven Weiss

Fitzgerald then asked about the policeman who came to his house and his handling of the gun. The young witness stated (with a disappointed look) that the officer touched the gun all over with his hands which bought out a bit of laughter in the courtroom.

Witness 36, Michael Watson, a Los Angeles police department officer, alleged receiving the revolver from the father of Steven Weiss. Under cross-examination he stated that he handled the gun and removed the shells.

Witness 37, Sergeant Robert Calkins, a Los Angeles police department investigator, testified to retrieving the pistol at the Van Nuys police station on December 16, 1969. He testified to the fact that the right handgrip was missing. Attorney Fitzgerald asked about the flyers sent out to different police agencies in the US and Canada looking for the gun. Prosecutor Bugliosi asked if a flyer had ever been sent to LAPD Valley Services in Van Nuys. The witness answered, "Not to my knowledge"

Witness 38, Sergeant Dudley D. Barney, a Los Angeles police department's robbery division officer, gave a description of bullet fragments discharged and removed from Steven Parent's car.

Witness 39, Sergeant William Lee, a Los Angeles police department firearms expert and investigator, gave testimony about the brand of ammunition found and fired from the pistol at the slayings and gave a detailed explanation of tests conducted to identify firearms and bullets. He identified the Sebring bullet as being fired from the pistol used in the slayings and linksed shell casings from the same gun to the Spahn Ranch.

At last, court was adjourned for the day.

The trial proceedings resumed after a longer than usual recess of five days. While waiting impatiently for court to reconvene, the jury had a respite from the monotony of hotel living by spending a day, escorted by the ever-present deputies, at wonderful Disneyland in Anaheim.

When court reopened on Thursday, September 10, 1970, prosecutor Aaron Stovitz was taken off the case. In his place two young deputy district attorneys, Donald Musich and Stephen Kay were selected to assist now senior prosecutor Vincent Bugliosi.

[EDITOR'S NOTE: Aaron Stovitz was removed from his role as lead prosecutor by then District Attorney Evelle Younger amid speculation that it was in reaction to an offhand remark he was overheard as making regarding Susan Atkins. Susan Atkins had to be taken to the hospital because of stomach pains. According to a story in the LA Times quoting UPI he is said to have stated: "She's putting on an act worthy of Sarah Bernhardt." Stovitz had already caused problems for the DA when he gave a supposedly "off the record" interview to Rolling Stone in which he gave details of the case in violation of a gag order. He claimed it was background information. Bugliosi was originally assigned the case during the investigation and was happy to take over although he was quoted as saying: "I consider it a personal loss that he will no longer be co-prosecutor with me on this extremely important murder trial."

The following Sunday, September 6 a time bomb exploded on the sixth floor of the Hall of Justice about 35 feet down the hall from the DA's office and directly beneath the courtroom where Manson and the co-defendants were on trial. It blew an 9 x 11 foot hole in a wall and ruptured a six inch water main. It had been placed inside the washroom with a timing device on it.

Although the jury was completely unaware, there was a hearing where Kanarek assumed the jury would be aware of the bombing and other news about the trial in spite of the sequestration. Although this is speculation, this could have been the purpose of the bomb since it was set to go off on a Sunday when no one was in the building.

Bugliosi brought up a related matter never heard by the jury:

BUGLIOSI: One of our witnesses, Barbara Hoyt has left her parent's home. I don't have all of the details, but the mother said she received a threat on her life if she testified at this trial, she would be killed and so will her family. I know two things. I know the threat did not come from the prosecution and it did not come from an aunt I have that lives in Minnesota. I think the most reasonable inference is it came from the defense.]

♦ ♦ ♦

The first witness of the day to be called was Edward Lomax, witness number 40 on the calendar. Mr. Lomax was a sports and firearms salesman. He identified the gun used in the killings, the type of gun, the manufacturer and pieces of a walnut hand grip found in the hallway and living room of Miss Tate's home after the slayings in August 1969 that matched the left grip on the alleged murder weapon.

The next Witness, number 41 was Thomas J. Walleman, an unemployed ranch hand. Mr. Walleman said that he stayed at the Spahn movie ranch in Chatsworth during July 1969, when Manson and members of his "family" were living there. Walleman testified that the .22 caliber revolver that Manson took with him on a trip to a Hollywood apartment was similar to the gun identified as the death weapon in the Tate killings. But he didn't know for sure if it was the same revolver, but he said it did look like it.

The following day, Friday, September 11, Witness number 42, Danny DeCarlo, a former Navy gunner's mate, was called to the stand. The witness, a drifter and a gunsmith, admitted frankly being a member of the Manson "family." He met Manson at the Spahn Ranch in March 1969 initially to go to fix a motorcycle there. Mr. Kanarek had many objections during this testimony. The cultist leader gave Danny DeCarlo the run of the ranch and access to his girls. DeCarlo stayed at the ranch until August 1969. DeCarlo stated that Manson asked him to have his motorcycle club move to the ranch, but that they didn't want to.

DeCarlo then gave the names of all of the persons living at the ranch. Prosecutor Bugliosi showed him a photo exhibit of a girl who the witness identified as "Gypsy." When asked by the prosecutor about how he supported himself while at the ranch the witness answered: "by turning in pop bottles, selling motorcycle parts, pooling money together with others and garbage runs." The witness said that Susan Atkins told him that Manson "knows all and could see all."

He declared that Charles Manson called the police "pigs" and used the term "white collar workers who work from eight to five." According to this witness, Manson wanted the blacks and whites to militate against each other; and the words "Helter Skelter" were often repeated at the ranch.

Court was adjourned for the day, and the trial was recessed for three days.

As the Manson trial concluded its 13th week in Superior Court, the jurors were adjusting remarkably well despite their limited activities and hotel seclusion.

We panelists looked forward to every Friday evening, not only because it was the start of another weekend of rest, but because it promised a welcome change in the dinner menu and a change of scenery.

Sheriff Deputy Ann Orr

Sheriff Deputy Ann Orr, who usually made all the pre-arrangements for dinner in various restaurants, tried to promote and sustain a happy family spirit among all the jurors. She made it a point to find out who had a birthday or a wedding anniversary coming up. Greeting cards were purchased, signed by all of us at the appropriate time, and then presented to the honored guest at the dinner hour.

I realize it goes without writing that none of us was a tenor like Caruso or a coloratura like Galli-Curci, but we enjoyed singing loudly and enthusiastically the favorite stand-bye for such occasions; "Happy Birthday to You" and "For He's a Jolly Good fellow."

This practice of remembering special days in our lives helped immeasurably to create good humor and clean fun for us jurors on many of our dinner outings.

Weekend visitations brought renewal of family fellowship, a time of chatting, laughing and reminiscing. Here in the United States we refer to all of this as "good fellowship." The French refer to it as camaraderie and the Germans as Gemutlichkeit. I just thought that you'd like to know!

Meanwhile, back at our spacious apartment, my wife always arranged to spend those short weekends with me. While we were separated, we not only exchanged short telephone calls each day after the dinner hour to inquire how things were going, but we also exchanged short letters; our "little love notes" as we liked to call them.

Once every other week when my paycheck arrived at home, my wife would enclose a little "billet-doux" and mail it to me. In response, I would endorse the check and enclose a little note back to her. We joked about this romantic practice, but the spark of love was always there.

On special occasions, like a birthday or a wedding anniversary, and all the holidays that went by while we jurors were sequestered; Thanksgiving, Christmas, New Year's Day, Valentine's Day and Easter, we invariably exchanged greeting cards.

The court trial resumed on Thursday, September 17, 1970; witness Danny DeCarlo was recalled to the stand. Defense attorneys continued with cross examination. DeCarlo, age 26, testified candidly about his lifestyle at the Spahn ranch, his excessive consumption of alcohol and his predilection for firearms. He said that Manson gave him the job of taking care of all of the firearms on the ranch. He then described the guns; a sub machine gun, a .30 caliber carbine rifle, a .22 caliber rifle, an M-1 military rifle, a 20-gauge shotgun, a 12-gauge riot gun, in addition to the pistol.

DeCarlo alleged that Manson acquired the long barreled, nine shot revolver by trading a pick-up truck, owned by him (DeCarlo), for the gun. The witness went on to say that he saw at the ranch about 10 buck knives, which "family" members wore around their waists.

Under questioning from Vincent Bugliosi, DeCarlo further testified that he saw the leather thong around Manson's neck on the night of the killings when Charlie related that he was "the devil on the loose." DeCarlo also said he saw Manson buy a white nylon rope in a Santa Monica war surplus store, a rope similar to the one found around Sharon Tate and hair stylist Jay Sebring at the scene of the killings.

In all honesty, I must confess that it seemed to me many of the questions by the defense attorneys were frivolous and ridiculous, they had no relationship to the direct testimony at hand; the rest of the jurors felt as I did. Furthermore, Mr. Kanarek's constant interruptions and his outlandish questions, apparently his tactics to confuse and irritate the witness as well as the jurors, didn't work.

Naturally we jurors became irritated, more than once I wanted to jump up and shout out "Let's get on with the Trial!" But we jurors kept our "cool" as we sat in the panel section in silence with composed resignation.

On Friday morning September 18, 1970 the witness DeCarlo testified that the motorcycle gang "Straight Satans" had come to the Spahn Ranch to free him from Manson, but instead they partied, drinking beer with DeCarlo and they eventually left.

Fitzgerald asked the witness why he didn't leave with the motorcycle gang. He said he liked it there (at the Spahn Ranch) and that "the family was good to me." He also said he had an allegiance to the "Straight Satans" and that he loved Charles Manson.

During the afternoon court session on Friday September 18, 1970 Charles "Tex" Watson made an appearance in the courtroom.

He was called into court at the request of Defense attorney Paul Fitzgerald so that the Witness Danny DeCarlo could identify him.

Attorney Kanarek objected to this move and called for a mistrial. Judge Older denied the request stating he saw no reason why Mr. Watson should not appear to have the witness identify him.

Fitzgerald asked the witness if he recognized Watson in court and he replied "Yeah, he's right over there" pointing at Watson. Watson was asked to stand by Judge Older and identify himself, the Judge asked him twice to state his name; Watson stood up but said nothing. He was soon led out of the courtroom. The three women defendants, laughed, smiled and waved at him.

Witness DeCarlo, was finally excused from the stand after he identified Charles Manson and all of the "family" members. Before court adjournment, the final witness of the day approached the stand, Mr. William Lee, a police sergeant; he described the empty shell casings found on the Spahn ranch, which matched, the empty shell casings from the death weapon.

The court was back in session on Monday, September 21, 1970. Recalled to the witness stand was Los Angeles police Sergeant William Lee. The witness ended his testimony with an account of the finding of shell casings at the Spahn ranch.

Exhibit drawings of the shell casings were shown to the jury.

Witness number 43, Eleanor Lally, a realtor and manager of a beach house in Santa Monica, gave short testimony about the occupancy of an apartment by Mr. Saladin Nader who eventually left the country.

[EDITOR'S NOTE: Saladin Nader was a former lover of Linda Kasabian. In her testimony she stated Manson had ordered her to kill him on the night of the La Bianca murders. She testified she purposely knocked on the wrong door. This witness was likely brought in to prove where Saladin Nader had lived to corroborate Kasabian's testimony.]

◆   ◆   ◆

Witness number 44, a stable manager at the Spahn ranch, told of how she worked for 20 years for the blind owner, George Christian Spahn, who resided at the ranch. The witness said she met Manson and the other "family" members in 1968.

On Tuesday, September 22, as court reconvened, Mrs. Pearl was recalled to the witness stand, and testified that she saw a weapon at the ranch similar to the Western style revolver used as the murder weapon at the Tate estate on the wall of the Ranch hand's quarters. The witness identified clothing worn by Manson and "family" members and saw the nylon rope (in the back of the dune buggy) and leather thong worn by Manson around his neck, and the Buck knives worn by his "family" members.

Witness number 45, David Hannum, a cowboy and ranch hand at the Spahn ranch, informed the court that he loaned his car, a

Ruby Pearl

1961 Volvo Sedan to Linda Kasabian on August 12, 1969. Attorney Bugliosi asked the witness if Manson had said anything about humans and animals. Mr. Hannum stated that Manson said he'd rather kill humans than animals.

The witness was arrested on August 16, 1969.

[EDITOR'S NOTE: This refers to the raid of Spahn Ranch that led to the arrests of seven men and 20 women on suspicion of auto theft. This included "family" members, members of the Straight Satans and Charles Manson. The arrest warrant alleged they were stealing Volkswagens, dismantling them and using the parts to create dune buggies. Those arrested were released after ten days due to the wrong date on the arrest warrant. Upon their return to Spahn Ranch, they were assumed to have killed Shorty Shea, a ranch hand they believed had turned them into the police. Manson family members Steve Grogan, and Bruce Davis were later convicted of the crime. Shorty Shea's body was not found until 1977. Steve Grogan alleged that Tex Watson was present at the murder and ordered him to hit Shea with a pipe wrench. Tex Watson was never charged with the crime.]

❖ ❖ ❖

Witness number 46, William Gleason, deputy sheriff of the Los Angeles police department, testified to making the arrest of Manson and "family" members at the Spahn ranch on August 16, 1969. Description was given of all vehicles impounded at the ranch.

Witness number 47, Ralph Marshall, a police officer of San Fernando

Valley, stated he booked Mary Brunner and Sandra Collins (also known as Sandra Good) on August 8, 1969.

Witness number 48, Samuel Olmstead, deputy of Malibu Station, said he saw Manson for the first time on July 28, 1969; that Manson made a statement to Police that he was Charles Summers and that black people were at the Ranch to kill them; that Manson wanted the police and his "family" members to team up and wipe out the Black Panthers. The witness alleged that 11 "family" members were armed.

Witness number 49, George Grap, a former deputy and real estate salesman, testified that on July 28, 1969, he had talked with Manson and other officers regarding Manson's tale about the Black Panthers.

[EDITOR'S NOTE: The relevance of this testimony is more apparent with the benefit of hindsight. It confirms Manson's state of mind before the murders. As Dianne Lake describes in her book *Member of the Family, My Story of Charles Manson, Life Inside his Cult and the Darkness that Ended the Sixties*, it was clear the energy at the ranch had changed. She describes Manson obsessively looking at topical maps to plot out escape routes. Olmstead testified that on July 28th, one day after the murder of Gary Hinman by Bobby Beausoleil, he met Charles Manson, who gave the name of Charles Summers, at the intersection of Santa Susana Pass Road and Topanga Canyon at about 1:00 am. From the transcript.

BUGLIOSI: What was Mr. Manson doing at that time?
OLMSTEAD: He told me he was looking out for the Family; he was the lookout at that point and he was watching for Black Panthers who he expected to attack the Family at the Spahn Ranch.

Part of Manson's paranoia might have been related not only to his increasing delusion, but the fact that he had shot drug dealer Bernard "Lotsapoppa" Crowe and presumed not only that he was dead but that he was a member of the black panthers. Between early July until the murders there was an escalation of intensity. After the murders the "Family" escaped to the desert, a plan they had in place for many months.]

Former Deputy Grap asked Manson why he had been hiding in the bush area close to the intersection in a dune buggy. He related that he was on lookout for the Black Panthers.

Spahn Ranch

George Spahn

MANSON: We got into a hassle with a couple of those black mother-fuckers and we put one of them in the hospital, and they said they would get us for that."

He further said to the deputy:

MANSON: "You know, you guys, you cops ought to get smart and join up with us. Those guys are out to kill both you and us. I know you hate them as much as we do, but if we join together, we could solve this. problem. Well, they are out to stop us, we should stop them first."]

CHAPTER FOURTEEN

BARBARA HOYT

On Wednesday, September 23, witness number 50, Barbara Hoyt, 18-years-old and a member of the Manson "family," told of living with the "family" from April to September 1969; that she heard about the Tate murders the day following the killing; that Susan Atkins turned to the news report in a trailer at the Spahn Ranch to listen to a description of the murders; and overheard Susan Atkins say that "Sharon Tate was the last to die and had to watch the others die first."

On Thursday September 24, witness Barbara Hoyt was recalled to the witness stand.

Attorney Kanarek, tried to prove that she can't see without her glasses. He asked Miss Hoyt to remove them and tell him how many fingers he was holding up. He moved from maybe 25 feet to about three feet away from the witness in his demonstration. Miss Hoyt said she lost her glasses in the hills near the Spahn Ranch and didn't wear them most of the time she was with the "family" there. She stated she can see fine without them.

Attorney Kanarek asked the witness how many feet it is from her head to the kitchen, she replied maybe 16 or 17 feet. Kanarek asked her how loud the conversation was with Susan Atkins and the others. Miss Hoyt said she was talking loudly. Kanarek demonstrated from about 40 feet away and spoke. Miss Hoyt said she heard all of his words and said she knew what Susan Atkins had said that day to others.

Miss Hoyt told of the attempt on her life to prevent her from testifying. She gave an account of how she was persuaded to go to Hawaii.

While she was there a hamburger was ordered and given to her by Miss Morehouse, a "family" member; and that shortly thereafter, she suffered an extreme attack of nausea and dizziness, causing hospitalization for several days; and that upon her return to the mainland, she stayed with her parents in the San Fernando Valley.

On Friday, September 25, redirect testimony of Barbara Hoyt resumed. Attorney Bugliosi asked Miss Hoyt if Charles Manson had ever ordered her

Juan Flynn

to engage in a sex act with Juan Flynn, a former member of the "family" while they were at the Death Valley Meyer's Ranch in September 1969. She answered "yes." Bugliosi asked her if she wanted to do it and she answered "no." He asked if Mr. Manson was present and she answered "yes." Miss Hoyt testified that she and another girl, "Simi Valley Sherri" (Sherry Ann Cooper) walked away from the Ranch. Attorney Bugliosi asked why she left, and the witness said she was scared to stay there anymore and that she feared Charlie.

In response to attorney Fitzgerald, Miss Hoyt did say that Charles Manson had caught up with the girls when leaving and gave them $20 for bus Fare. Miss Hoyt was ordered to return to court on October 16, 1970

[EDITOR'S NOTE: The jury was unaware that Bugliosi had informed the Court ahead of time that witness Barbara Hoyt had received an anonymous phone call threatening her life. Approximately two days after that hearing in chambers Barbara Hoyt was found in Honolulu almost dead.

BUGLIOSI: It was a member of the Family that gave her an overdose and I state to defense counsel again, because I am going to do everything within my power to get this out in front of the jury, and this particular member of the Family is going to be prosecuted either by our office or by Honolulu.

I just tell the Court this because I ask the Court for some type of help. Apparently, the defendants and members of their Family will stop at nothing.]

❖   ❖   ❖

Witness George Grap was recalled to the witness stand and he described briefly the path driven by Manson and the police to the Spahn ranch.

Witness number 51, Donald Dunlap, deputy sheriff, outlined details pertaining to the arrest of Manson at the Spahn ranch on August 16, 1969. Photograph entries were shown to the jury. Court adjourned for the day.

It could be very well expected, as the week came to a close, that due to the large number of witnesses to be called during the trial, the process of examination and cross-examination would require, many, many weeks. I think we realized we were not as far along as we had hoped. We spent time putting the trial out of our minds. We were always admonished each time we left the courtroom that we were not to discuss the case with each other but would have time for that during deliberations. It was a welcome change to be at our hotel socializing and I would not have wanted to discuss the case or think about it when not in the courtroom. We did everything possible to unwind so we could begin again on Monday.

The trial proceedings resumed on September 28, 1970, Monday morning, with the jury assembled in the courtroom fresh and relaxed.

Witness number 52, Juan Flynn, alias John Leo Flynn, age 25, was the first to be called to the witness stand that day. The witness, a part time actor and former ranch hand at the Spahn ranch testified he met Manson in 1968; he related the conversation that took place after the Tate La Bianca murders and told of remarks made by Susan Atkins that "We're going to get some fucking pigs." Flynn identified the car used in the La Bianca slayings on the evening of August 9, 1969; and said he saw Linda Kasabian, Susan Atkins, Patricia Krenwinkel, Leslie Van Houten, Clem Tufts, Tex Watson, and Charles Manson, the driver, leaving in the car one evening. He said he couldn't remember the exact date.

Flynn testified that he recognized the .22 caliber revolver used in the Tate killings as the one he saw Manson and others fire at the Spahn ranch. Flynn then said he recognized the white nylon rope found tied around the necks of Sharon Tate and hair stylist Jay Sebring as the same rope as was carried by Manson in the rear of the dune buggy. Flynn also told of a conversation that took place in the kitchen at the ranch after the seven Tate La Bianca murders.

He stated that "Manson grabbed me by the hair and put a knife on my throat and then he said, "Don't you know I'm the one that's doing all these killings?" The witness stated that Manson also made the statement that he wanted to show "the black man how to kill these white pigs."

On cross-examination the witness admitted that while he didn't agree with everything that Manson did, he said "He has a right to do whatever he does." He also said he became very cautious around Manson. He stated, "If I didn't go along with him, I'd be hanging from a tree and everyone would come and stick knives in me."

On Tuesday, September 29, witness Juan Flynn was recalled to the stand. He stated that he became afraid of Manson after realizing that he was telling the truth about being behind the seven Tate La Bianca murders. When cross-examined by Kanarek the witness told of carrying a shotgun or a long stick to protect himself from Manson. He also said he had taken LSD seven or eight times while at the Spahn Ranch. The witness stated that at one time he was a very mixed up man.

The witness described again the incident when Manson grabbed him by the hair and put a knife on his throat and then he said "Don't you know I'm the one that's doing all these killings?"

Kanarek also asked Flynn why he didn't tell police about the admission from Manson. Flynn said, "I didn't want to believe him." Kanarek then told the witness that he thought he fabricated the whole story and that the incident did not occur.

Prosecutor Bugliosi and Kanarek then exchanged words; the word "liar" was used. Judge Older ordered them to stop. Kanarek asked Flynn if he was trying to further his movie career by appearing at the trial to gain publicity. The witness replied, "The kind of publicity I am getting here now, I can tell you I don't need, you big catfish." Court was adjourned by Judge Older immediately.

CHAPTER FIFTEEN

HAPPY BIRTHDAY

The dawn loomed forth bright and sunny the morning of Wednesday September 30, 1970. This was an outstanding and memorable day for me. With humble and sincere gratitude, I recall fond memories for the warm friendship and affection of fellow jurors, deputies and others.

The downpour of birthday greetings started the first thing in the morning at breakfast. Seating myself at the table, I noticed an envelope tucked under my plate; a birthday card from my fellow jurors. I tried to express my thanks, when everyone burst out with "happy birthday to you!"

Halfway through breakfast, our waitress appeared with a candle lit cupcake for me. Soon waitresses, busboys, and other kitchen help gathered around our table and gaily sang out "happy birthday to you."

Riding in the sheriff's bus to the courthouse, jurors and deputies started harmonizing the happy birthday refrain.

Upon entering the court room, some news reporters held up a happy birthday poster.

Taking my seat in the jury box and looking around, I saw Charles Manson across the room gazing at me. To my great surprise, he made a motion and silently mouthed "happy birthday."

Judge Older and some of the attorneys, as they entered the court room, looked in my direction, smiled pleasantly, and nodded their acknowledgement.

When court recessed for lunch, the jurors took a short drive to the

Hilton coffee shop to eat. About midway through our lunch, our waitress approached our table with a small candle-lit birthday cake. Waitresses, bus-boys and jurors all joined in with "happy birthday to you."

In the afternoon, as court recessed for a fifteen-minute break and the jurors retired to their secluded waiting room upstairs, the Manson girl defendants passing our door could be heard singing "happy birthday to you."

Driving back to the Ambassador hotel after court adjourned for the day, the jurors began to harmonize again. I was feeling a little uneasy thinking perhaps someone might be getting a little fed up with the old birthday song, but the atmosphere seemed to be permeated with jovial and social spirit.

That evening the jurors assembled downstairs in the Ambassador coffee shop dinner. Before we finished eating, our waitress appeared with a large tray of cupcakes, birthday treats for all present! Once again everybody joined in with "happy birthday to you."

The day was not over yet, however. This was bowling night for a small group of jurors, a sport in which I participated. All was peace and quiet when we arrived at the bowling alley. We started our first game and as I approached the bowling lane with ball in hand, a voice thundered out through the loudspeaker; Happy birthday, Herman." That prompted the group to sing the most famous of all birthday anniversary songs yet one more time.

When, finally, the day ended and all of the jurors retired to the gratitude of their hotel rooms, all had had their fill of "Happy Birthday!"

There was testimony from the witness Juan Flynn on this day. The witness said he was intimidated, meaning; "the telephone would ring in the middle of the night and the voice on the other end would go oink, oink, snort, snort, oink, oink, snort, snort, they were pig sounds."

The witness also said that two weeks ago, two hippie cult members, a man and a woman, came to him at the Spahn ranch where he was chopping wood. "They said they were going to do me in right there." The witness said he had an ax and he told them "to help themselves." He said "They told me someone downtown wanted to see me. And they said if you are not going with us, then we are going to get you right here. When they saw I wasn't going to do what they wanted, the girl started crying." He said also that he had received two threatening notes, one said, "How big a change does it take to scrub away from the face of the earth, a lazy image like you." The other said, "This is an indictment on your life."

Manson, during the testimony said something like "man, it's all prosecution here, there's no defense here."

Judge Older did caution the jurors that much of what the witness was testifying to related to Mr. Manson only and not the others.

The witness acknowledged that it was a year before he told Los Angeles authorities about the fact that Manson had told him he was behind the seven killings. Prosecutor Bugliosi asked him if it was because he feared for his life. The witness answered "partly."

The witness also said that one day he went with Manson to an ice cream parlor and afterwards they drove to some of Flynn's relatives where Manson suggested they go inside and cut them to pieces. The suggestion was dropped immediately.

The number one song on the "Billboard" charts on September 30, 1970 was *Ain't no Mountain High Enough* by Diana Ross. Today it felt that we the jurors were climbing a huge mountain, and it was hardly over.

The Tate La Bianca trial was now in its sixteenth week.

On Thursday and Friday, October 1 and 2, 1970, Juan Flynn, the part time motion picture actor, took the witness stand to deliver further testimony. Under cross examination carried out by the defense attorneys, Flynn told of threat notes which were given to him by "family" members and which he put in his pockets. But the notes were destroyed when his lady friend washed his clothes. Manson had approached him in the ranch kitchen, grabbed him by the hair, tilted his head back, stuck a knife blade to his throat and declared, "Don't you know I'm the one who's doing all these killings." The witness then told of threats made by Manson when he made jail visits to the cult leader.

Prosecutor Vincent Bugliosi questioned Mr. Flynn about Manson's belief in "programming" of children by their parents and society, and how people could be "un-programmed." Flynn testified that Manson said, "To un-program yourself you must get rid of all the egotism, all your wants, give up your mother and your father, get rid of all your inhibitions, just blank yourself out." Flynn said the cult leader talked about "un-programming" members of the "family" by getting rid of their sexual inhibitions through perverted acts.

Under cross examination by the defense, the witness was questioned about his service record in Vietnam. Flynn said that he served 11 months and 29 days in Vietnam, was wounded and received two purple hearts.

On Friday morning, as court reconvened and witness Juan Flynn was recalled to the stand, the proceedings were disrupted by Charles Manson and the three women defendants. The 35-year-old Manson and his girls caused a disturbance with outbursts, chanting and singing.

Superior Court Judge Charles Older ordered Manson and the female trio removed from the courtroom. The trial continued with the defendants listening from nearby rooms by means of loudspeakers.

Prosecutor Vincent Bugliosi was held in contempt of court after an outburst at Kanarek. He was the fourth attorney to be held in contempt of court since the beginning of the trial. The others were Kanarek and defense attorneys Ronald Hughes and Daye Shinn.

Court proceedings resumed with witness number 53, David Steuber, a police officer and CHP (California Highway Patrol) investigator from Fresno, California. Officer Steuber testified to meeting Juan Flynn for the first time on December 19,1969 and taking a tape recording of Flynn's knife incident story as told to him on that date. The witness was allowed to play the part of the taped interview dealing with Manson's admission of the killings. The panelists heard Juan Flynn say "Then he was looking at me real funny, and then he grabbed me by the hair like that and he put a knife to my throat and then he said, 'Don't you know I am the one who is doing all these killings.' "

Finally, trial testimony ended for the day as court was suspended for another weekend.

The first weekend of October was very warm and sunny, and many of the jurors took full advantage of the enclosed Ambassador Hotel courtyard and swimming pool.

On many Saturday mornings I would participate and enjoy a fast game of paddle ball with fellow jurors. Some of the younger fellows would joke around and rib me about keeping up with them on the court. But after a few games they soon learned that I could hold my own. They would laughingly wisecrack and ask: "how old are you, Herman?" I would clown around and say, "Don't let this gray hair fool you. There is still a lot of life left in the old man!"

Our morning play sessions were great fun and just the thing to relieve tension and provide some physical exercise. Some of the fellows went ahead and made their own wooden paddles, saving on the cost of hotel rental equipment.

This Sunday a trip to the Los Angeles international airport was scheduled and arranged for the jurors and their spouses who wished to participate, and for our buddies and ever-ready companions, the bailiffs.

The group enjoyed a guided tour through the spacious and luxurious 747 airplane, which was one of the highlights of the day

[EDITOR'S NOTE: At this time in 1970, the 747 was new state-of-the-art technology. The first 747 flew on February 9, 1969 over Western Washington. Pan Am took delivery of its first 747 on January 15, 1970.]

❖   ❖   ❖

Later, we went up to the sky room, the radar tower, the pilots dispatch quarters and the baggage conveyer lanes. We were permitted to observe the working crew behind the scenes. It was fascinating and intriguing to see the timing and precision of flight operations.

Later in the afternoon we went to the Proud Bird restaurant near the airport for dinner. While we dined, we watched the beautiful scenic view of planes taking off and landing. It was a most enjoyable and relaxing experience for all of us.

The following Monday morning, October 5, 1970, the jurors marched diligently into the court room with notebooks and pencils in hand and prepared to hear further testimony in the Tate La Bianca murder trial.

The first witness of the day, number 54 was Sergeant Paul Whitely, a detective with the Los Angeles sheriff's homicide department. Sergeant Whitely briefly testified to making the arrest of Robert Beausoleil on August 7, 1969.

The cult leader, Charles Manson, disrupted further court proceedings by making a threatening outburst to Superior Court Judge Charles Older. Manson, first used threatening words, and then he leaped over the counsel table and headed for the Judge with a pencil in one hand. Bailiff William Murray tackled Manson from behind and Deputy Sheriff Digby (Dick) Rowe leaped forward, knocking Manson to the floor; and with the help of another bailiff Robert Weekley they subdued Manson and carried him from the courtroom.

The three female defendants then stood up and began singing and chanting, but their words made no sense. They were also removed from the courtroom to the adjacent lockup, where with Manson they could listen to the trial proceedings over a sound system.

[EDITOR'S NOTE: Detective Paul Whitely testified to arresting Robert Beausoleil which greatly upset Manson. The jury would have had no awareness of the connection between Beausoleil's arrest two days before the murders and Manson. It is still unclear why he responded as he did but here is what happened in open court:

MANSON: May I examine him, your Honor?

COURT: No, you may not.

MANSON: You are going to use this court to kill me?

COURT: (to the witness) You may step down.

MANSON: Are you going to use this courtroom to kill me? Do you want me dead?

COURT: Mr. Manson!

MANSON: The minute I see you are going to kll me, you know what I am going to do.

COURT: What are you going to do?

MANSON: You know. You have studied your books. You know who you are talking to?

COURT: If you don't stop, Mr. Manson--and I order you to stop now—I will have to have you removed as I did the other day.

MANSON: Order me to be quiet while you kill me with your courtroom? Does that make much sense? Am I supposed to lay here and just let you kill me? I am a human being. I am going to fight for my life, one way or another. You should let me do it with words.

COURT: If you don't stop, I will have to have you removed.

MANSON: I will have to have you removed if you don't stop. I have a little system of my own. (Court ignores him).

MANSON: Do you think I'm kidding?

Manson then jumped over the counsel table towrd the bench until he was subdued by the bailiff. The Judge ordered him removed.

MANSON: Don't let me get the jump on your boys. In the name of Christian justice someone should cut your head off.

Then the co-defendants began to chant in unison "noem be oro decaio," something that still today remains undefined. The co-defendant's lawyers tried to move for a mistrial but the Judge said they would not benefit from their wrongdoing. He thought it was obvious they were taking their cue from Manson and fully intended to disrupt the proceedings.]

❖   ❖   ❖

The next witness, number 55 was Sergeant Manuel Gutierrez of the Los Angeles Police homicide department. Sergeant Gutierrez, who was a courtroom spectator, told what he observed when Manson first carved an "X" on his forehead and the three girl defendants marked their foreheads the following day. The witness said that Manson made a threatening motion with his fingers across his throat to Linda Kasabian when she was on the witness stand. The witness identified an exhibit photograph of the words "Helter Skelter," which was like the words on the poster which was on the cabinet door out at the Spahn ranch.

Witness number 56, Sergeant Albert Lavallee of the Los Angeles police department, testified briefly about taking aerial photographs of the Spahn ranch.

Witness number 57, Lt. Jack Holt, deputy sheriff of Los Angeles County, told of booking and arresting Sandra Pugh (Sandra Good), and Mary Brunner on October 8, 1969.

Witness number 58, DeWayne Wolfer, criminologist and firearms expert from the Los Angeles police department, testified to making firearms tests of sounds and noises at the Tate residence on August 18, 1969.

The following day, October 6, Sergeant Wolfer was recalled to the witness stand. The witness described briefly the test of sound discharging firearms when stereo music was on and when stereo music was off at the guest house adjacent to the Tate residence.

Witness number 59, Jerrold Friedman, age 26, gave short testimony about receiving a phone call from Steven Parent on August 8, 1969 at 11:45 p.m.

The next witness (number 60) called to the stand, was Mrs. Gloria Hardaway, a clerk in the jail of the women's division in the Los Angeles sheriff's department. Mrs. Hardaway gave a short testimony about the booking and release of Sandra Pugh (Sandra Good), on August 12, 1969.

Court reconvened the following day, October 7, with witness number 61, Mrs. Rachel Burgess, deputy sheriff of Los Angeles County. Mrs. Burgess testified briefly concerning the document record of booking and the release of Mary Brunner on September 23, 1969.

The next witness was Sergeant Michael McGann, who was recalled to the witness stand. He estimated the mileage from the Tate residence to the Webber home as 1.8 miles, and from the Tate residence to the Weiss home as 2.6 miles; and that the death pistol was found about 5.4 miles from the Tate residence.

The following witness was deputy sheriff William Gleason, who was recalled to the stand. Mr. Gleason stated the number of persons arrested at the Spahn Ranch as 27 adults and five or six minors.

On Thursday, October 8, the jury retired to the jurors' room, while Judge Older and court counsel went into chambers for further discussion.

CHAPTER SIXTEEN

JUROR JOHN ELLIS HAS THE FLOOR

As the trial continued the jury panel had to accept unforeseen hardships and problems which might have been expected had we truly understood our length of sequestration. First and foremost, of course the jurors had to forfeit the freedom of normal activity, and secondary, we had to become resigned to hotel cooking and to a restaurant diet which was a big change from home cooking.

[EDITOR'S NOTE: In 1970, home cooking was more the rule rather than the exception. People did not eat out on a regular basis but rather left restaurants for special occasions such as anniversaries or birthdays.

Burger joints with car hops did exist, especially in California, but drive-throughs, a staple for many busy families of today were just beginning. In fact, Wendy's Hamburgers is said to have opened the first drive-through restaurant in Columbus, Ohio in 1970. Young women were expected to learn to cook in home economics classes and family meals were expected to be eaten together at home. So, for Herman Tubick and the other jurors, the novelty of restaurant food was wearing thin.]

❖   ❖   ❖

At the Ambassador hotel the daily menu was always the same, the first few weeks everyone enjoyed eating out, but as the days stretched into months, it became quite depressing.

The jurors were always at a loss; what to order that would provide a balanced and nutritious meal and still be appetizing, the outlook on the small selection was bleak, never tender or tasty, in desperation we tried switching to hamburger, but that too was a disappointment. In addition to our distress, the service was slow and so many of our meals were cooked lukewarm.

Little wonder then, that some of the jurors resorted to the use of an electric hot plate in their rooms on weekends when families would bring a prepared dish for a fast warm up. Sometimes readymade hamburgers, tacos or hotdogs were brought in.

Whenever the jurors dined out in various finer restaurants, we enjoyed the change as well as the better food and selection, but because of the large group we still had a problem in slow-paced service. The jury panel had to be segregated from the general public, therefore, we usually would have one waitress that was available to serve us, and by the time half of the group was served and began eating, the other half was still waiting to be served.

It was no surprise, when some of the jurors became frustrated at the dinner hour. Most of us learned to accept the situation with good humor, a few would complain bitterly, and some even joked about it. Amazingly enough, no one ever blew their top during the long ordeal.

The deputies dining with us were concerned and well-aware of our unhappy meal situation, and finally, as the days stretched into months, it was reported to the Judge. The Judge, wishing to relieve tension and promote relaxation for the jurors at dinner time, permitted an order of a cocktail if anyone requested an alcoholic beverage.

Later, when the jurors went home and the long ordeal was over, we learned that the press had released a story about the Tate La Bianca jurors having highballs at dinner. Defense attorney Irving Kanarek tried to discredit one of the jurors, Mrs. Evelyn Hines, by commenting that she might not be fit to carry on as a juror, since she never drank at home. I felt the implication was ridiculous. Accordingly, the public was under the impression that the Manson jurors were "wined and dined and had a ball." They didn't know the pressure we were under. We may have been able to tolerate the time away from our families with the extra efforts made, but the presumption that we were remotely having a fun time was absurd and farfetched!

During the long confinement there were many occasions when I held periodic meetings and discussions in the jury room when court was recessed. Of course, this was not to discuss the details of the case but rather to check in on how everyone was holding up under the pressure. I encouraged those talks, feeling that if the jurors voiced their frustrations and grievances, brought them out in the open and got them off their chest, they would not only feel better, but it would ease some of the strain and stress and help to build moral support as we went along.

The major complaints that were brought out by members of the panel were; the short court sessions, the many delays in the court hearings and the prolonged tactics of the defense attorneys.

Some of the jurors requested that I speak to Judge Older to ask if anything could be done to step up the court hearings, possibly, have the court sessions start earlier in the morning and have shorter lunch periods with longer hours in the afternoon, any feasible change that would promote a faster pace in the trial proceedings would be welcomed. I listened, expressed my own concern and stated that I understood well their anxiety and their impatience. I tried to reason with the jurors, emphasizing that it was not my place to tell the Judge how to run his courtroom, urging them to have patience; after all I pointed out, the trial should be more than half over.

Some were unhappy about the limited family visitations, they wanted the privilege to see spouses and families during week days in the evening, and a few who had pets at home, suggested that they be allowed to be brought to the hotel once in a while, so that they could see them.

There were further complaints about the evening walks which were discontinued; unfortunately, some of the jurors were to be blamed for that. An incident occurred one evening while some of the members were out walking, escorted by two deputies. It appears that a few panelists felt too exuberant and started singing and whistling and began to scatter out a bit too far from each other. They were seen by a newspaper reporter and the jurors' "improper conduct" was reported to the Judge. They were probably simply expressing cabin fever. Letting off steam was better than people losing their minds. However, the jury panel was now only allowed to take walks around the enclosed Ambassador grounds, escorted by the deputies for a bit of air and exercise.

The jurors were not allowed to use the hotel gym at first, but later, restrictions were lifted. Also, some felt abused that they were restricted from talking with anyone on the Ambassador grounds, not even to discuss the weather, as one put it! They were craving human contact from those other than their jury peers.

Some of the women and a few of the men said they were just dying to do some honest to goodness shopping.

Amid all the loud griping and chatter of trivial complaints it was obvious that sharing feelings resulted in a more relaxed atmosphere. it appeared everyone felt better. Whereupon, I reemphasized my desire not to take it to the Judge. Griping felt better but our many complaints were very petty compared to the magnitude of the task at hand. I reminded them that we had better be resigned to the situation.

After one of our jury room gripe sessions a deputy entered and told the jurors to take their places in the court room. This witness would remind us why we were there. As was so frequent during the court procedure, Judge Older and court counsel returned from private conference. A lot of discussion was held out of the earshot of the jury as it pertained to points of law and we were there to determine the facts. It was likely the Judge and attorneys were discussing motions and the admissibility of evidence. These had

Virginia Graham Castro

to be out of our purview as we were not to consider it in our deliberations unless it was allowed through testimony or stipulation. Stipulation was when the attorneys agreed to the facts without having to have testimony. This rarely happened.

When the testimony resumed on Friday October 9th, one of the more important witnesses in the Tate La Bianca trial was called to the stand. Witness number 62 on the list, Mrs. Virginia Graham Castro, age 37, who was a cellmate of Susan Atkins at the Sybil Brand Institute for Women, in November 1969.

Mrs. Castro testified about the conversations with Miss Atkins when they were both in the dormitory at the Institute. According to her testimony, Susan Atkins related that she stabbed Sharon Tate to death and took part in the stabbing of Jay Sebring and another man who ran through the living room at the Tate residence. Mrs. Castro related that Miss Atkins confessed to her that she did not know any of these people at the Tate residence, but "all were to die." The witness then told of meeting Ronnie Howard, another inmate at the Sybil Brand Institute, who confirmed Susan Atkins' story to the witness.

The witness stated; about November 6, 1969 Susan Atkins sat down next to her in Dormitory 800 and talked about the Tate murders. She said to her "You know who did it, don't you? Well you're looking at her." Virginia Castro said that Susan stated that Sharon Tate and Jay Sebring were in the bedroom and they were taken into the living room where another man (Wojciech Frykowski) ran past her and as he ran past her, she stabbed him four or five times. He got to the front door screaming "help, help." Miss Atkins then said, "And would you believe he was screaming help, help and nobody came?"

The witness said that Susan said she was holding Sharon Tate's arms behind her and a crying Sharon Tate said, "Please don't kill me, I don't want to die, I just want to have my baby."

She continued that Susan then said, "Look bitch, you might as well face it right now, you're going to die, and I don't feel a thing behind it."

Bugliosi asked her if Susan Atkins had said she had killed the actress and the witness said "yes, Susan Atkins said "I killed her."" Bugliosi asked her about the blood and Virginia stated that Susan said she looked at her hand and put it to her mouth and said, "To taste death and yet give life, wow what a trick." Virginia said that Susan said she got quite a thrill out of the soft feeling of a knife as it entered a body. The witness said, "They wanted to do more, like take their eyes and squish them against the wall, cut their fingers off, but they ran out of time."

The witness, Virginia Castro, stated when asked by Bugliosi about how Miss Atkins felt after the murders; "Susan stated she was tired but felt elated and was at peace with herself and seemed excited about telling me about it and showed no remorse." Susan Atkins was then bought in to the courtroom and was identified by the witness. None of the defendants had been in the courtroom since their disruptions.

Daye Shinn cross examined the witness and asked if she'd been convicted of two felonies using different names, the answer was "yes." Shinn asked what she thought of Miss Atkins when she first met her. The witness replied that "she looked like a teenager who shouldn't be there." Shinn asked the witness if she had made "advances" towards Susan Atkins and the answer was "no." Mrs. Castro was excused for the day and court testimony was once again delayed for another day with a holiday on Monday, the commemoration of Columbus Day.

As was so often in the Tate La Bianca trial, the jurors were unhappy with all the delays, even for holidays. They grumbled and complained and they at times became discouraged, but not defeated. I knew that the real test was yet to come. We had to persevere to reach the end, and for this, I prayed and hoped for the best outcome.

The jury panel would have to overlook the many court delays, the constant interruptions and the repetitious objections from Kanarek, the prolonged tactics of the defense, and even the short court hearings. We had to, to reach our goal. Despite the odds against all the jurors persevering and lasting out the long ordeal, it seemed each of us was up for the challenge.

I first heard the news from one of the deputies that one of our alternates John Ellis, had lost his father. Johnny, as I called Mr. Ellis was a young bachelor, a quiet and modest fellow, somewhat on the shy side. He was employed by the telephone company as a repair technician, and he had served in the armed forces during the Korean War.

John and I became good friends during the long confinement; we exchanged tales of our service days, mine as a Marine and his in the Army. During our leisure hours at the hotel we enjoyed a good work out in the courtyard, playing table tennis, paddle ball or we swam in the pool. Many evenings we would sit and watch the sports events on the television and share our comments and views in the world of sports.

As it was with many of us during the long trial, we had our depressing and frustrating moments with which each one of us had to cope. This troubled moment was now facing John Ellis when he received the news about his fathers' death. I expressed my concern and sympathy, and I asked John what he intended to do. He told me his father had passed away in San Francisco and since the funeral and burial would take place there, he had decided not to attend the funeral. He felt his first obligation was to stay with the jury panel, his attendance at the funeral wouldn't help his father any. I expressed my admiration for his noble gesture. I completely understood his choice, having faced it when I lost my brother. We had made a commitment and were going to see it through.

John's discipline in the Army served him well in the grueling experience of the Tate La Bianca trial. On many occasions when the court was in recess, the jurors would be sitting around, waiting in the jury room, wondering when we would be called back into open court. Many times, we sat and waited all day, until finally, we would be driven back to the hotel only to return the following day.

It is not surprising that when the jurors became edgy and frustrated, they continued to air out their complaints. After all, nothing could be done about them. John Ellis would sit there in silence and shake his head in dismay, until finally one day he suddenly got up and said, "quiet everyone; I've got the floor now!" Imagine, here was John; naturally shy, getting up to make a speech. It was beautiful to hear and see him, he was suddenly animated, his boyish face lit up in sober seriousness, gesturing with his hands, his words went something like this; "Ladies and Gentlemen of the jury, do you realize how lucky you are, nothing to worry about, we've got police protection around the clock. Just stop and think, right this moment there are hundreds of people on the outside world who are being attacked, robbed, beaten or even killed. Some are wandering in the streets, with no home and no place to go.

Here we have an elegant hotel to live in, a lovely room, a clean bed, our meals are served and cooked for us, no dirty dishes to do, no beds to make and no rooms to clean. In the morning we are awakened by a gentle tap on our door, in case our alarm does not go off. We have our own private bathroom, no one yelling at us to hurry up and get out! Then we go down to breakfast, our deputies and protectors greeting us with a smile and a cheery "good morning." We never get lonely at mealtime; there is always lots of company. Then we have a nice ride in a chauffeured bus, the windows are smeared but that's so no one can take a pot-shot at us. We can sit back, relax and enjoy the drive, with no worry about the congested freeway traffic, the hustle and bustle of getting to work on time. Once we get into the court room, we have front row reserved seats to the most sensational and international murder trial of the year. We are surrounded by news reporters and the television media. Later we are escorted to the elegant Hilton coffee shop for lunch, and in the afternoon, we have a few hours of court hearing. We get $5.00 a day, room and board and our laundry is done; we never had it so good! No worry or fretting about cutting the grass or doing house-work. No wondering if the car will start in the morning. So, relax and enjoy it, you're on a nice long vacation!"

As Johnny came to the end of his speech, we were laughing, and the tension was broken. I couldn't help thinking his loss had made him see what was important, and perhaps the seriousness of the trial was also giving us a bit of perspective. We had difficulty being taken out of our lives. Many things were inconvenient. But he was right, we were the lucky ones. We still had lives to go back to. No matter the result of the trial, the victims were never going home and their families never to be the same. Although we never discussed it, I know some of us were praying at night and giving thanks that we were observers and there would be a time we would return to our waiting loved ones.

We now returned to keeping busy. We sought whatever activities were at hand to pass the time. Some brought along reading material, playing cards, puzzles and some of the women brought along their knitting and sewing items. The fellows had a couple of golf balls they putted around the room. Some would set up facial tissue boxes across the table to serve as a net and play table tennis; a few tried their hand at throwing darts. We invented games to help pass the time and to help us compartmentalize. In our off hours we were people, not jurors. We were friends by the nature of being thrown together into a situation only we could understand. We tried to make the best of it.

Throughout the course of the trial, there were many instances when John Ellis proved to be an advocate among us, spreading humor and cheer by his earthy characterization of events. I was happy he was there.

On Monday's holiday, the jurors and our deputies went on a picnic; it was a beautiful day for an outing, very warm and sunny. We left in the early morning, driving into the San Fernando Valley and up into the hills. I felt a great appreciation for the beauty and the green freshness of the countryside. I know we were all feeling more grateful. The driver took the sheriff's bus into an isolated park grounds deserted except for a couple of caretakers.

This was calculated, I'm sure to give us a chance to roam around freely and relax away from the everyday turmoil and the strain of the trial. The jurors seemed childlike, grilling hamburgers and hot dogs out in the open, and even wading barefoot in the cool and sparkling brook that was discovered nearby.

The deputies brought picnic foods and some playing equipment, a soft ball, a bat and a Croquet set, just what was needed for a bit of exercise. When finally, we rode back to the hotel, everyone seemed relaxed and carefree; it was the end of a perfect day, a gift that almost helped us forget what was still ahead.

CHAPTER SEVENTEEN

THE 18TH WEEK

The Tate La Bianca murder trial was now in its 18th week. The jurors assembled into the courtroom on October 13, but we remained only a short time.

Witness Virginia Graham Castro was recalled to the stand and declared that she related the confession story of Susan Atkins to Ronnie Howard when both were inmates at the Sybil Brand Institute.

After a brief re-direct questioning of the witness by prosecutor Bugliosi, Miss Castro was excused, and the jury was also excused for the day.

On Wednesday, October 14, the jurors reconvened in open court and the 63rd witness took the stand. Ronnie Howard, age 31, also known as Veronica Hughes, testified that Susan Atkins told her that she stabbed Sharon Tate in the chest over

Ronnie Howard

and over again until she killed her; and that the conversation took place in the Sybil Brand Institute when both were cellmates in November 1969. The witness stated that Susan Atkins said that stabbing the actress was a form of sexual release. Miss Howard told of reporting to the police, the conversation of the Tate killings, on December 19, 1969, and stated that a reward of $25,000 would be given for information in connection with the Tate murders.

At that time she said that she and Susan Atkins were separated at the Institute but Susan managed to get a letter to her, telling her at first when she found she was the informer that she wanted to slit her throat, but then she realized that in fact she (Susan) was the informer and held no ill feelings toward the witness.

Defense attorney Daye Shinn cross-examined the witness with personal questions relating to criminal record and convictions for extortion and forgery, and various assumed names.

Judge Older motioned to sheriff deputy William Murray to remove two bearded male spectators from the courtroom.

On Thursday, October 15, the jury remained at the Ambassador hotel waiting to be called for further court hearings.

The jurors were once again becoming edgy with anticipation and impatient wondering about the reason for the delay. Most of us indulged in card playing and reading to pass the time.

Trial testimony resumed on Friday, October 16, with the jury back in open court.

Gregg Jakobson

The court council made an announcement that former witness Barbara Hoyt would return to the witness stand on November 19, 1970.

The next prosecution witness, number 64, was Gregg Jakobson, age 30, a Music Record Producer for Terry Melcher. Prosecutor Bugliosi questioned Mr. Jakobson.

The defendants were still not back in the courtroom for being disruptive about two weeks ago. The defense attorneys said each time they were asked if they would come back and behave themselves the answer was "no."

The witness stated that he first met Charles Manson in May 1968 at the home of Dennis Wilson, a member of the *Beach Boys*. Jakobson stated that he believed in Charles Manson's potential ability as a musical performer.

The witness told of Manson's beliefs and philosophy (and how he had talked with him about this many times) that there was no such thing as right or wrong, no good and no bad, and that pain and death are only concepts in man's mind; and that it is all right to kill human beings. Pain does not exist.

Defense attorney Shinn made a motion that this testimony was limited to Manson and the jury was so instructed by Judge Older.

He said Manson told him that he had died a long time ago and that he had experienced death many times, that it was beautiful, that it was only a physical change of the body and the spirit went on. Therefore there is no such thing as death. Time and death didn't exist; it was only a concept of man.

Jakobson claimed that the cult leader told him of being Jesus Christ and the Devil; and that Manson declared that "Helter Skelter," between the blacks and the whites was imminent, and that blacks would take over the establishment, but in the end would seek him out to rule when they found out that they could not rule.

Manson's attorney Kanarek had many, many objections during this testimony. Jakobson told of seeing Manson after the Tate la Bianca murders, about August or September 1969 and that Manson "moved like an animal in a cage. The electricity was coming out of him. His hair was on end and his eyes were wild." The witness said that the cult leader told him the "family" was going to descend into a "bottomless pit" in the Death Valley area by means of a special nylon rope and remain there until the blacks destroyed the whites. Manson believed that blacks would not be able to handle the reins of power and would give it back to the whites that were left alive and who Manson believed would be the "Manson family." Manson didn't want anything to do with the current establishment because he felt it was coming to an end. He said, "Manson had a face or mask for everyone he dealt with, he had a thousand faces."

The prosecution witness testified that Manson derived his beliefs from passages in the Bible and from lyrics of the Beatles (who he believed were prophets) songs as *Helter Skelter*, *Revolution 9*, *Piggies*, *BlackBird* and *Sexy Sadie*." Prosecutor Bugliosi showed an exhibit to the witness which was the Beatles *White Album* and asked if he had seen it at the Spahn Ranch, the answer was "yes." The prosecutor read the lyrics from other exhibits from some of these songs to the witness. The witness said that Manson said the meaning of *Helter Skelter* was Armageddon, *Piggies* was the white establishment, *Revolution 9* was the same as *Revelations Nine* in the *Bible* and *Blackbird* was a song about the black man with his broken wings learning to fly.

The witness said that Manson would occasionally use a line from the song *Helter Skelter* and insert it into his own song. He said the words Helter Skelter were written also on a mural near Santa Susanna Road near the front buildings at the Spahn Ranch.

Prosecutor Bugliosi introduced an exhibit which is the *King James Bible* reading verses from *Revelations* and referring to the "bottomless pit." The prosecutor asked the witness what the language about the bottomless pit means.

"The bottomless pit was the bottomless pit in the desert, Death Valley which was where Manson intended to go and escape Helter Skelter." Among the many questions and answered given from the *Revelations* verses, the prosecutor asked about this verse; "Saying to the sixth angel who had the trumpet, release the four angels who are bound at the great river Euphrates." He then asked, "Did Manson say who the four angels were?" The witness stated that "the four angels were the Beatles."

The witness also stated that he was producing Charlie in the studio and produced some of Manson's songs, stating that he was a friend of Manson during this time.

Attorney Paul Fitzgerald cross-examined the witness. The witness stated that he thought Manson showed musical talent. Jakobson was impressed with Manson's songs and said he sang and played his own music. He described Manson as a truthful man who was interested in protecting children and teenagers from the evil of the world. The witness also said he was a close friend.

Another weekend was upon us, after an abbreviated week of trial proceedings that seemed to drag at a slow pace with a holiday in-between and only two full days of court testimony for the jury to hear. It was time again for family members and jurors to get together, visiting, reminiscing and sharing meals. The families routinely arrived on Saturday afternoon and departed the following day mid-afternoon.

This weekend the jurors noticed a posted announcement on the bulletin board; "a tour to the Natural History Museum of Los Angeles County on Sunday right after lunch."

The next day, all the jurors were ready and waiting, eager and delighted for a chance to get out and see some of the outside world. Soon we were riding into Exposition Park, the site of the famous Natural History museum which is one of the outstanding attractions in Los Angeles County for tourists and Los Angeleans. We disembarked from the sheriff's bus and walked through a beautiful rose garden.,

Here at this huge museum, one was keenly aware of man's great achievements and nature's pre-eminent beauty. The many famous exhibits displaying natural and historical art were truly priceless and irreplaceable.

Many of the jurors and families participating in the tour, previously visited the museum at one time or another, but we were grateful for a change of scenery. We assured everyone that in a building of this magnitude a person is certain to have missed seeing something worthwhile during the first time around.

The hours sped by quickly and soon we were boarding the bus and on our way. Driving a short distance, we arrived at one of our old familiar spots, the Hilton coffee shop. Here we had dinner before we were whisked off back to our "lockup" quarters at the Ambassador hotel.

On Monday morning, October 19, the jurors were back in the courtroom, filing into the familiar jury box.

The Tate La Bianca murder trial resumed with the cross examination of prosecution witness Gregg Jakobson. The witness stated that his boss, Terry Melcher, went to the Spahn Ranch twice in late May 1969 and listened to the songs of Charles Manson, but Terry decided that they were not worth commercial recordings. Manson later asked the witness for Terry Melcher's phone number, but he gave him the one for his answering service.

Defense attorney Kanarek suggested to the witness that he was putting on or leading Manson on, in his hope that he would become a recording star, so that the witness could have sexual relations with the family member girls at the Spahn Ranch. The witness stated this was not true.

The witness said that Manson once spoke of the "Negros ripping off some white families." Kanarek asked how he could remember that so well; the witness replied that he remembered the sky, the sun, the girls, the motorcycles, the hills, the music and the guitars and thought what a wonderful scene this could make in a movie.

On Tuesday, October 20, witness Gregg Jakobson was recalled once again to the stand. The witness testified that Manson had scouted the home of Beach Boy musician Dennis Wilson, the night he was looking for a murder victim and ended up at the home of Leno and Rosemary La Bianca. The witness identified an area near Will Rogers State Park as the home of the recording star. The witness also said that all the girls at the Spahn Ranch loved Manson and that Manson loved them also.

After a brief re-direct testimony in which the prosecution witness stated that Charles Manson believed in the "Nietzsche Theory," or the "Master Race," this being Manson's philosophy, the witness was finally excused.

There were so many questions asked of this important witness, so many answers from him, so many defense objections along the way and so many meetings at the bench that at times it was hard to follow. All the jurors were extremely perturbed at the constant defense objections, especially from defense attorney Kanarek, as so many of them seemed frivolous.

Witness number 65 was called; Shahrokh Hatami, an Iranian born photographer who was Sharon Tate's personal photographer, who identified a picture of Charles Manson as resembling a man he saw at the actress's home in late march, 1969, about five months before she and four others were killed at the rented estate.

Hatami stated that Miss Tate came out of the house and could easily see the man he was talking to. The witness testified that he went to Miss Tate's house in late March 1969, to film the blond movie star as she packed for a trip to Rome. The witness related that when he saw a man through the window approach the house, unsure and hesitant and walking without permission, he challenged the man and angrily told him to take the back alley if he wanted to visit the guest house in the rear.

The witness described the man as being about 30 to 32 years of age, short and thin with long dark brown or nearly black hair, and stubble of beard. The witness was then excused.

Before court adjourned for the day, Superior Court Judge Charles Older made an announcement. The court day would be lengthened by an hour and a quarter, the Judge apparently being concerned about the slow rate of progress in the trial.

In my opinion it was an excellent move, and the rest of the jurors felt the same way, trusting now that the trial procedure would move along considerably faster.

From now on, court would be in session from 9 A.M. to 12:00 noon and from 2:00 P.M. to 4:30 P.M., with a fifteen-minute recess during the morning and during the afternoon.

On Wednesday, October 21, court was in session at 9:00 A.M., and the first witness to be recalled was Shahrokh Hatami. A brief re-direct examination by prosecutor Vincent Bugliosi, related to the description of the man confronted at the Tate estate. Hatami stated that Manson's picture bore a resemblance to the man he saw.

The next witness, number 66 was Rudolph Altobelli, owner of the Cielo drive property and friend and landlord to Sharon Tate and before her, to Terry Melcher. Mr. Altobelli also is a manager of professional talent and was a personal agent of Sharon Tate.

Mr. Altobelli told of renting his home to Terry Melcher from 1966 to 1968, and later to Sharon Tate in March 1969. The witness testified that on March 23, 1969, Manson approached him at the Cielo Drive address, then inhabited by Sharon Tate. He said Manson came to the back guest house and asked about Melcher, a record company producer. Mr. Altobelli said he recognized Charles Manson during their first meeting in musician Dennis Wilson's house in the summer of 1968 and listened to a tape recording of Manson's singing and guitar playing. The witness identified Manson in the courtroom.

Terry Melcher

Defense attorney Irving Kanarek took Rudolph Altobelli under cross examination, with questions being argumentative and personal.

Recalled to the witness stand was Los Angeles Police Sergeant William Lee. The sergeant gave a short testimony of shell casings from the death weapon compared with a test of firing and shell casings found at the Spahn ranch.

The next witness was Charles Koenig, number 67, a gas station attendant at a Standard station. Mr. Koenig testified that he had found a wallet in the water tank at the restroom of the gas station on December 10, 1969. He said that he called the police and turned the wallet and contents over to them. The witness said a watch, coins and some papers belonged to Mrs. La Bianca.

On Thursday, October 22, Judge Older gave permission for Charles Manson and the three women defendants to return to the courtroom and hopefully, to listen quietly to testimony in the Tate La Bianca murder trial.

Witness Charles Koenig was recalled to the stand for brief re-direct testimony. He gave the location of the gas station in Sylmar off the Golden State

Roseanne Walker

freeway on Encinita Boulevard.

The next witness number 68 on the list was Roseanne Walker, who was an inmate at the Sybil Brand Institute for Women from July 23, 1969 to November 1969. She said she met Susan Atkins (Susan Glutz) at the Institute.

The witness testified that when the news of the Tate La Bianca murders was broadcast, and a comment was made on the glasses found Sadie said could solve the murders. Miss Atkins made a statement, "That ain't how it went down." Miss Walker stated that Susan said "I'm in more trouble than you know about. I was in on those other murders." When they were separated in November 1969 Susan cried and said, "I know I'll never see you again."

Defense attorney Paul Fitzgerald asked the witness if the reason she was talking so slowly was because she had taken tranquilizers. She denied that and said she was nervous.

Harold True

The next prosecution witness number 69 was Harold True, age 30, a student who resided with three other men at 3267 Waverly Drive, next door to 3301 Waverly Drive, the home of the wealthy grocer, Leno La Bianca, and his wife Rosemary.

The witness testified that Manson was a friend of his since their meeting in March 1967, in a Topanga Canyon house; that he saw the defendant and visited perhaps five to ten times at the Spahn Ranch in Chatsworth; and that he knew the other "family" members.

CHAPTER EIGHTEEN

TERRY MELCHER AND MANSON'S MUSIC

The witness today would prove to be significant to the larger picture we would be called to analyze in the deliberation room. For now, he was simply another brick in the building the prosecution was attempting to build for us.

Terry Melcher, the 28-year-old son of Doris Day, and the State's 70th witness, took the stand. He said that he lived at the 10050 Cielo Drive estate from 1966 to January 1969, prior to the time that the Benedict Canyon house was leased by Miss Tate and her movie director husband, Roman Polanski. I know many of us were scrutinizing Mr. Melcher to see any resemblance to his famous mother.

Melcher testified that he met Charles Manson, the hippie cult leader, at a party in Dennis Wilson's home during the summer of 1968, and later, on May 18, 1969, auditioned Manson, a self-styled soul singer and guitarist; and that another session at the Spahn ranch followed a few days later.

Melcher was the owner of a record company and was the executive producer for his mother's television series. The witness said that he was unimpressed with Manson as a singer and musician. There were no plans ever made to record or publish Manson's songs. He said he was more impressed with what he saw at the Spahn Ranch while auditioning Manson. He said there seemed to be a great deal of unity and that Manson seemed to be the focal point of it all. He said he listened to Manson sing about 15 to 20 songs while "family" members hummed along while Manson played his guitar.

Stephanie Schram

The next witness number 71, Stephanie Schram, age 18, testified briefly that she met Charles Manson on August 3, 1969, near Big Sur, CA, and became one of the "family" members and went into Death Valley in the fall of 1969. Under re-direct testimony, the witness declared that Manson beat her up in the desert. She was feeling home-sick and Manson asked her if she wanted to go home. She said "yes." Manson then took a rifle and hit her in the head with it and told her she better forget about going home.

The witness also said that she and others went to Devil's Canyon early on August 9. But she also said that she thought Manson left the camp at dark that night but came back during the night or the early morning. Miss Schram was then excused, and the court session was adjourned for the day.

On Friday evening, we were given a surprise. Deputy Ann Orr, our social organizer did not tell us where we would be dining.

Upon arriving at the Ambassador hotel after our day ended in the court-room, we had plenty of time to shower, relax a bit, groom and dress for dinner. We always tried to make Friday nights a little festive. Then when we were ready and dressed, we went out into the parking lot and started to board the sheriff's bus. We were startled to see all our spouses, beaming happily and dressed elegantly, seated in the back. "Surprise, surprise," every-one shouted.

Then Deputy Orr stepped in and announced that this was a special cele-bration for wedding anniversaries for the month of October, for the months in the past, and for the ones to come. A few persons on the jury had their wedding anniversary in October. My wife and I would be celebrating ours on October 25.

It felt good that everyone could be excited for everyone else. We were jovial and even sang in harmony to a happy anniversary refrain.

We drove through town and up into Chinatown and stopped at Little Joe's Italian Restaurant. Once inside, we had to wait a short while before we were all seated in a group. Indeed, Little Joe's was a busy place.

Each of us had a choice in the dinner menu. We had traditional Italian dishes of spaghetti and meat balls or of ravioli which were very authentic. We were also given a glass of sparkling burgundy wine.

The court had to make sure the spouses paid for their own dinner tab. We were already being closely scrutinized and assumed to be wined and dined. There could not be even the appearance of something improper or it would be brought to the attention of the Judge. It was only in hindsight that I realized why the spouses had to pay their own way. At the time we were just happy. My wife surprised me and the rest of the jury with a large anniversary sheet cake, which she had purchased and concealed in the sheriff's bus under the driver's seat. Deputy Ann Orr brought in the cake for everyone to see before it was cut up and served for dessert, a piece being distributed to everyone present.

Our evening of celebration and social gathering with jurors, wives, husbands and a few family members was not only welcome and gratifying, but it gave everyone an opportunity to know one another a little better and helped to bring about a closer friendship.

After our arrival at the Ambassador Hotel, everyone retired to their rooms. The spirit of gaiety was still with me as my wife and I retired for the night and it was easy to forget why we were there. I remember remarking to my wife Helen, "Here we are sweetheart, a private room at a famous hotel after a wonderful anniversary dinner. All that is missing is the melody of violins on our balcony!"

On Sunday, October 25, our daughter, Sister Paulynne, came to visit me and my wife. She came well prepared to extend happy anniversary greetings to us. She carted along her accordion to play for us, brought several brightly wrapped and beribboned gifts, and a big colored poster that she made and tacked on my wall, big enough so that I couldn't miss seeing it as soon as I entered my room. It covered half of one side of the wall with huge cutout letters announcing, "Happy Anniversary, Mom and Dad!" My daughter also gifted us with a free-hand cartoon sketch of my wife and me, and brightly colored scenic pictures, cut out from magazines of our favorite sports. These would help me through the long days and nights that I would still be sequestered for the remainder of the trial.

The jury was back in open court, Monday morning, October 26, and the trial proceedings resumed with witness number 72, Janet M. Owens, alias Kitt Flecher, former inmate at the Sybil Brand Institute for Women, from October 1969, to November 11, 1969.

Miss Owens told briefly of meeting and knowing Susan Atkins at the Institute and receiving a letter from her.

The next witness called to the stand, 73rd on the list, was Deputy Sheriff Lila Koelker, a house officer at the Women's Institute. Deputy Koelker stated briefly that she picked up Susan Atkins' letter at her cell in December 1969, and after a photostat was made, it was mailed to Miss Owens.

The following witness number 74 was Lieutenant Deputy Sheriff Carolyn Alley, an officer at the Institute. A brief statement was made by Lt. Alley; that she received Susan Atkins' letter in December 1969 and made a transfer to Joseph Stevenson for a Photostat copy, according to the rules and regulations at the Sybil Brand Institute.

Recalled to the witness stand was Sergeant Gutierrez, who stated that he picked up the Photostat copy of Susan Atkins letter on December 15, 1969.

The court clerk called the next prosecution witness number 75, who was Sergeant William McKellar, a detective from Alabama. Sergeant McKellar testified briefly of making the arrest of Patricia Krenwinkel, December 1, 1969, who gave her name as Montgomery. The witness identified Miss Krenwinkel in the courtroom.

The following witness number 76 was Sergeant Frank Patchett, of the Los Angeles Police Department. Sergeant Patchett told of removing the leather thongs from Charles Manson's boot and trousers which were found under the seat of a 1959 white car when the vehicle was impounded.

The Sergeant's testimony corresponded with the previous testimony given by Linda Kasabian.

Brooks Poston, 21, and the state's 77th witness, took the stand to testify that in June 1968, he met Charles Manson at Dennis Wilson's residence, and in October 1968, went to live at the Spahn ranch.

Poston, a Texan and former "family" devotee, said that Charles Manson predicted in 1969 that a black-white race war, called Helter Skelter, would erupt when Negroes would slaughter the whites in their neighborhoods.

The witness testified that cultist Charles Manson derived his theory of impending racial warfare from the Beatles in the lyrics from the *White double Album* produced by the British group. Brooks Poston quoted Manson as saying that the victims would be stabbed, cut up, and "pig" would be written on the walls in their blood. After the killings the whites were going to go into the black ghetto and kill, but then the blacks would wipe out the white survivors. But after that the blacks would then turn over the responsibility of governing to Manson. The witness said that Manson thought the Beatles were talking to him through their songs.

Poston said that he had many conversations with Manson at the Spahn and Barker Ranches during which the defendant told him that he had to "get through the fear of death. Acid can take you through it." The witness believed that Charles Manson was Jesus Christ, and that he was completely subservient to his will.

According to the witness, the cult leader experienced death on a "drug trip." Defense attorney Paul Fitzgerald asked the witness if Mr. Manson told you, you had to die, would you have died, and the witness stated he was working on it.

The following day, Tuesday, October 27, Brooks Poston was recalled to the stand, and under cross examination by Defense lawyer Ronald Hughes, the witness said that Manson told him to get a knife and kill the Sheriff of Shoshone.

Prosecutor Vincent Bugliosi on redirect examination, asked for a more detailed recollection.

The witness related, that Manson said, "If you're with us, you'll take this knife, sneak into the sheriff's house in Shoshone and cut his throat."

The next witness, number 78, was Paul Watkins, 20, a former "family" member, who told of his experiences recruiting young girls for Charles Manson, one of which was Leslie Van Houten.

Watkins said that Manson discussed "Helter Skelter" constantly at the Barker Ranch, and quoted Manson as saying, "I'm going to show Blackie how to do it." The witness admitted to taking LSD between 150 and 200 times, beginning when he was 16 years old. Both witnesses on the stand, Watkins and Poston, testi-

Paul Watkins

fied that they once thought that Manson was Jesus Christ, and the defendant was always talking about death. Both testified that the cult leader preached that a black-white race war was imminent, but Manson and "family" members would escape it in the bottomless pit in the desert and return to rule.

The court clerk called the next witness to take the stand, Frank H. Fowles III, District Attorney of Inyo County, witness number 79. The District

Attorney testified to the photograph exhibits that were taken at the shack at the Meyers Ranch, and pictures and measurements of the interior, the distance from the kitchen door to the bedroom wall. Photograph exhibits were shown of the Barker ranch, Goler Wash, Lotus Mine, and the school bus once occupied by the "family."

The next witness number 80 was Officer James Pursell of the California Highway Patrol and Frank Fowles assistant. Officer Pursell told of making the arrest of Patricia Krenwinkel, Susan Atkins and Leslie Van Houten at the Barker Ranch, on October 10, 1969, and the arrest of Charles Manson on October 12, 1969.

The panelists were presented with special court exhibits 8, 9 and 11, stipulations of letters written by Susan Atkins in mid-December 1969.

Exhibit 8, Atkins admitted being in the first house, not in the second house when murders were committed and threatened to cut throats.

Exhibit 9, Atkins admitted to cell mate to seven counts of murder.

Exhibit 11, Atkins' explanatory remarks on "why she did it, why she talked to cell mate about the murders" and "I did what I did because I had to do it."

The court session was concluded for the day and the trial was adjourned for the next five days.

The Tate La Bianca murder trial was now in the final day of the 20th week. The panelists made their daily appearance at the Hall of Justice, going up into the jury room and waiting to be called into the court room for further testimony hearings.

For the next three days, the jurors sat around, secluded on the upper floor of the courtroom, restlessly waiting, and trying to pass the time. Each one brought something along to amuse them. Some brought playing cards, crossword puzzles, jig saw puzzles, ping pong balls and paddles, a few golf balls, and a putter. The women brought their knitting and crocheting, a few novels and even jacks and a ball.

One more day went by, Tuesday November 3, was Election Day in Los Angeles; court was not in session.

CHAPTER NINETEEN

THE LAST WITNESS FOR THE PROSECUTION

On Thursday, November 5th, a key prosecution witness, number 81 on the list, was called to the stand; Miss Dianne Elizabeth Lake, age 17, alias Diane Bluestein, sometimes called "Snake" by the "family" members. Miss Lake joined the group at the age of 14, in 1967. The witness told of a conversation with Leslie Van Houten at Willow Springs in Death Valley, when they were both "family" members. Miss Van Houten told Dianne that she had stabbed someone who was already dead; that she didn't want to do it, but she did it anyway. She said that Van Houten told her that "She wiped fingerprints around the rooms of the La Bianca home on the night of the murders."

Dianne "Snake" Lake

According to the witness, the time was early August 1969, when Miss Van Houten came in about 7:00 a.m., and within a few minutes, a car drove up and a man walked towards the house. She (Miss Van Houten) said, "don't let the man in or see me because he just gave me a ride from Griffith Park." Then, Miss Lake stated, the defendant hid under the sheets on a mattress until the man left. Dianne, the teenager, also testified that Patricia Krenwinkel once told her that she had dragged Abigail Folger from the bedroom to the living room of the Tate residence on the night of the murders.

Miss Lake also told that Manson ordered her to do certain chores like housework and taking care of the babies at the Spahn ranch. And Manson held "family" meetings for the entire group and gave assignments to each one.

Under direct questioning by Bugliosi, Miss Lake said that Manson talked about killing people for at least a year before the seven Tate La Bianca murders in August 1969. He (Manson) said, "We had to be willing to kill pigs to help the black people start the revolution, "Helter Skelter." According to the cult leader, "pigs" were the white Establishment, the white-collar workers.

Dianne Lake admitted, under cross examination, that she had taken LSD about 50 to 100 times and was committed to Patton State Hospital in San Bernardino from January 10, 1970 to August 30 the same year.

The defense began cross examination of the witness when finally, court was adjourned for the day.

On Friday, November 6, because of illness of one of the jurors, Mrs. Thelma McKenzie, court was not in session.

Whenever one of the panelists complained of not feeling well or a sign of illness was noticed amongst us, everyone was concerned.

It goes without saying, that living under one roof after all these weeks; we became a big family, trying to look after each other giving advice and counseling on what to do and what not to do. When anyone ran out of aspirin or other medicinal home remedy, everyone was obliging and willing to lend a hand, loaning whatever he or she had in supply of medicine. And the deputy sheriffs who were assigned to guard us, kept a watchful eye upon the jurors, any sign of serious illness was never neglected.

During Thursday's court proceedings, one of the jurors, Mrs. Thelma McKenzie, felt ill and had a fainting spell. After completion of the trial session, the ailing panelist was taken to the County USC Medical center for a brief examination, but the nature of the illness was not considered serious.

The long weekend for the jury at the Ambassador Hotel, sequestered since being impaneled 17 weeks ago, was spent quietly on the premises, visiting with spouses and family members.

On Monday, November 9, 1970, the jury of the Tate La Bianca murder trial was back in the court room. And the ailing juror, after a four-day weekend of rest was well enough to make an appearance. The final major prosecution witness, Dianne Lake was recalled to the stand.

Under cross examination by Paul Fitzgerald, Miss Lake admitted that she lied to the Grand Jury in December of 1969 when Charles Manson and his three girl defendants were indicted, because she was afraid of Manson and the "family" members.

The witness testified that she was threatened, and the Manson "family" would kill her if she said anything to anyone of authority.

The young woman also admitted that she lied regarding when she first heard of the Tate La Bianca murders, whether she had lived at the Spahn Ranch and about her name and age. During the Grand testimony Lake had testified that she had not heard about the murders until her arrest when in fact she had learned about the crimes from Tex Watson before going into Death Valley where she was arrested with Charles Manson on October 12, 1969.

On redirect examination, prosecutor Vincent Bugliosi asked questions designed to show that the District Attorney's Office had decided not to prosecute Dianne Lake because she was a juvenile when she testified before the Grand Jury, and her lies did not materially affect the Grand Jury's indictment of Manson and the others.

According to the witness, on one of those occasions, late August 1969, at Willow Springs in Death Valley, when she, Manson, and other members were on LSD, Charlie got up and slugged her in the mouth, and many other times would beat her up.

The 35-year-old cult leader interrupted court procedure and cried out at Superior Court Judge Older, time and time again.

After several admonishments, Manson was removed from the courtroom by the bailiffs, and led to a speaker equipped holding room. As he was led away, Manson muttered, "You've got your flunkies. It would be different if it was just you and me."

In the past, the three women defendants, Susan Atkins, Patricia Krenwinkel and Leslie Van Houten, had quickly followed Manson's lead when he created a disruption, but this time, however, the young women remained quiet through the rest of the afternoon session.

On Tuesday, November 10, the jury assembled into their assigned seats and court was called to order in Department 104. Charles Manson was back in the courtroom with the female defendants. The court clerk called Dianne Lake to the stand, the teenager's third day of testimony.

The witness under cross examination by defense attorney Irving Kanarek related once again being afraid of Manson and his "family" members and feared they would kill her. Miss Lake referred to the time of the roundup of Manson and his members by Inyo County authorities in October of 1969.

The young teenager said that she shared a jail cell with the four members of the Manson "family" when she was threatened. The statement was made that "I'm going to kill you."

During re-cross examination by defense attorney Ronald Hughes, Miss Lake said that she had taken LSD from 40 to 50 times and had smoked marijuana.

Special exhibits were shown to the court; documents and statements of Miss Lake, presented by Officer Sartuche. Court adjourned for the day.

On Wednesday, November 11, 1970, the court was not in session; it was a national holiday, Veteran's Day on the calendar.

The following day, November 12, the court trial resumed with a recall of witness Dianne Lake.

Under re-direct testimony, Miss Lake told how Manson had hurt her on many occasions. "He hit me with a chair leg, and he kicked me, and he whipped me with an electrical cord."

The witness repeated her earlier statement that Manson threatened to kill her in September or October 1969, when she was still a member of the hippie cult.

Miss Lake said she saw Leslie Van Houten burn a rope, a purse, and her clothes when she returned to the Spahn Ranch in early August 1969. Miss Van Houten also gave her some foreign coins and Canadian nickels.

Special exhibits of Dianne Lake's statements and documents were presented to the jury in the courtroom.

The next witness, number 82, was Dr. Blake Skrdla, a psychiatrist, who was appointed by the court to examine Dianne Lake and verify her competency.

Dr. Skrdla testified that he examined Miss Lake on October 26, 1970 and found "no impairment of memory," and she, Dianne Lake is able to recall her 1969 conversations with Miss Van Houten and the other "family" members, despite her use of the drug, LSD.

Under cross examination, Dr. Skrdla presented an exhibit of a medical report of Dianne Lake, while she was at the Patton State Hospital.

The next witness was Dr. Harold C. Deering, a psychiatrist, who was witness number 83 on the list. Dr. Deering testified that he had examined

Dianne Lake on October 26, 1970 and found Miss Lake sane and in good health. The doctor also stated that despite Miss Lake's use of drugs, her memory would not be impaired.

It was disclosed by the two court-appointed psychiatrists, and several Patton State members, that Dianne Lake had recuperated from severe drug induced psychosis. They stated Miss Lake is now living in a foster home after being treated at Patton State Hospital from January 12 to August 30, 1969. The defense concluded with its cross examination, and court was adjourned for the day.

Chapter Twenty

Prosecution and Defense Rest

The jury panel was experiencing a feeling of frustration and weariness as the slow, tedious procedure of the Tate La Bianca murder trial was nearing the Thanksgiving Holiday. That hopeful anticipation, nevertheless, remained in the hearts of the jurors. That possibly, in the month of December the trial would be coming to a close and a Christmas holiday would be celebrated at home with family.

An incident occurred about this time which touched me deeply. I was fully aware, of course, of the grueling experience the jurors were facing as the trial dragged on into months, but in this moment of anguish of one woman juror, however, reflected the full impact of strain and frustration that many of us were struggling with. I will not mention the woman's name, for I do not want to exploit her personal feelings of mental distress.

That afternoon, hearing a knock at my door, I went to see who it was. Standing there was a woman juror, weeping in anguish, a deputy was with her. The deputy anxiously asked me, "Herman, will you please talk with her!?"

"Yes, of course, do come in," I replied. As the woman entered my room, out of the presence of the deputy, she broke down and sobbed. "I can't stand it, I can't stand it any longer, and it's driving me crazy! I miss my husband and kids so much; I want to be with them. How in God's name can you stand it, Herman, don't you feel anything?" she cried out.

"Of course, I do, it's all bottled up inside of me," I said. "God only knows I have my bad moments when I get uptight," I confessed, "but I turn to prayer and ask God for patience and strength to go on. I leave my room and get busy, do something, go and talk to someone. We're all in the same boat, it's a real struggle for all of us, and it takes a lot of guts and courage to keep going."

As she continued to sob, I added, "But I believe we can make it if we stick together. Anytime you want to talk, please feel free to knock on my door. I'll be glad to sit and visit, if I'm not around, visit with one of the other jurors, or go and talk with one of the deputies."

"Oh, talk about the deputies" she replied airing out her complaint. "I really got mad at one of them; I swore at him and told him a thing or two. Who in the hell does he think he is ordering me around like that!" When she stopped sobbing, she said, "You know, I am ashamed to face him now, it's going to be embarrassing."

"Don't worry about it, and don't take it to heart," I replied trying to console her. "It really could have been any of us. We all have our ways of letting off steam. Haven't you watched the fierce competition between Zamora and McBride during paddle tennis? That was instead of someone resorting to violence. Thank goodness for sports."

She was becoming calm. "The deputies realize that we are under terrible strain, that there will be frustrating moments when some of us will lose patience and blow our top, and I am sure they were expecting it a lot sooner than this. I am sure they will overlook it and won't hold it against us. You must consider that the deputies have a job to do and a responsibility to face, just as we do; they are here to protect us and tell us what to do and what not to do."

"I never really thought of it that way," she said thoughtfully, composed and now at ease. "Try and take it easy, hold your head up and relax" I said smiling at her.

"If you can take it, I guess I can too" she replied, "I hope to God to have the patience and courage to see it through. Thanks Herman, for talking to me, your words and advice is as encouraging as can be, please say a prayer for me, now and then."

"I will, I promise," I assured her as we walked to the door.

Another week ended, and a hotel break was planned for the jurors, a tour was scheduled for early Sunday morning, right after breakfast. Our deputy Ann Orr, who usually arranged the outings for various sightseeing tours for the jurors and families, went to great lengths to come up with something new for us that would suit our differences in age and interests. We needed the break in the monotony. This week it was a ride and trip to the Navy Yard in Long Beach.

This was to be a guided tour aboard the Navy Vessel U.S.S. Denver. We breezed along into the picturesque Vincent Thomas Bridge to Terminal Island; the view of the sea and blue of the sky was beautiful to behold and the sailboats in the far distance looked like miniature toys.

[EDITOR'S NOTE: The Long Beach Naval Shipyard, which closed in 1997 was located on Terminal Island between Long Beach and the San Pedro district of Los Angeles. It occupied half the island, the other half occupied by the Terminal Island Federal Correctional Institute. Of course, the jurors had no idea that Charles Manson had spent quite a bit of time as an inmate there. The first time Manson went to Terminal Island was for a probation violation due to a stolen car taken across state lines. Manson was sent to Terminal Island for a second time in 1966 from McNeil Island, Washington where he had a sentence for violating probation for a check-cashing charge. He was released on March 21,1967 after spending half of his then 31 years in prison or institutions. He is said to have requested to stay in prison as it had become his home. The jurors had no idea of the irony that Terminal Island had represented a safe harbor for Manson before he formed his "family."]

❖   ❖   ❖

Eventually, we were winding our way into the Navy Yard and up to the parking lot. Leaving the bus, we walked on to the pier towards the huge naval vessel and up the gang plank.

Some of the fellow jurors, who were familiar with naval regulations, saluted the flag and greeted the Officer of the Day (Signal granting permission to board the ship). One of the Officers introduced the Captain of the Ship and his staff to the jurors and their guests.

The guided tour began from the top side deck to the bottom side. First view of the top deck looked very intriguing with the torpedo tubes and the mounted anti-aircraft turret guns, and a small flight deck for helicopter landings. As we looked up one could see the "Crows-Nest" and the lookout observation post.

We followed our guide to the Captain's bridge. Here was the main commanding post, a dispatch center for giving orders to all points of the ship as well as to all personnel. Here also was the navigation room with radar screens and telephones. We went through the mess hall, all neat and clean with long rows of dining tables, and we viewed the large spotless kitchen, the huge kitchen utensils and coffee urns. Those reminded me of large cement mixers!

The bottom deck looked like a huge warehouse. Here were many machine shops, equipped for making repairs for ships at sea and those offshore. One could see huge forklifts and overhead there were numerous tracks that were running every which way for the crane-lifts.

Finally, our tour completed, we followed our guide up to the Officer's Mess Hall. The rows of dining tables looked inviting, neatly set with white linen and silver.

The jurors and guests were delighted to join the Captain and his staff for lunch. They made us feel right at home. After our brisk exercise in walking and scaling up and down the ladders of the ship, we relished lunch.

We were also treated to a film, a comedy.

The trial ground on, and we made our appearance in open court on Monday November 16, 1970. After a short session in the courtroom Judge Older informed the jurors that defendant Patricia Krenwinkel had refused to submit an example of her printing and handwriting so that it might be compared by an expert, or experts to the blood writing on the wall at the La Bianca home. Miss Krenwinkel, then stood up and repeated to the jury, "I respectfully refuse on the advice of my counsel, (Paul Fitzgerald) to make exemplars of my printing."

Whereupon prosecutor Vincent Bugliosi rose and announced, "The People of the State of California rest their case."

After all the anticipation this almost seemed anticlimactic. Of course, there was still a great deal ahead of us. This was only the prosecution. If Kanarek's cross examination was any indication, we would be here for a long time.

Judge Older advised the jurors to return to court Thursday, November 19, as the day for the defense to begin presentation of its case and adjourned the court.

On Thursday, November 19, the jurors were back in the courtroom, when Paul Fitzgerald, stood up and informed the court that "The Defense rests."

I was taken by complete surprise, and most certainly, so were the rest of the jurors. The thought ran through my mind, this "no defense" must be some kind of legal maneuver, perhaps to seek a delay or an appeal in the case. The thought also crossed my mind that the defendants might want more time to produce witnesses for their defense. As I reflected on these things, Patricia Krenwinkel stood up and addressed Judge Older that she wished to testify. Then Susan Atkins and Leslie Van Houten quickly joined in with the same request.

Patricia Krenwinkel   *Susan Atkins*   *Leslie Van Houten*

Miss Atkins' defense counsel, Daye Shinn, refused to question the defendant, saying that it would incriminate his client. The defense counsel for Manson, Miss Krenwinkel and Miss Van Houten quickly joined in opposing such testimony for their clients, despite orders from Judge Older to question the "family" leader and the girl trio. The jury recessed early for the day.

On Friday, November 20, the panelists assembled in the court room, but only for a short session. After the Judge and attorneys returned from chamber consultation, the jurors were informed that both sides rested their cases. Superior Court Judge Older recessed the jury for the Thanksgiving holiday and advised them to return on November 30, 1970.

[EDITOR'S NOTE: On the morning of Friday, November 20 there was a hearing outside the presence of the jury that was key to the trial. The female defendants, Patricia Krenwinkel, Susan Atkins and Leslie Van Houten insisted that they wanted to testify and disagreed with the defense attorney's decision to rest the case. Bugliosi was in agreement with the defense attorneys who were against this.

BUGLIOSI: I think everybody knows the whole story and I have evidence that Mr. Manson has asked the three girls to take the stand and confess and exonerate him.

The Court asked what difference it made why they wanted to testify.

BUGLIOSI: because I still feel the defense counsel's position not to call them to the stand to confess should prevail over their doing what Mr. Manson wants them to do.

Kanarek pointed out to the Court that by allowing them to do so it would be a defacto confession and would constitute a change in plea. Manson interjected:

MANSON: We are not talking about a change of plea, Irving, that is in your mind. Don't mention a thing like that.

KANAREK: What they are in effect doing is changing their pleas.

VAN HOUTEN: How do you know. Jesus, you are all making all kinds of pretrial—

COURT: Let me just review what I consider to be at least the theoretical alternatives to proceeding in view of what has occurred, and then I will tell you what I have decided to do. (Manson then addressed the Court)

MANSON: I would like to testify too, if these people testify, because then I feel obligated to do the same, and I also feel obligated to explain this to the Court; that it is our intention to not divide a house and all stick together and offer one defense to the Court and be able to control our defense in the respect that it could be understood. In many cases through this trial there has been miscommunication between attorneys and client, there has been miscommunication between clients and your Honor.

Respectfully, we wanted to come and abide by all the rules.

I know I have kind of made a little boy out of myself two or three times in jumping and screaming and shouting, but I felt that it was appropriate at the time.

I do think that we are capable of offering a defense to this Court. We are capable of establishing communication with the jury and the Judge and behaving ourselves and doing what we should.

We want very much to defend ourselves, but under the circumstances, we have been kind of pushed in a corner to where we have to pretty much do what the attorneys say.

Not selling the attorneys short, I think the attorneys are very capable but I also think the magnitude of this thing is beyond proportion, and that the philosophies and the generation gaps and the LSD, and the things that most common people have no knowledge of, it is hard to explain with words and symbols our understanding and our belief, you know, and the way that we reflect on each other, to the point where, like, if they get up and say something, they have got it generally from me, as when your children get up and say something, generally it is what they got from you.

So, the information and the data in their heads is mine and I am responsible for them as much as you are for yours. Right and wrong is relative to the way we think, and I think with the positive thought that if your Honor would appeal and reconsider, to let us stumble through with the assistance of these counsel and prepare a case in the proper way, we can paint a nice picture.

Although this is only theory, it seems consistent with Manson's desire all along to be able to convince the Court of his own innocence. He might have even believed he could reshape the reality of the jury. Or it is possible he was simply delusional much as we have seen with other psychopaths who have believed they could outsmart a Judge and jury as we saw in the late seventies trial of Ted Bundy. The Court tried to find a solution to weighing a defendant's right to testify and the attorney's vehement and appropriate objections on behalf of their clients. The defense attorneys for the three women knew they were planning on exonerating Manson. Attorney Ronald Hughes made a statement to the Court regarding not wanting to participate in his client's testimony.

HUGHES: I believe that it is clear that this Court has, on the one hand, wanted the defendants to hurtle themselves out the window, but has always demanded that someone be there to push them as they go. Your Honor, I refuse to take part in any proceedings where I am forced to push a client out the window.

Judge Older suggested the defendants, including Manson testify in a narrative outside the presence of the jury so it could be determined what they would be saying. The idea was to avoid violations of the rules of evidence. The only one who testified in front of the judge and lawyers was Manson himself. He was permitted to ramble on for hours. Eventually the Judge suggested he try to relate to the case at hand. He attempted to address the evidence against him. For example, he responded to Paul Watkins's testimony regarding asking Paul to take a knife and kill the sheriff of Shoshone.

MANSON: I am not saying that I didn't say it, but if I said it, at the time I may have thought it was a good idea.

Whether I said it in gest or whether I said it in joking, I can't recall and reach back in my memory. I could say either way. I could say: Oh, I was just curious. But to be honest with you, I don't recall ever saying; Get a knife and change of clothes and go do what Tex said. Or I don't recall saying: Get a knife and go kill the Sheriff. I don't recall saying to anyone: Go get a knife and kill anyone or anything. In fact, it makes me mad when someone kills snakes or dogs or cats or horses. I don't even like to eat meat because that is how much I am against killing.

So, you have got the guy that is against killing on the witness stand, and you are all asking him to kill you. You are asking him to judge you. Because with my words, each one of your opinions or diagrams, your thoughts, are dying. What you thought was true is dying. What you thought was real is dying. Because you all know, and I know you know, and you know that I know you know. So, let's make that circle."

This is just one example of the kind of typical double talk Manson used when he got permission to speak. The Judge was surprisingly patient and allowed him to continue the narrative for as long as he liked. I suspect that even the Judge was curious about the inner workings of the mind of Charles Manson. When asked if he would want to repeat his testimony in front of the jury Manson declined indicating that the pressure was relieved. He had spoken his piece.]

CHAPTER TWENTY-ONE

A SEQUESTERED THANKSGIVING

At this time the trial was nearing its 160th day; and I wanted to include a few reflections from my wife, Helen. Although we couldn't speak for the other spouses or family members of the sequestered jurors, I could imagine their experiences must have been similar.

I had ample opportunity to become well acquainted with the jurors and the spouses they had left on the home front during the lengthy Tate La Bianca case, as I continued with my weekly visits to the Ambassador Hotel to see my husband.

In our private conversations, whenever I met the wives of the male jurors, we aired out our views and grievances; how slow the trial was proceeding, the tedious boredom and emotional strain on our spouses which increased our admiration for the courageous stability of the jurors. And we, here at home, were faced with the hardship of loneliness. There were also inconveniences like constantly reorganizing our weekend plans so that the hours would be free to spend with the jurors, and the tiresome weekly chore, packing and unpacking suitcases. We sympathized with each other because to complain to those not walking in our shoes would likely not be met with the same understanding. As much as we tried to be brave and supportive, it was an ordeal for everyone.

When we heard that the defense rested their case and the attorneys were preparing for final arguments; we all felt a sense of profound relief. We couldn't help but predict that the trial would soon be coming to a close. Perhaps by Christmas the jurors would be home. As for myself, I tried not to raise my hopes too high. I had learned to live day by day, and to accept and be resigned to whatever may come to pass.

The work and the problems around the apartments managed to get done somehow, with a helping hand from others. I was amazed how well I could handle a hammer and screwdriver when it was necessary. I was proud when I learned to adjust the automatic timers for the outdoor house lights, and with a little practice, to unscrew the iron guards on the flood lights when light bulbs had to be replaced. This gave me a sense hat I could get the job done.

On weekends when visiting my husband, I had plenty to talk about (without mentioning the trial); there was the humorous and serious side to everyday events around the apartments, and there were letters to be read from our daughters, relatives or friends.

It was now mid-November, and I noticed the look of strain and fatigue on my husband's face and the loss of weight. I was concerned but when I questioned him, he brushed it off. He attributed everything to the sitting around, lack of exercise and the grave responsibility facing each juror. I know we only learned a small portion of what is happening inside the courtroom in the news, but from what I could see, he was bound to lose his appetite.

On one occasion, a Saturday evening, I invited a group of jurors and their spouses (eight people) for a buffet dinner in my husband's spacious hotel room. I tried to reciprocate for the many invitations that were extended to us from the other wives.

I tried to make this a special gala affair. Saturday morning before my departure to the hotel, I prepared one of my favorite recipes, lamb kebabs; a leg of lamb, boned and cubed, seasoned lightly with onions and garlic, and pan roasted in the oven. The cooked lamb was put into a large electric skillet, easy to reheat on a plug-in socket. To accompany the lamb, a fresh salad, and a fruit salad for dessert, all stored in plastic bowels. Fresh buttered rolls and cookies completed the menu. And I was determined to serve hot coffee, so the electric coffee pot, china cups and saucers had to be packed in a box along with the silver. I even packed my pretty colored plastic fruit cups for the fruit salad.

I finally arrived at the Ambassador hotel and pulled into the parking lot and started unloading, trying to carry as much as I could up to the 6th floor and into Herman's room.

After the fourth trip down, all exhausted, I realized this task was bigger than I had anticipated. Once I had everything inside, my husband was able to help. We borrowed a few card tables and chairs from the recreation room, and managed to have everything ready and set up when our guests began to *arrive at 8:00 p.m.*

Some of the guests brought cold beer and cokes; one juror brought his guitar. It was a pleasant and relaxing evening with everyone sitting around, talking and eating. The lamb kabobs and the fresh salad were a hit with everyone, the pretty transparent fruit cups looked elegant, and the hot coffee with crispy cookies was met with applause. I was thrilled with the success of the evening, but I was bone tired.

Later, some of the guests started a card game, sipping on a coke or beer, our guitar player strumming a few popular tunes, and some of the brave ones responding and trying to harmonize.

Finally, when everyone had gone, we still had to clean everything up. I had to laugh when I realized we had to wash the dishes and utensils in the wash basin in the bathroom.

We finished after midnight, and when the last piece of silverware was washed and put away, I heaved a sigh of relief. Then and there, I made up my mind this would be my first and last attempt at private room service.

On Thanksgiving Day, Thursday, November 26, 1970 the jurors and families had a choice. We could have dinner at the Queens Arms restaurant or the Ambassador Hotel in the cafe.

The day before, wives and husbands at home were notified by the deputies and told about the dinner arrangements and the price per person.

Most of the jurors and their families planned to go out and eat at the Queens Arms restaurant, glad for a change of scenery and menu, and even a ride in a bus; I shared their feelings. I loved my wife's dinner party, but we were still cooped up in the hotel.

My wife joined us, and we had dinner reservations scheduled for early afternoon. The day was clear and sunny and pleasantly cool.

We all enjoyed the ride as the sheriff's bus breezed along the freeway on to the little city of Encino. We tried to seem happy and appreciative, but I'm afraid we all failed miserably.

Our driver pulled up to the Queens Arms restaurant, a nice place decorated like a royal queen's palace; the front entrance with an overhanging canopy, braced with large pillars, vivid in red and gold.

The deputies escorted our group through several carpeted and cushioned dining rooms, luxurious in its elegant décor into a private banquet room in the back. It had round tables set with bright red linen and heavy silver. Waiters soon appeared in their sleek uniformed red jackets and gold trousers.

Some of the guests ordered wine before dinner, served in beautiful goblets. The dinner included large slices of turkey, stuffing, sweet yams and cranberry sauce. Amidst the luxurious setting, the excellent service and the quietude of privacy, it was fit for a queen, but somehow all of this couldn't take the place of the good old-fashioned traditional Thanksgiving at home.

At least for me, Thanksgiving conjured images of family and relatives happily gathered around the dinner table with wonderful aromas of roast turkey and fresh baked apple pie. I longed for the intimacy of people who knew us best. We jurors had bonded together but it was through circumstance. This was the day that got under my skin the most of all the days of sequestration. I had lost my brother. It hit home how fragile and unpredictable life could be. I surmised that by the somber expressions on the guests and jurors, and the feeble attempts at conversation, others shared these feelings.

It was still early in the day when we departed; the bus driver took us into downtown Los Angeles and stopped at a small delicatessen store. The deputy made a purchase of assorted cold cuts and food snacks, a surprise planned for us, a little variation for the evening meal. We would have a buffet spread in the recreation room. It wasn't the same as turkey leftovers made into sandwiches, but it was thoughtful and welcomed.

Jurors and guests sat around wherever space was available, on chairs, sofas or on the floor, eating, chatting and joking. It helped me feel better and at least for a time there was a sense of warmth, unity and fellowship. Later we pushed aside tables and chairs and watched an old movie on a homemade screen.

The Sunday after Thanksgiving brought another special visit from our daughter, Sister Paulynne. Those few hours together, the three of us, was worth everything. It brought a renewal in family love, giving me the strength to continue the arduous journey ahead. The jury now had to go back and hear the instructions so we could deliberate and make our decision about the fate of the four accused.

It was a welcome distraction to hear stories of my daughter's experiences teaching elementary school children. It helped to hear stories with such innocence associated with them. My daughter also brought me two books to help me clear my mind; *Thoughts for Daily Living* by Bishop Fulton J. Sheen, and a mystery novel. Like in a mystery novel, we would be putting together clues to reach an answer. Only this was real life.

CHAPTER TWENTY-TWO

RONALD HUGHES IS MISSING

On Monday November 30, 1970, we, the jurors were anxious and expecting to go into court to resume the trial, and when we were not called, we began to wonder why.

On Friday, December 4, the jury was called into the recreation room and we were informed by Superior Court Judge Charles H. Older, that defense attorney Ronald Hughes was missing. We were told that an intensive search was being made for his whereabouts.

The jurors commented how considerate and thoughtful it was of Judge Older to come to the Ambassador Hotel to make an informal statement explaining the situation.

After the Judge departed, the jurors had many thoughts running through their minds. I don't know that we understood the implications of the announcement. We were concerned about the welfare and safety of Mr. Hughes, and prayerfully hoped that he would be found safe and unharmed. In truth, we were also concerned that the trial wouldn't be delayed for too long.

Several days later, Honorable Judge Older once again made an appearance at the Ambassador in our recreation room, a court clerk with him. We were instructed that attorney Maxwell S. Keith was appointed co-counsel to the missing Hughes, and by December 16, court session would resume after the new defense attorney had time to study the transcripts of the trial.

We were all disappointed, of course, to hear about the delay, but none of us complained too drastically, at least not in front of each other. I think we realized that the turn of events was out of our hands, and we might as well be resigned to the fact and make the best of it. The jurors were also becoming aware that Christmas, most likely would not be at home. And in a week or so, the deputies confirmed our beliefs; Christmas would be at the Ambassador.

[EDITOR'S NOTE: Court was to resume at regular time on Monday, November 30, 1970. Here is what transpired in chambers:

COURT: The record will show all counsel are present except Mr. Hughes. I understand from talking with counsel that no one has heard anything of him this morning or knows of his whereabouts.

    If I am mistaken, please so indicate. The clerk has also indicated that no message has been received from Mr. Hughes this morning. Bugliosi said he had heard Hughes on the radio that morning but did not know when the interview had taken place. It was about the Court interfering with the relationship between-"I think he was referring to the defendants taking the witness stand or something like that. It was almost incoherent."

    The Court listened to discussion about jury instructions. Later the Judge asked again about Mr. Hughes and if anyone had received word.

MR. KAY: I understand from Mr. Kendall of the Los Angeles Times that he checked with the Ventura Sheriff's Department and they tended to discount the fact that Mr. Hughes was in Sespe Hot Springs, at least that is the information he implied to me last night. He said they had been flying people out of there all day yesterday, and Mr. Hughes was not one of the people. They were bringing them out by helicopter. They had no word he was there.

COURT: I tried to call Sespe Hot Springs last night, but the Phone Company did not have any listing for it.

    If anyone has any information about him or obtains any, I would appreciate getting it because it may be possible for us to have a sheriff's helicopter pick him up if we know where he is. But in the absence of some definite location there isn't much point in sending a helicopter up there just to fly around the area.

KAY: Mr. Kendall also went to Mr. Hughes' home yesterday afternoon. He said it was in complete disarray and his mattress, which he sleeps on, which was on the garage floor, was completely soaking wet from the rain.

COURT: Who is this, John Kendall of the Times?

KAY: Yes, the Los Angeles Times.

COURT: The Clerk has indicated that he has some information regarding his efforts to contact Mr. Hughes. Will you state what you have been able to find out.

CLERK: First I contacted Rancho Sespe, as indicated by you. They referred me to the Filmore Police Department. The Filmore Police Department referred me to the Sheriff's Department. I talked to the Watch Commander of the Sheriff's Department who indicated that he had information that Mr. Hughes was in the Rose Valley area. Yesterday the helicopter flew 17 people out. Ten people hiked out. But they had not had any personal contact in any way with Mr. Hughes whatsoever and they have no information other than what I have indicated.

During another meeting in chambers the Judge once again asked about Hughes.

ATTORNEY FITZGERALD: No, your Honor, I might ay that I am beginning to become concerned, and I am actually becoming worried about him.

By and large, he kept in relatively close contact with me. He would call me every weekend, frequently at nights; and because he didn't have secretarial service, my secretary did his legal work for him; and frequently, if there were problems in connection with the instructions and problems in connection with legal documents and motions, I assisted him in preparation, and my secretary actually prepared them for Hughes. I haven't heard from him and I 'm concerned.

COURT: As I indicated yesterday, the Clerk did get an anonymous phone call from somebody saying he was up at Sespe Hot Springs; and I understand that you got some kind of message.

FITZGERALD: I did. My secretary, unfortunately, became ill with the flu about 10:00 in the morning. But the answering service received a call at 1:33 yesterday afternoon, indicating that a man who identified himself as Ronald Hughes—and the answering service, although they have heard Hughes' voice on a number of occasions, was unable to state whether it was Hughes or not—they said it sounded like a young voice, approximately 21 years of age. They said it, 50-50 could have been Hughes, and it could not have been Hughes. Anyway, this person who identified himself as Ronald Hughes said that he was marooned in the Sespe hot Springs area of Ventura County and was going to remain there until the police allowed them to leave when the roads were open. And that is the only information I have. He has not attempted to call back the answering service or my office or my home, and I have absolutely no further information.

Fitzgerald said Hughes had gone to Sespe Hot Springs in the past, but he had no knowledge that he was going there the previous weekend and thought it might have even been inappropriate to go there because of the rain. He had talked to him either Friday or Saturday morning about jury instructions and he seemed to be calling him from a local phone. They were discussing legal issues for the case so he had no indication Hughes wouldn't be in court. He was very concerned. The Court said it would send a helicopter to look for him.

On the morning of Thursday, December 1, 1970 the Judge updated counsel and the defendants in chambers about attorney Hughes:

COURT: The Sheriff's Department indicated to me last night that one James Forsher had informed the Sheriff's Department that he was the one who accompanied Mr. Hughes to the Sespe are last Friday along with some young lady whose name is undisclosed, in I believe the car belonged to the young lady.

Mr. Forsher was flown out, I believe, on Saturday, but according to what he told the Sheriff's Department, as related to me, Mr. Hughes said he wanted to stay.

The Sheriff's helicopter crew was unable yesterday to locate Mr. Hughes or anyone who had seen him. However, I was also informed that the Ventura Sheriff's Department had talked to somebody in Piru, California, who said that a storekeeper there had informed them that Mr. Hughes was in the store on Monday, buying supplies and was with, I believe he said, two hippie types.

After it was determined that Mr. Hughes could not be found, at least for the moment, the Judge suggested appointing a new attorney to represent Leslie Van Houten. Once again Manson and all of the defendants said they wanted to put on a defense and call and question 21 witnesses. After denying the motion once more, Manson said, "Your Honor, do you think it might be possible to obtain an attorney that will do and ask the questions we tell him to ask rather than tell us how we should—The Judge did not address his statement. Manson then said, "and if you people cannot see what is going on, you'd better open your eyes."]

CHAPTER TWENTY-THREE

THEY CRY OUT FOR JUSTICE

The jurors who had been sequestered since the Tate La Bianca murder trial began on July 15 were back in the courtroom in Department 104, Monday morning, December 21, 1970.

[EDITOR'S NOTE: Leslie Van Houten did not want Maxwell Keith appointed as her attorney. He was Princeton trained and tried to argue that Manson brainwashed his followers. She, like the others, resisted any defense on their own behalf. The defendants were still trying to put on a defense for Manson. In front of the jury Patricia Krenwinkel disrupted the court by saying, "Are you so afraid of hearing the truth? We are trying to give you a defense. You have an innocent man that you are trying to crucify. You are going to have to start…

Then the Judge cautioned them as Leslie Van Houten was engaged in a physical altercation with a bailiff. He said he would have them removed from the courtroom.

KRENWINKEL: We have a defense to put on.

MANSON: We have a defense to put on.

VAN HOUTEN: The fact is that we exist, yet you are going to somehow justify it in your mind that you are a judge. God is going to judge you.

COURT: I am going to have you removed from the courtroom if you don't stop.

KRENWINKEL: We are going to remove you from the face of the earth.

COURT: I want all the defendants to sit down so we can resume.

VAN HOUTEN: I am not sitting down. I am not doing anything you say until you do what I say.

Their behavior was escalating and when the new attorney tried to sever Van Houten's case from the others, Manson said, "All you are trying to do is divide the house, old man." Manson confronted the Judge to look at him when he was talking to him and the Judge had him removed.

Before closing arguments began the Judge agreed to allow the defendant's back into the courtroom but that did not last.] 18488

◆ ◆ ◆

As prosecutor Vincent T. Bugliosi began a meticulous summation in final argument through the testimony of the seven killings, the trial was disrupted time and time again, first by Charles Manson and then by the three girl defendants.

Attorney Bugliosi stated in his introduction "When the prosecution finally called its last witness to the stand a few weeks ago and rested, the defense also rested."

Then Charles Manson interrupted by shouting, "The defense never rested. The lawyers, the Judge's lawyers, rested."

Bugliosi did not acknowledge the interruption and continued explaining the law that although the evidence showed that Charles Manson was the leader of a conspiracy to commit the murders there is no evidence, he actually killed any of the seven people in this case. Then he explained that the joint responsibility rule of conspiracy makes him guilty of all seven murders.

Manson continued to interrupt with side comments as Bugliosi was reviewing the evidence.

Finally, Judge Older had the cult leader and his three disciples removed from the courtroom to an adjacent room allowing them to listen through a speaker system. Miss Van Houten displayed her temperament by cursing and slapping a female bailiff on her way out and Susan Atkins made a grab at Bugliosi's sheaf of yellow legal sized paper as she walked between the rostrum he was using and the jury box, and Manson threw a paper clip at the Judge and missed.

The surprised prosecutor grabbed the papers with both hands and tried to ward off Miss Atkins' hand away from his notes and transcripts, calling her a "little bitch."

Prosecutor Vincent Bugliosi began his argument, speaking in a quiet, calm and self-assured manner, suggesting that the jurors take notes. He smiled and commented, "Even I can't remember all of the details of this trial." Then he proceeded to describe Manson's formation of the family as described by witness Paul Watkins, a former follower, and the clan's arrival at the Spahn Ranch as described by Ruby Pearl, a former stable manager at the ranch.

The prosecutor quoted testimony that the cult-leader, Charles Manson had visited the Tate residence at 10050 Cielo Drive at least twice, and had possibly seen Sharon Tate and knew Terry Melcher, a former resident who previously leased the estate.

Attorney Bugliosi said Melcher, the son of actress Doris Day, had "subtlety rejected" Manson's attempts to record for the record producer and thus became an object of the cultist's anger. Charles Manson, the conspirator, ordered Susan Atkins, Patricia Krenwinkel, Charles Watson and Linda Kasabian to the Tate residence to take vengeance on the "establishment."

When the four returned from the killings, according to a statement attributed to Manson, there was no remorse. "After all, why should they have remorse? All they had done was kill five human beings. And human beings are pigs, that don't deserve to live. Birds' yes, rattlesnakes yes. But not human beings." The prosecutor reminded the jurors the five Tate victims "had been savagely massacred" to satisfy their master, Charles Manson.

Bugliosi argued that the defendants had three main motives for the slayings.

The first, "Charles Manson's hatred of human beings and his lust and passion for violent death."

The second motive was "Manson's extreme antiestablishment hatred."

And the third motive, the "Principal" motive, was Charlie's Helter Skelter idea. The blood written words, Rise! War! Plus, Death to Pigs at the scene of the crime left not only their motive, but their identification. Charles Manson, the cult leader, master minded and preached his "sick philosophy" to his "family" members, *Revolution 9*, "the bottomless pit," and "Helter Skelter," in an attempt to start the black-white race war.

For the next two and a half days, the deputy district attorney proceeded to summarize the evidence and testimony, with a flare of self-confidence and a display of incredible memory even though at times he referred to portions of the trial transcript. His argument was organized, and he recalled names, dates and places, reconstructing the high points of testimony into brief detail, resulting in a logical recitation of the events leading up to the murders. I know I was grateful for this reiteration. Although I had taken notes of what stuck out in each witness's testimony as significant, having it put into a narrative was extremely helpful. There were so many counts and so many outcomes to consider that without some kind of guidance it would be all but impossible to evaluate the case.

Time and time again, the prosecutor was interrupted by objections from defense attorney Kanarek, the familiar tactics displayed by the defense attorney, so well-known by now and tolerated by everyone. At this point I think we were all ignoring him, but finally, the profound patience of the Judge ran out, and he sentenced Mr. Kanarek for contempt of court.

Between interruptions, Bugliosi went over testimony about the victims' wounds, the defendant's fingerprints at the murder scene, the long barreled .22 caliber revolver identified as the murder weapon. He then reiterated the total number of stab wounds in the five Tate victims. There were 102, and the La Biancas had 67 stab wounds inflicted between them.

The prosecutor, boldly called for a first-degree murder conviction for the three female members; "a closely-knit band of vagabond mindless robots," and Manson, "the dictatorial master of a tribe of bootlicking slaves."

Bugliosi described Manson as a "vicious, diabolical killer." Manson, in his penned-up cell called out "Grrrrrrr!" loudly enough for us to hear. Charlie's frequent outbursts added a bit of humor to the tension in the courtroom more than once.

The prosecutor sarcastically cited the coincidences found within the testimony about the Leno and Rosemary La Bianca murders. "Manson's visits next door several times before the killings."

"In addition," he added, "it just simply can't be coincidence that Danny DeCarlo, a former member of the Manson family, testified that he saw a gun, rope, and clothing at the Spahn Ranch similar to those found at the murder scene or near the Tate residence."

The deputy district attorney had not yet completed his final summation on Wednesday, December 23rd when court was adjourned for the day. The Tate La Bianca trial was recessed for the Christmas holiday.

CHAPTER TWENTY- FOUR

CHRISTMAS AT THE AMBASSADOR

Christmas at the Ambassador Hotel, for the sequestered Tate La Bianca jurors went far better than many of us could have anticipated. We were all disappointed that we would be spending the holidays away from home and our extended families. However, I think the success of Thanksgiving helped us see that we could get through it as a group. We all tried to show the holiday spirit through our decorating attempts on the 6th floor of the rambling hotel. Our hearts and spirits were at low ebb, but I truly believe everyone was trying to make the best of it.

This jury of ten men and seven women had submitted to the longest sequestration in the annals of American jurisprudence. On June 15, 1970, we entered into a different world, suspended from our normal busy and comfortable lives, to embrace a challenging experience.

For me, and many of the jurors, it was the first time we were called to serve our civic duty; learning the basic constitutional rights, the judicial process, courtroom procedure, all while facing a grave responsibility. I know that through this experience we each learned to know ourselves better, seeing our character traits reflected back at us by our behavior in this challenging environment. We also gained new insights into the judicial system.

It is remarkable, how well the panelists adjusted to the many delays in the long trial and faced the hardships with courage and a sense of humor. The days of waiting and the inherent boredom were at times difficult and frustrating. Time passed and blurred. We lost track and measured our days and weeks by meals, occasional outings and the unreality of the court-room. There were moments when one felt like climbing the walls; in those moments I would turn to prayer. As was my practice at home, I would pick up a rosary and meditate on the mystery prayers of the holy rosary, the bitter chalice of Christ our Lord; it brought me calmness of spirit, a renewal in patience and I was able to face another day.

I was never one to be confined to my room for too long. Some jurors made model airplanes or engaged in other hobbies. Reading for an hour or two was my usual limit, and when I became restless, I'd join fellow jurors in the recreation room, playing cards, watching television and sharing superfi-cial comments. Whenever the weather permitted outdoor playing, I would participate with the group in paddle ball or swimming in the enclosed pool. When the jurors were not around, I would sit and talk with the deputies; we'd discuss sports, politics and our families. We watched televised boxing bouts, the football and basketball games, the horse races or a movie.

To cope with the boredom, we also resorted to inventing practical jokes and harmless pranks. A "rubber chicken" made the rounds, placed under bed sheets, pillows, toilet seats, and one morning it was found under the warm chafing dish at breakfast. (The chicken was given to Judge Older at the end of the trial). We came up with novel stunts like removing a juror's door when the room was unoccupied (one with a good sense of humor), hid the door and posted a sign "OPEN HOUSE." We short sheeted the deputies' mattresses and placed a tape recorder set to play reveille under the beds, timed to go off at midnight. (Larry Sheely and Anlee Sisto were good at this).

We varied the pranks and were able to break up the tension with our laughter. A few of the jurors became a little annoyed with the mischievous capers, but most were happy to join in. The fun-loving panelists adopted me as the father of their group, being that I was the oldest jester, the clique stuck as "Herman's Kids." (Jurors Jean Roseland, Larry Sheely, Anlee Sisto, Evelyn Hines and Robert Douglass, an alternate juror was part of this group).

The deputies tried to lighten the long court delay in mid-December for the jurors, by scheduling a weekend outing to Big Bear and a visit to Santa Claus Village. I had come down with a mild case of the flu so didn't partic-ipate in that trip. The jurors brought back a collection of pinecones to be gilded or silvered for Christmas decorations.

I thought I would be fine, but when a fever and annoying cough devel-oped, the watchful and concerned deputies took me to the Medical Center for a checkup. The condition was not serious so they simply prescribed medication for the fever and the cough.

The jury members, despite their disappointment in not being able to go home for the holidays, made the best of the situation. Everyone tried to create a glow of Christmas spirit in their private dormitory. We worked together to prepare for the holiday in the recreation suite by displaying evergreen sprays, silvered pinecones, mistletoe and brightly colored Christmas decorations. We each tried to make unique Christmas decorations for our doors. My work was the traditional evergreen wreath, with red ribbon and mistletoe above. We put a lot of effort into our crafts. I think we were grasping at our identities which were being merged into a unit.

The doors were a true expression of personality and ranged from the novel to artistic, from Santa's red stockings, green wreaths and red holly to the Christmas card posters, "Jingle Bells" sheet music, cardboard sign lettered "Help" to the parsley draped Ambassador menu (posted by William McBride who by now was exasperated by the hotel menu) punctuated by the critique; "Bah Humbug!" I suppose he was summing up our feelings, but he was the only one willing to say it.

The deputies participated and shared in our Christmas spirit, presenting each juror with a bottle of champagne. I don't know if they had any idea how much we appreciated the large evergreen tree they brought for us to put in the recreation room. They helped us decorate it and for the few hours it took to cover it with streamers and ornaments I know many of us felt more serene than we had felt since the trial had begun. We transformed our home away from home into an environment of holiday cheer. We covered mirrors and doorframes. We had miniature Christmas trees, mock fireplaces, Santa's reindeer, the nativity crib, Christmas card displays, and brightly wrapped presents.

One of the best surprises of the season was when the deputies escorted us on a Christmas shopping spree to purchase gifts for our families and small tokens for each other. I never enjoyed shopping, but even I found it to be exhilarating.

Then we were being called back to court after a long recess and needed to concentrate on the matters at hand even with the holiday only a few days away.

Christmas Eve was upon us and we were still sequestered. The time of the year when hearts mellowed, and the spirit is reawakened towards "Good Will" to all. It was difficult to make the transition away from the closing argument at first, but we had all been looking forward to this day.

We had already become reconciled to spending Christmas at the Ambassador and were making the best of the situation. We exchanged greeting cards and small gifts and the deputies were also included in our token of friendship.

The day before Christmas my wife and daughter arrived at the hotel in the early afternoon with a few brightly wrapped gifts, and Sister Paulynne brought her accordion.

We had our own private celebration exchanging cards and gifts. And our daughter described the fun everyone had when her fourth-grade pupils put on a Christmas play for the Sisters.

Before departing, our daughter, trying to help us experience the joyous Yuletide spirit, played a few Christmas carols on her accordion. Finally, just before leaving, Sister Paulynne told us the surprising and unpleasant news, keeping it to the very last so as not to spoil our few hours of joyful celebration. She informed us that she would be entering St. John's hospital the day after Christmas for a week in traction to correct a slipped disk in the lower lumbar vertebra.

"What a Christmas," my wife Helen moaned at dinner that night. "Our daughter in the hospital in traction, and you locked up and isolated from society."

On Christmas Eve, my wife's two sisters and family arrived at the hotel. All the jurors were given a Christmas Eve party in the Ambassador Embassy room. We joined the others and their guests for cocktails and hors d'oeuvres. There was dance music with a record player and the evening was more than we expected.

We took a few flash-bulb pictures as we all grouped around the banquet table, a monumental keepsake for this special event. The children of the younger families were in an adjacent room, trying bravely to look happy as they attempted to trim a Christmas tree. Santa Claus appeared, and the hotel provided punch and cookies.

On Christmas Day, the jurors and their families were treated to a festive holiday dinner. At two in the afternoon, everyone was escorted into the Embassy banquet room, the large tables beautifully decorated for the season.

We were served a traditional meal of a colorful fruit cup, chilled in a silver bowl, french salad, turkey and stuffing with glazed yams and carrots, and for dessert, a decorative sliced ice cream cake roll. We savored the time together. My wife commented on how quiet I was being, but I couldn't tell her what we would be facing upon our return to court. The trial was now in the final arguments and soon we would be called upon to deliberate on the evidence. As much as we would want to embrace theories. we would need to re-examine the evidence to determine what we believed were the real facts behind the crimes. Only then could we render a just decision.

CHAPTER TWENTY-FIVE

FINAL SUMMATION AND
DEFENSE CLOSING ARGUMENTS

It was a long, drawn out holiday weekend of nervous anticipation, when finally, on Monday, December 28, 1970, we were back in Department 104, taking our familiar places in the jury box.

The deputy district attorney, Vincent Bugliosi resumed his final closing arguments in the Tate La Bianca murder trial.

Entering the fourth day, Mr. Bugliosi finished his enormous task of crystalizing into condensed relevant form more than 18,000 pages of testimony given by 83 prosecution witnesses.

Prosecutor Bugliosi approached the jury box and commenced his final summation with a flare of elegance and colorful forcefulness. He reminded the jury of the "unbelievable orgy of murders," in which the accused participated.

"It was perhaps one of the most inhuman, horror filled hours of savage murder and human slaughter in the recorded annals of crime. The helpless victims begged and screamed out in the night for their lives; their life blood gushed out of their bodies forming rivers of gore! If they could have, I'm sure, Watson, Atkins and Krenwinkel would have gladly swum in the river of blood with orgasmic ecstasy on their faces!"

"But Charles Manson made one mistake," Bugliosi remarked triumphantly, "he sent out one human being on that mission of murder: Linda Kasabian. She cried, you saw her, when she told you about the brutal murders." Then the prosecutor, called for a first-degree murder conviction for the three female defendants and "the dictatorial master and leader, Charles Manson." After a brief pause, Mr. Bugliosi went on to list the twenty-seven counts against the defendants.

The atmosphere in the court was tense, as Mr. Bugliosi paused, turned to the jurors, and carefully listed each name of the murdered victims his voice raising with each one. "Sharon Tate, Abigail Folger, Wojciech Frykowski, Jay Sebring, Steven Parent, Leno La Bianca, Rosemary La Bianca are not here with us now in this courtroom, but from their graves they cry out for justice." The room was silent. He then added, "Justice can only be served by coming back to this courtroom with a verdict of guilty."

The deputy district attorney ended his closing summation by reminding the jury, "The People of the State of California are the plaintiffs in this case. I have every confidence that you will not let them down."

Defense attorney, Paul Fitzgerald, proceeded to make the first defense closing argument on behalf of one of Manson's co-defendants, 22-year-old Patricia Krenwinkel. The poised, lanky and tousled-haired attorney resorted to dubious tactics in the search for something of substance on which to base his plea for her innocence at least of the charge of first-degree murder.

The defense attorney tried to point out to the jury that, "mindless robots cannot be guilty of first-degree murder." Fitzgerald made attempts to impeach Linda Kasabian's testimony, referring to "Five knives and a gun," in the car driven by Tex Watson.

Linda Kasabian's testimony referred to only three knives. There were other discrepancies all throughout Fitzgerald's argument; perhaps this was his way to confuse the jurors.

Defense attorney Paul Fitzgerald climaxed his argument on a complaint against the prosecution tactics. "They have absolutely no evidence against Manson." The prosecution was reaching for excessive testimony about "his lifestyle and attitudes." He ended his presentation by imploring each juror to consider the evidence and acquit the defendants.

Fitzgerald concluded his final argument during the afternoon of the second day, December 29, 1970.

Attorney Daye Shinn proceeded with his brief closing argument on behalf of Susan Atkins, for approximately one and one-half hours. Mr. Shinn aimed his argument at the two former cellmates of Miss Atkins; Virginia Graham and Ronnie Howard.

Shinn reminded the jurors about Susan Atkins confessing to participation in the Tate slayings at Benedict Canyon, stating that they were convicts with criminal records, "and now they want to share the $25,000 reward."

In the late afternoon, on Tuesday, December 29th, defense attorney Irving Kanarek began his closing arguments on behalf of his client Charles Manson.

Mr. Kanarek, the stocky obstructionist began his snail's pace, eight-day argument, with the claim that the prosecution in the Tate La Bianca murder trial is "trying to lynch" Charles Manson via prejudice and publicity. Manson's attorney argued that the testimony of Linda Kasabian, the State's key witness, had not been corroborated to show "any wrongdoing on the part of Mr. Manson."

Kanarek tried to point out that even the prosecution did not claim that Manson was present at the time of the five murders at the Tate estate or the slayings of Leno La Bianca and his wife the following night.

The attorney told the jurors that Mrs. Kasabian may be protecting Watson; according to her testimony, as we know both of them were at the Tate estate the night of the slayings.

According to Mr. Kanarek's contention, "it is Tex Watson who is the "real power" behind the murders, whereas, the prosecution maintains that Manson masterminded the killings."

On Thursday, as Irving Kanarek evoked Mr. Magoo and a circus of ancient Rome in final arguments, linking Linda Kasabian to Magoo, the near-sighted cartoon character who creates havoc wherever he goes but escapes unscathed, the court hearing was then disrupted.

A woman who identified herself as Nancy Jo Davis, 34, walked down the central aisle, talking aloud. "I have come to defend my brother," she said. "I came here to defend my Christian brother."

She was quietly escorted outside by the bailiffs. Superior Court Judge Charles Older admonished the jurors to disregard the women's remarks, saying that she had nothing to do with the trial.

The Judge adjourned the trial for the day and wished the jurors a "Happy New Year."

New Year's Day at the Ambassador Hotel was one of quiet serenity for the Tate La Bianca jurors and their families.

The night before, on New Year's Eve, the sounds of music drifted up to the 6th floor as hotel guests celebrated downstairs in the Embassy Ballroom. Therefore, it was no surprise when the next morning almost everyone took advantage of the holiday by catching up on lost sleep.

In the late morning, the jurors and families shared a leisurely buffet breakfast in the recreation room and watched the Rose Parade on the television screen.

On Saturday, many of the jurors went to the Calico silver mining town in Barstow. For many of the jurors and guests, it was a new spot to see and explore. I was still fighting a cold, so I stayed behind. My wife was with me during the long weekend, and she provided good company.

We were pleasantly surprised, when on Sunday, Miss Connie Stevens, who was staying at the Ambassador Hotel and performing at the Coconut Grove, extended a personal invitation to the jurors and their guests to see her show that evening. It was a sparkling performance made even better by her warm personality. After the show, we went backstage to thank Miss Stevens for her kindness and extend congratulations for her fine performance. Many of us felt star struck but it wouldn't have surprised me if she would have liked to ask us about our experiences with what was surely to the outside world, a fascinating trial. Of course, she didn't refer to the case or why we were traveling in such a close-knit group.

On Monday, January 4, 1971, the 12 regular and five alternate jurors, after the long weekend holiday, took their seats in the jury box. We were prepared to hear further arguments from Charles Manson's attorney, Irving A. Kanarek as he showed no signs of slowing down. Mr. Kanarek, offering final arguments for the fourth day, claimed that the prosecution is "hell bent" to convict Manson because the cultist represents confrontations in the nation today. The trial is "political" and a "lynching." Manson's attorney charged that the prosecution "programmed" witnesses to produce prejudicial testimony.

And, it is not "inconceivable" that the .22 caliber pistol identified as one of the murder weapons is a "fraud."

Mr. Kanarek said it is "almost unbelievable" that a camera crew from KABC-TV discovered clothing supposedly worn by the Tate killers. He claimed it might be "a publicity stunt."

Pausing for a few moments, Kanarek began once again to show the ghastly photographs of the murder victims, saying, "We might as well face the prejudice here, you're going to see them in the jury room."

The jurors were shown a series of pictures of actress Sharon Tate's Benedict canyon home, photos of other figures in the case such as Charles (Tex) Watson, and pictures of the victims. Once again Kanarek asked how they corroborated Mrs. Kasabian's testimony of two nights of murder.

For the rest of the week, Charles Manson's attorney, slowly working his way through more than 18,000 pages of transcript, described the Tate La Bianca case as a "political trial" and claimed his client is innocent. Kanarek belittled the suggestion that Manson ordered the seven Tate La Bianca killings to start a black-white race war.

"If this was a start to a black-white war, why did it stop on the second night?" he asked. "Why wasn't there a third, fourth and fifth night, if that was what was supposed to take place?"

Mr. Kanarek discredited the testimony of Juan Flynn, a Vietnam veteran who testified that Manson once held a knife at his throat at the Spahn Ranch and said, "don't you know I'm the one responsible for all these killings?'

Kanarek asked, "What killings? All sorts of philosophical discussions were going on there at the Spahn Ranch." The attorney argued that the statement doesn't resemble anything near a confession because no "ascertained human beings" had been named in the words of "all these killings."

Finally, on Friday, January 8th, Irving Kanarek, like other defense attorneys, concluded his final arguments. He had used the opportunity to reiterate and attack a good portion of the trial transcript and case presented by the prosecution. He also attacked the validity of the evidence and prosecution exhibits.

Mr. Kanarek apologized to the jury for the lengthiness of his argument and told the jurors that he "cut out great chunks" in an effort to shorten his presentation.

It was still early in the afternoon around 2:30 when the defense attorney completed his closing argument and Judge Older adjourned the court for the day.

It was now the weekend of January 9 and 10. The jurors at this point were anticipating the next phase of deliberation. I missed the Sunday trip to Palm Springs and remained at the Ambassador with a few other panelists. We were still having our bout with colds and coughs.

My cold developed into a hacking cough. The deputies were concerned so on Saturday, I was taken once again, to the USC Medical center for a physical checkup. The examination disclosed nothing serious, only an inflammation of the bronchial tubes. Medication for a cough suppressant was prescribed, and the doctor advised me to drink plenty of fruit juice and water.

Friday evening my wife telephoned, telling me that she wouldn't be coming to the Ambassador for the weekend. She had torn a muscle in her right arm and was unable to drive her car.

The deputies heard about my wife's predicament and after duty hours, they stopped by to look in on her to see if she needed medical attention or a supply of groceries. We were both grateful for their thoughtfulness, and we extended our sincere thanks to Deputies Ann Orr, Elaine Slagle, William Murray and Odin Skupen for their kind consideration.

On Tuesday morning, January 12th, the jurors were back in the Hall of Justice, Department 104, taking our places in the jury section; the Tate La Bianca murder trial was in session.

Maxwell Keith, defense attorney representing Leslie Van Houten, began his closing argument. Mr. Keith, 46, was appointed by the court to replace Ronald Hughes, who disappeared in the Sespe Hot Springs area of Ventura County during a storm two days after Thanksgiving.

[EDITOR'S NOTE: There is still speculation that attorney Hughes was killed by order of Charles Manson. Hughes was inexperienced but was in tune with the hippie culture. He was the first attorney for Manson but was replaced by Irving Kanarek. Ron Hughes became the attorney for Leslie Van Houten and to zealously represent his client, as per the mandate for attorneys, wanted to separate her interests from those of Charles Manson. He planned to show she was not acting independently but was completely controlled by Manson. The speculation is that this strategy is one of the reasons why he was killed and that his death was not an accident as claimed. Although he was presumed dead, his body was not found until March 29, 1971. Ironically this was the same day all of the defendants, having been found guilty were sentenced to death. No one was ever charged with the crime.]

❖ ❖ ❖

The defense attorney's approach was sincere and courteous as he began arguing his case. He told the jurors he felt hampered because he had not had the time to establish a closer conformity with jurors during the lengthy trial or to have observed witnesses as they testified.

But after a study of a 20,000-page record of the case, Keith argued, it shows that "Leslie Van Houten is not guilty of the offenses charged against her."

Maxwell Keith reminded the jurors that the court would instruct them that Linda Kasabian's testimony is to be regarded with distrust because she is an accomplice.

Mr. Keith argued that Dianne Lake's testimony against Leslie Van Houten was "thread thin," resting solely for corroboration on the testimony of "this little girl." He maintained that it is "impossible to accept" that young girls went out to kill people they never saw or heard of before. Mr. Keith implied that the defendants' minds had been "totally controlled by someone else," reminding jurors of Rasputin as a historical example.

"I think" he argued, "the relationship between Charles Manson and the "family" was something mystical and occult. They all thought Manson was God."

The defense attorney concluded his brief argument, urging jurors to consider that there is no evidence to convict his client, Leslie Van Houten, of conspiracy to kill the La Bianca's in the murder of the couple.

Prosecutor Vincent Bugliosi began his final summation in rebuttal, Wednesday January 13th, charging that the defense in the Tate la Bianca murder trial tried to conceal the guilt of Charles Manson and the three women defendants behind a smokescreen. Bugliosi, his manner forceful and confident, told the jurors that the defendants are "guilty as sin," but like the octopus, their attorneys tried to let them escape in a cloud of ink. He argued that the defense tried to create an impression that the prosecution's case in the seven killings was based solely on circumstantial evidence, when in fact, it rests on direct evidence; the eyewitness testimony of Linda Kasabian and other physical evidence, such as fingerprints at the Tate residence and a .22 caliber revolver used in the killings.

The prosecutor defended his statement of "robot" by pointing out that it was a "figure of speech," meaning "someone who is slavishly obedient to someone else."

Bugliosi turned and pointed to Mr. Kanarek, and shouted, "It was your client, Charles Manson, who ordered the commission of these horrible murders. The "family" was not suffering from any diminished mental capacity, they suffered from diminished hearts and diminished souls."

As the prosecuting attorney slowly turned and approached the jury he declared, "I'm not going to be like Mr. Kanarek and show you all of these pictures," picking them up from the council table. "But the unbelievable orgy of murder, in which the accused have participated," declared Bugliosi, as he flipped through the murder pictures of all seven victims, "is all here."

Kanarek interrupted Bugliosi's summation time and time again, the Judge told him to sit down and refrain from comments. Finally, after the fourth or fifth time, the Judge stopped him, and Mr. Kanarek was cited with contempt of court.

Prosecutor Vincent Bugliosi resumed with his closing summation, pointing out that "the ingestion of LSD has no relevance in this case, stressing that its use has crossed and penetrated all social and economic classes." The drug-oriented issue had been brought up by Kanarek and the other attorneys regarding Linda Kasabian and other "family" members.

Bugliosi spent a lot of time focused on what he said was the defense attorney's misstatement of the facts. He made it sound like Fitzgerald wasn't paying enough attention, but he made it clear he thought Kanarek was making things up.

Bugliosi cited more than two dozen specific examples of Mrs. Kasabian's account about the Tate murders which he said had been corroborated by either physical evidence or the testimony of other witnesses. He also made clear that the burden on the prosecution to prove the guilt of each defendant beyond a reasonable doubt meant to the exclusion of all reasonable doubt, not all possible doubt. I know I found this to be an important distinction. He explained that the Judge would instruct us the prosecution does not have the burden of offering the degree of proof which excludes all possibility of error and produces absolute certainty but rather a degree of proof which produces conviction in an unprejudiced mind. moral certainty.

"Charles Manson," the deputy district attorney told the jury, "had total dominance over the members of the Family. Manson is on trial because he is a cold blooded, diabolical murderer. As sure as I am standing here, as sure as the night follows day, these defendants are guilty."

Chapter Twenty-Six

Deliberations

After lunch on Friday, January 15, Judge Older swore in the five male and three female bailiffs charged with the care of the jurors. The jurors were escorted to the jury room and he read his instructions to the jury.

[EDITOR'S NOTE: Quoted from transcript he said in part:

JUDGE OLDER: It is my duty to instruct you in the law that applies to this case and you must follow the law as I state it to you. As jurors it is your exclusive duty to decide all questions of fact submitted to you and for that purpose to determine the effect and value of the evidence. In performing this duty, you must not be influenced by pity for any defendant or by passion or prejudice against him. You must not be biased against any defendant because he has been arrested for this offense, or because a charge has been filed against him, or because he has been brought to trial. None of these facts is evidence of his guilt and you must not infer or speculate from any or all of them that he is more likely to be guilty than innocent.

In determining whether any defendant is guilty or not guilty you must be governed solely by the evidence received in this trial and the law as stated to you by the court. You must not be governed by mere sentiment, conjecture, sympathy, passion, prejudice, public opinion or public feeling. Both the people and the defendants have a right to expect that you will conscientiously consider and weigh the evidence and apply the law of the case and that you will reach a just verdict regardless of what the consequences of such a verdict may be. For the full jury instructions see addendum.]

❖   ❖   ❖

The Jury instructions took over an hour and explained in great detail how we were to apply the law to the facts. We needed to be clear on the meaning of conspiracy especially as that was a key factor in determining the guilt or innocence of Charles Manson.

The time was finally here, the deliberations; the very serious and grave responsibility of passing judgment on four human lives. The lifestyle of these people didn't matter at all, that they were hippie types, long haired, short haired or drug oriented, or even their moral beliefs. I would pass judgment solely on the evidence that I had heard from the witness stand and the case as presented by the attorneys.

It was already late in the afternoon near four o'clock, on Friday January 15, 1971 when the jurors of the Tate la Bianca murder trial cast their first ballot for a jury foreman.

The panelists were tired and weary after the close of the courtroom proceedings and Judge Older's final instructions to the jury to begin deliberations. All of us, with the exception of William Zamora, wanted to wait until the following day before we elected a foreman. But Mr. Zamora, nevertheless, kept insisting that we go ahead with the election of a foreman.

The jurors were all for keeping peace and harmony, and so we agreed to go ahead and cast a ballot. The first selection in votes was as follows: John Baer received one vote, William Zamora had two votes, Larry Sheely had two votes, Alva Dawson had three votes and I received four votes.

However, our juror William Zamora refused to accept the results, saying that the foremanship should have the majority of the panel of twelve.

Mr. Dawson spoke up and said that he wished to concede and suggested that I be the foreman since I would then have received the majority of the votes. It was my wish, nevertheless, to strive for peace and final acceptance, so I suggested casting another ballot. On the second try, Dawson had six votes and I had six votes, whereupon Mr. Dawson wanted to concede again, suggesting that I take over.

Trying to gain final approval, I said, "Let us toss a coin for the final decision." Mr. Baer tossed a dime piece; it rolled across the table and landed on the floor and rolled against the water cooler and came to rest on its edge. On the second toss of the coin, it was in my favor. I believe most of the jurors were pleased that I was elected foreman, some in the group applauded and gave a cheer, but that may have been because it meant we could all go back to our hotel for the evening. I know I was glad and relieved this part was over even though it meant I now had the responsibility of foreman.

Our "discontented juror" (William Zamora,) however was not pleased at all; he looked aggravated and was so upset he wouldn't speak to anyone.

The bailiff was called and notified that I was elected foreman, and the news was given to the judge and the press. The thought crossed my mind that It was all over, the long waiting, the many court delays, it was finally coming to an end, and most certainly the panel felt the same way. As one bailiff put it, "The fun and games" were over, and now we were down to the "brass tacks," the serious business, and of utmost importance the deliberation and the solemn responsibility of passing judgment on four human lives. We remained in the jury deliberation room for about 70 minutes.

That evening the jurors, escorted by two deputies went down to dinner to our usual spot in the hotel's cafe section, we seated ourselves in groups in several small tables.

Our "provoked juror" still harboring resentment, sat at a table by himself, and ordered a cocktail and dinner. When he finished his drink and before his dinner was served, he asked the deputy to take him up to his room. This cleared the tense atmosphere, so the rest of us sat back and enjoyed our dinner, as we exchanged casual talk and shared a few jokes in an effort to prepare for what was ahead. We noticed an increase in security around us. I don't think any of us realized any potential danger, but we found out later that the Sheriff's department had reports that friends of Manson might try to disrupt the deliberations. That could have meant anything.

I barely slept the night before deliberations began. I was worried and deeply concerned. I knew we would have trouble with one juror (William Zamora). and now that I was elected foreman, it was up to me to guide and instruct the jury in the best way possible. Above all I would need to maintain an atmosphere of harmony. I meditated and prayed, asking God for guidance, strength and understanding, and that his Holy will be done.

The court gave no basic rules nor regulations to follow, nor any formality as to the methods for the jury to use in deliberating. It would be the job of the foreman to act as a leader and set up some method of rules or guidelines for the jury.

The most common rule used and practiced is that of the secret ballot. I decided on oral discussion and open rebuttals. I didn't write any notes of instructions whatsoever, deciding to speak outright to the jurors on rules and guidelines on the following day.

It was Saturday morning, January 16, 1971; when we began. The early winter day was still cold and gray at 8:30 a.m. when the sheriff's bus pulled into the parking lot behind the courthouse. We were escorted into the jury room and the jurors took their familiar places around the long table. I suggested that we begin and end our deliberation with a silent prayer. Everyone agreed, which I took as a good sign we might be able to work together. We bowed our heads for a moment, and each one of us, in his or her own way of faith asked God to guide and direct us.

I began explaining to the jury my instructions, a series of rules and a method on guidelines we would follow. Amid the course of my explanatory speech, I felt a sense of great confidence and in those moments, I was deeply aware that the Holy Spirit was guiding me. The special words of my instructions to the jury were simple and precise as I outlined each detail very clearly, and slowly and without hesitation. I recall telling the jurors that each one must form his or her own opinion and decision on all the major issues of court testimony.

There were over 500 issues in the Manson case to consider. It would be a tremendous task for us because we were all in agreement that we would not render any decision without completely reviewing everything. It would have been easy to react from gut feelings but that was not what we were tasked to do. It would have been a violation of the sacred trust that had been given us to be the arbiters of the facts. We were to determine what we believed to be true and then were to apply that to the law as it was given to us by the judge. Our personal prejudices had to be set aside. It was my job to do my best to see that we were deliberating in good faith. I believed in the capacity of my fellow jurors to do this. I had gotten to know them over time. I even believed that aside from his disgruntled nature, even Mr. Zamora would do the right thing. There was so much to ponder that I knew the process would become exhausting. We all decided we would take our time. We would discuss the issues openly, listen to "devil's advocate" arguments and rebuttals and thrash through any doubts.

The jurors, apparently, were impressed with my detailed instructions for deliberating as everyone gave their full attention, and many in the group commented on the excellent method guidelines.

As might be expected on the first day, during the course of my speech, our disgruntled juror, sat back in gloomy silence not responding to anything in our morning session of deliberations. We were given a fifteen-minute break in the hallway.

As we walked out of the room, I tried to recall the words of my instructions to the jury panel, wanting to jot them down in my memo-pad, but try as I may, I couldn't remember the words; it was if they were erased from my memory.

After our leg stretch, the jurors filed back into the jury room to begin the serious decisions on the guilt or innocence of Charles Manson, Susan Atkins, Patricia Krenwinkel and Leslie Van Houten.

As we gathered around the long jury table, we examined the color photographs of the murder victims. I know I had only taken a cursory view of them during the trial. I understood now why the defense kept insisting they were too prejudicial. The photographs were horrible. I might even say they were ghastly. They depicted a brutality I am not sure any of us truly expected. Even so, we still had to consider the evidence and testimony. We knew these crimes happened. Our job was to determine who was responsible for them and to what extent they were guilty.

We discussed the photographs by going clockwise around the table. Each juror took a turn sharing his or her views. I could see how difficult it was for us to talk about the photographs unemotionally. We tried to be objective. Everyone gave an opinion which opened our discussions on the issues of the case.

When it came to the dissentious juror's turn to speak, he said he was not ready, and the second time around he again declined saying, "I'm not ready." It was obvious, to all of us that our panelist was defiant and was not responding as a statement.

I was deeply concerned, and realized it was time for me to act; somehow, I must seek a way, to get the man to cooperate with us. We must have unity and harmony before we could go on with any further deliberations. I waited, planning to approach him at the right time and in the right place.

On Sunday morning, after we returned from Church services and breakfast was over, the jurors went up to their rooms. I went directly to the man's room and knocked on the door (William Zamora in room 680). He looked surprised when he opened the door and saw me standing there. "May I come in?" I asked.

He invited me in, and I came right to the point. I asked, "Are you sick?" "No" he replied, "I'm not sick." "Well," I responded quickly, "if by any chance you're not feeling well and you are not able to go on and deliberate with us, just say so, I'll speak to the Judge and have you replaced. We can always get one of the alternate jurors to take your place who will cooperate with us. With or without you; we are going to finish this case."

"No, no" our juror began to plead. "Please don't say anything to the Judge, I'm feeling fine, I'll go on and deliberate. You know" he interjected, accusingly, "you're all against me, eleven against one, a lot of the jurors are making fun of me, of my accent and the way I talk."

I had seen no evidence of that, so it appeared he was trying to cover up his actions by blaming everyone else.

"Look" I said, "we are not here to criticize each other's faults and actions, nor are we here to scrutinize each other's personalities. We are here on serious business, trying to deliberate and to pass judgment on four human lives. It is a grave responsibility for all of us, and we can't waste our time and our energy on petty personal things, so let's stop the foolishness and get down to the business at hand." I felt that ended the confrontation so I turned and walked out of the room before he could reply.

On Monday morning, January 18, the we were back in Department 104, and once again, we assembled in the jury room to resume deliberations in reaching a verdict in the guilt or innocence phase of the case.

We gathered around the jury table and opened our session with a silent prayer.

We discussed the details of the case and exchanged opinions about the credibility of the evidence. We were now in full swing of weighing the facts and the arguments as presented by the prosecution and defense. The evidence was presented by the prosecution, but each side had a different interpretation of its meaning and validity as it pertained to his client. It was quite apparent to all of us, that our perturbed juror (William Zamora) was now in a better frame of mind and was finally cooperating with us. I experienced a feeling of profound relief and thankfulness that harmony was now abiding with us.

We discussed the case openly proceeding at a steady pace. Each panelist took his or her turn to speak and to express an opinion of guilt or innocence of the four defendants. In one instance, when our respondent juror had the floor, a lady panelist looked up (whom at times found things amusing) and her mischievous smile was breaking out. To preempt an outburst I quickly put my hand to my mouth, making a motion for silence. I could not take any chances on provoking our speaker.

At another time, a female juror was concentrating out loud. She was deep in thought and trying to decide on the guilt of one defendant, and she kept saying. "I don't know, I just don't know."

Apparently, another woman juror, who was very outspoken, became a little annoyed and she burst out with, "What do you mean, you don't know, what have you been doing in that courtroom day after day, month after month, sitting on your brains?" She realized what she had said and tried to backtrack but not before we all joined in general laughter.

Then as the procedure of our sessions went on, even our reluctant juror began to loosen up as he put on a little demonstration for us. After one made a comment and asked, "How could it be possible for Charles Manson to break in so easily and enter a private residence?" Zamora responded, "Easy." He then sprang up quickly from his seat, ran out into the adjoining room, the lounge, then he dashed back in, and remarked, "See how easy it is for Manson to break in!" We all laughed until it became difficult to restore decorum.

During the deliberations from January 16 until January 24 we discussed many things. After all, we had heard the testimony of 83 witnesses. I was grateful that I had notes on what I felt was relevant in the testimony as did most of the other jurors. Otherwise we would have been completely lost.

One main subject was whether to believe the testimony of Linda Kasabian. She had given the longest testimony and was considered a key witness. Even though she had not been with the family as long as the last witness, Dianne Lake, she was present on both nights. After much discussion we were all in agreement that she was telling the truth. Some jurors stated that it was impossible not to believe her.

If what Linda Kasabian said was to be believed, it would be impossible not to tie together the prosecution's case regardless of the motive for the killings. We continued to examine all of the evidence.

On Tuesday, January 18, 1971, the jury requested a nighttime visit to the two homes where the crimes occurred; that of Sharon Tate and the four other victims and the La Bianca's. Judge Older refused this request.

The jurors discussed how the murders happened and who committed them on the first and second nights. We viewed photos, drawings and diagrams during our deliberations.

We requested a record player to hear the Beatles *White Album*. This request was granted. On January 19, the jury listened to the album. We also returned to the courtroom to hear the court reporter read three letters written by defendant Susan Atkins to former cell mates.

The jury made another request during the deliberations for a list identifying some of the 297 exhibits introduced by the State and some of the photos. The requests were granted but later the jury withdrew the 297 exhibits request and said it had done its own coordinating.

We discussed the testimony of many of the witnesses including Gregg Jacobson, Shahrokh Hatami, Rudolph Altobelli, in relation to seeing Charles Manson at the Tate residence.

We had heated discussions on Leslie van Houten and whether she was guilty of first-degree murder. We all finally agreed that she was. There were some harsh statements made between some of the jurors while discussing Leslie Van Houten.

[EDITOR'S NOTE: Bill McBride, a juror during the trial recently shared his views of the experience to us. He stated that he had a huge problem with believing Leslie Van Houten should be found guilty of first-degree murder. He focused on the coroner's report that the stab wounds made by Leslie Van Houten were inflicted after the victim was already dead. The coroner said there was no blood related to those wounds. McBride didn't know how you could convict someone for killing someone who was already dead. He said, "I was the only one who had doubts about Leslie." The other jurors eventually convinced him by pointing out that she could not have known for certain that the person was already dead. As far as she was concerned, she must have been alive when Tex told her to stab her, so the requisite intent was there.]

❖   ❖   ❖

We had a minor sheriff's bus accident with another police vehicle. The bus side swiped it in the parking lot and then went the wrong way on a one-way street.

We resumed deliberations a little shaken. We deliberated forty-two hours and forty minutes; we were unanimous in our decision on the guilty verdict for the four defendants. I had no doubt in my mind, as to the guilt of the trio of women defendants. In the end we all agreed that that there was absolutely no evidence that would have set Charles Manson free. We, the jury panel, were certain that Charles Manson was the leader and conspirator of the "family" members and he ordered the killings of the Tate and the La Bianca victims. This was very evident through the court testimony. Tex Watson and the three convicted female defendants went out to do the cult leader's bidding; they committed seven bizarre slayings with no remorse, whatsoever.

It was my strong personal belief that Manson was evil. His total dominance over the members of his "family" was incredible. Tex Watson, Susan Atkins, Patricia Krenwinkel and Leslie Van Houten meekly followed Manson's most demanding emotional and physical dictates. And there was no question that Charles Manson, who as the leader and instigator, was a dangerous influence, not only to the "family" group but to society as well.

We voted at about 10:30 on Monday morning, January 25, 1971. We reached a verdict; all were guilty. As the panel filed into the courtroom and took their places in the jury section, Judge Older asked if the jury had reached a verdict. "Yes, your Honor, we have" I answered, and I handed the forms to the bailiff.

The Judge, after reading through the twenty-seven sheaves of paper, passed the small paper to clerk Eugene Darrow, asking him to read the verdicts. They were as follows; Charles Manson, guilty of seven counts of murder of the first degree and one count of conspiracy; Susan Atkins and Patricia Krenwinkel each were guilty of exactly the same, and Leslie Van Houten was found guilty of two counts of murder of the first degree and one count of conspiracy.

As the verdict was read, the four defendants displayed no glimmer of contrition, and after the reading they appeared seemingly unmoved and flighty. Only Manson spoke out after the clerk had finished. Facing the jury, he blurted out "You're all guilty." And to the Judge, he exclaimed, "We weren't allowed to put on a defense, old man. And you won't forget for a long time!"

In the emotion charged atmosphere of the crowded courtroom, Judge Older adjourned with the sound of his gavel.

[EDITOR'S NOTE: Juror Bill McBride provided some more insights into the trial and deliberations. He was only 24 years-old at the time of the trial and remembers it well.

"We believed Manson was the leader. He was a Christ-like figure in their eyes. He was doing the preaching and they were doing the listening. They were followers."

He also described the demeanor of the defendants and Charles Manson in the courtroom.

"You could see the glances from the three girls to him (Manson) and he would look at them. It was something you could feel over the months. He would stare at the jury and at the witnesses. He would stare them down until they broke the gaze. He would start with the first juror and go down the line. I held the gaze longer than anyone else because I felt I had to show I was not afraid of his staring. When Linda Kasabian testified, he was staring at her the whole time. He did a swiping movement like cutting the throat while she sat alone on the stand. (the attorneys were either at the bench or in Judge's chambers) and I was surprised he did that in front of the jury."

McBride explained that Linda Kasabian's testimony was strongly considered in the deliberations.

"She was present on both nights and testified to everything that led up to the it (the murders). She was credible, and we believed her. We didn't buy the defense efforts at discrediting her. She was a soft-spoken young woman. She said she was upset with what she had been a part of. She knew the whole story and we felt she was telling the truth."

"We also felt the testimony by experts and other family members, especially the coroner's testimony was very powerful." (He specifically referred to the blood type evidence and whose blood was found where).

McBride discussed the testimony regarding motive as bizarre but under- stood its relevance in tying together circumstantial evidence. The prosecutor had explained that there were several possible motives but the one he presented the most was that Manson wanted to start a race war and blame it on the blacks. He said that according to the testimony Manson felt the black people would win and take up the reins of power. Then 144,000 followers of Manson would come up from the bottomless pit to "take the reins of power from blackie and tie them on their curly heads."

McBride explained that with or without the motive testimony the jury would have reached the same result based on the evidence. However, the motive narrative made a few more pieces fit into place in some perverted, crazy way.

"They were a bunch of hippies in the day of love-ins," he explained. "How they could think killing was doing someone a favor so they would be reincarnated as more beautiful people, such as themselves, was crazy. These girls were not murder- ers without having come into contact with Manson. They were convinced it was the right thing to do."

McBride described the women as "appearing kind of nuts," at the trial. "They tried to interrupt things. One time they sang the old gray mare ain't what he used to be, to taunt the Judge."

He also said Leslie Van Houten would look at him in the jury box. It made him uncomfortable. She once mouthed to him, "my life is your life."

In describing the deliberations McBride said, "We bounced feelings off each other and talked about the evidence. It took us seven days rehashing not because we were hung up on anything but because we did it thoroughly and not in a hurry.

We were all clear soon after deliberations begun that we were all of similar mind about whether or not they did what they were charged with. We reviewed the evidence as it related to each defendant singularly.

We knew how serious the decision was. Our decision happened naturally as we combed through the evidence. We took written ballots. We all unanimously agreed all four were guilty of each and every count. We had taken seven or eight days to reach our final unanimous decision.

Herman signed the verdict forms. We were nervous.

When we were brought into the courtroom the room was jam-packed and the energy was supercharged. There were many people waiting who thought we were not going to convict. After the verdict was read, we were polled and taken out of the courtroom. The penalty phase would be next. We were allowed to go home for a few days but were then sequestered in a different hotel because Manson had made threats against us." (Interview with Bill McBride, 2019)]

◆   ◆   ◆

Now once again a few reflections from my wife Helen at home.

The spouses and families waiting at home were experiencing many feelings of mixed emotions at this crucial time of the jury deliberations. First and utmost in my opinion was that of profound relief the Tate La Bianca murder trial would soon be over.

There would be many mixed emotions; anxiety, joyful anticipation, contemplation, and there would be moments of disappointment. While the jury deliberated, the majority of society, on the outside was making predictions, and I'm certain, the feeling that we all experienced; not only the families, but the news reporters, the television media and Judge Older as well, was how the time drags when one waits. The hours of the day somehow seemed a little longer than usual.

I hadn't seen my husband in several weeks prior to the deliberations because of my mishap, the torn muscle in my right arm. Now that I was able to drive again, the jury was in deliberations and that meant no personal communication at all.

The deputies were very obliging and considerate. One would phone after the dinner hour to inquire if all was well, and to say, "Herman sends his love."

I responded with my usual short message, "All is well, I'm fine. Tell Herman my love is with him and my prayers embrace them all"

The days passed very slowly; Thursday, Friday, Saturday, the radio and newspaper were my constant companions. Like everyone else, I was getting a little on edge wondering how much longer the jury would deliberate.

It was Sunday evening, January 24, 1971. I received a phone call (how well I recall the day) from my daughter, Sister Paulynne. She usually made the evening phone call once a week to enquire about my health and how things were on the home front.

Our oldest daughter, Sister Gabriella was still in Australia, we corresponded frequently, and between the two of them, they helped to keep my spirit aglow.

This evening, Sister Paulynne's voice had a ring of excitement. "Well Mom," she burst out heartily, "I know how anxious you are for the Manson jury to bring in the verdict. Tomorrow is the day; keep tuned to the news at noon. I don't mean to sound mercurial, but it will be a verdict of first-degree murder for Manson and the three girls."

In great amazement, I asked "How do you know?"

"I made a novena to Saint Paul," my daughter went on to explain, "and my premonition is so vivid; it will be Monday, on the Conversion of Saint Paul, the Apostle."

On the following day, preparing lunch as time hung suspended in tense expectancy, I had my ear glued to the radio station KPOL. It was 11:45 a.m. The news was starting to come on. The announcer said, "The Manson jury has reached a verdict; guilty of first-degree murder and conspiracy for Charles Manson and the three female defendants!"

Hearing the news of the verdict was of little surprise, but I was overwhelmed with the accuracy of the prediction. I experienced deep emotions on this day; first of relief that it was over but there were also feelings of sorrow and sadness.

I felt sorry for Manson and the three girls; those wretched souls lost in the web of evil. I especially thought about the women, so young, at that age, like of our daughters, in the flower of life. Had they chosen another path, they could have contributed to society, as it was, their road led to the inevitable self-destruction.

I thought of the parents, the anguish of heartaches and self-reproach they must be going through. And I thought of the waste upon society, the monies, the time and the long ordeal for everyone connected with this sensational murder trial; not to mention the grief of the families of the deceased.

Who is to blame? Undoubtedly, there were many explanations, but it all boils down to one point; Manson and others like him who plot and plan the destruction of others, they will always be snarled in their own web of evil.

I thought of my husband and the jurors, what a grave responsibility they had to face, passing judgment on four human lives, weighing all the facts and making the final decision of guilt, murder in the first degree. I know my husband to be a man of compassion, but firm if need be; he could not let his heart rule his head.

The jury deliberated 42 hours and 40 minutes, the verdict was reached on the eighth day, Monday, January 25, 1971. I checked the date on my Catholic calendar; it was the Conversion of Saint Paul, the Apostle. That eventful day, Monday January 25, 1971 just before the noon hour, the Tate jurors reached their final decision on the guilty verdict of first-degree murder and conspiracy for Charles Manson, Susan Atkins, Patricia Krenwinkel and Leslie Van Houten.

During this day of extraordinarily tense emotions, I had several calls from news reporters. They were surprisingly considerate, first asking if I'd mind answering a few questions; giving my views on sequestration. "How did the long separation affect me and my husband?" "How do I feel, now that the end is near?" And, "Am I planning a special dinner tonight for my husband?" I was happy to express some of my thoughts.

First, I believed the sequestration was necessary because of the impact of publicity on a murder trial so sensational, and also for the safety of the jurors. The long separation brought us closer together. We realized how much we meant to each other and how much one depends on the other.

We were both rejoicing that the end was near, and it was difficult to express how much we were yearning to get back to normal. I was assuming the jurors would be released after the guilty verdict was brought in, so I was preparing one of my husband's favorite meals; leg of lamb, baked potatoes, cauliflower au gratin, salad and apple pie.

Apparently, some of the news reporters, as well as families at home and I learned later, that some of the jurors were assuming that the jury would be released after the guilt phase was finished.

During the week when the jury was beginning to deliberate, I had several phone calls from the television networks. They asked if my husband would mind making a personal appearance, a telecast interview after it was all over. A representative from Life Magazine left his business card at our door and asked if we would permit an exclusive story for the magazine after the close of the trial.

I couldn't make any promises or commitments for my husband until I had the chance to discuss it with him, so phone numbers and business cards were filed away. I had my doubts about my husband making any television interviews, I knew that he didn't care for publicity and he would shun the limelight.

On Monday, after the guilty verdict was announced, an agent from KHJ Channel 9 phoned and asked me for permission to hold a brief home interview. The voice was courteous and kind. I didn't have the heart to say "no."

The three-minute interview covered just a few high lights on the emotions and experiences of the spouses at home.

"I believe all of us realized that sequestration was necessary, the nature of the crime and the exposure to the spectacular publicity. Like many others, I thought the trial dragged on far too long. During the long ordeal, we all experienced hard times which we managed to endure; undoubtedly it provided a challenge for us all. There were moments when we experienced fear and when times became really difficult, we turned to heavenly Father and asked for courage and strength."

The telecast was shown on Channel 9 television, on the early 5 PM news. Very much later in the evening, after the dinner hour, I was pacing the floor waiting for some word from my husband; finally, the phone rang. As my husband's voice came through, I burst out with excitement, "Are you coming home!?" My husband, taken by surprise answered, "No, I'm not coming home, we have yet to pass the penalty phase."

"Penalty Phase?" I replied. "I thought the Judge took care of that?" And with my next breath, "How long will that take?"

"I really don't know," my husband replied calmly. "Maybe two or three weeks; it shouldn't be too long." Then he went on to explain that the jury was told right from the start of the trial, that there would be two phases on which to pass judgment; the first phase was the "innocent or guilty phase," and the second, the "penalty phase"; life imprisonment or death.

To say I was disappointed is putting it mildly, but soon the moment passed and with determined resignation and hopeful expectancy I kept thinking; "It shouldn't be too long now."

CHAPTER TWENTY-SEVEN

THE PENALTY PHASE

The weary jurors were anticipating that the verdict was the conclusion of the trial, and the majority, as I could readily see, were experiencing a feeling of profound relief that the long confinement was finally over. Apparently, almost everyone had forgotten the final speech in the chamber (which seemed so long ago) given by Judge Older at the beginning of the murder trial; as well as the jury instructions that said if the verdict was guilty of first degree murder we would have a second phase to determine a penalty of life imprisonment or death.

Upon arriving at the Ambassador Hotel, the jurors were in a state of confusion, many in the group came to me asking questions;

"Doesn't first degree murder carry an automatic death penalty?" "Doesn't the Judge pass judgment on the Penalty Phase?" "Were we to remain sequestered and hear further testimony of defense witnesses?" The deputies were also confronted with many questions from the jurors. I gently reminded the jurors of Judge Older's final instructions on the second phase of the murder trial.

An explanatory pamphlet was presented to the jurors on California's trial system. It read as follows: "California's bifurcated (double) trial system, on penalties in capital cases has been in use since 1957, and since that time has been adopted by five States; Connecticut, Georgia, New York, Pennsylvania and Texas. Its purpose is to permit the jury to judge the accused and not their crimes. Under the California system, the defense is permitted to select

for presentation to the jury in the penalty phase and all favorable or mitigating evidence concerning the offense and relating to the backgrounds of
the defendants.

The jurors need not find ameliorating circumstances to impose the death
penalty. The jury is not permitted to consider any evidence relating to other
crimes which many have been committed by the defendants unless they are
proved beyond a reasonable doubt. In the guilt and innocence phase of the
trial, the prosecution is not bound by this requirement, and may introduce
evidence of other crimes without proving guilt beyond a reasonable doubt,
only by preponderance of evidence."

[EDITOR'S NOTE: Mitigating factors are those extenuating circumstances presented by the defense during the penalty phase of a capital crime that can help reduce
the potential sentence. For example, evidence of mental illness, abuse in childhood,
drug addiction, hardship or a show of remorse can be used to try to convince a
jury the defendant deserves a lower sentence. In an article titled "When mitigation
evidence makes a difference: effects of psychological; mitigating evidence on sen-
tencing decisions in capital trials" (Michelle E. Barnett, M.A., Stanley L. Brodsky
Ph.D., and Cali Manning David, Ph.D. https://doi.org/10.1002/bsl.591 2004) a
study showed that when mitigating evidence was presented, the mock jury was less
likely to sentence the defendants to death.

Aggravating factors would include lack of remorse, the amount of harm to the
victims, which would lead the jury to support the stronger penalty.]

❖   ❖   ❖

In this case the penalty phase would be a time for the defense to present
evidence to convince the jury to sentence the defendants to life in prison
rather than a sentence of death. There was at this phase no question of guilt
or innocence. This had already been decided in the main trial.

After a debate of questions and answers, the jurors were finally aware that
we would remain sequestered, and would be hearing testimony of defense
witnesses, possibly for weeks.

Amidst an atmosphere of gloom and depression, the disgruntled jurors
complained freely, the comment most frequently made was, "I wonder how
much longer this is going to take?" Several in the group were composing letters of protest to give to Judge Older. I tried to discourage them, reminding
the panelists that a few more weeks of isolation wouldn't hurt us. We did a

fine job so far and accomplished so much, why not stick it out and really be proud of our endurance.

On Thursday, January 25th, the composed and reconciled jurors were back in crowded Department 104, taking their places in the jury box; the penalty phase of the murder trial of Charles Manson, Susan Atkins, Patricia Krenwinkel and Leslie Van Houten resumed.

The jury would be hearing evidence to determine only one issue; whether the defendants were fit to live.

The purpose of the penalty phase for the prosecution was to reinforce that the crimes called for a death sentence and not life in prison. As prosecutor Vincent T. Bugliosi called the first witness in the penalty phase, a musician, Bernard (Lotsa Poppa) Crowe, age 28, to the witness stand, Charles Manson disrupted the courtroom with violent objections.

"We wish to put on a defense," Manson told Judge Older who had granted the defendant permission to make a motion. "We have wanted to put on a defense since we were arrested."

Whereupon the Judge told him he would be allowed to call the witnesses he wanted, but through his attorney. Manson snapped "There's no justice here Older! Damn it, look at it!"

Once again, the Judge warned Manson that he would have him removed from the courtroom if he persisted in the disruptions and advised him that it was in his best interest to sit down.

"My best interest," Manson fumed, "I've already been convicted of something I didn't do." Manson struck and shoved his attorney Mr. Kanarek, several times and said "I can't do anything with you. I can't communicate with you." Judge Older had the defendant removed from the courtroom.

The first witness, Bernard Crowe testified that Manson shot him on August 1, 1969 (at his girlfriend's apartment) with a long barreled .22 caliber revolver similar to the death weapon used in the Tate murders, and he still carried the slug lodged near his spine. The shooting followed an argument over a payment for and then non delivery of marijuana, Crowe said, and he was hospitalized for 18 days and nearly died.

Defense attorney Irving Kanarek cross examined the witness; the questions were related to the narcotics trade. Much of Kanarek's questioning was objected to by prosecutor Bugliosi. and sustained by Judge Older. Court was adjourned for the day.

On Friday, January 29, Kenneth Daut, one of the five alternate jurors was dismissed during the penalty phase of the trial by Superior Court Judge

Charles H. Older. Mr. Daut's wife was involved in an automobile accident and received painful injuries. Mr. Daut gave some of his views and reflections on the Tate trial in a press statement. Leaving the trial, a slightly bitter man because of the length of it; a "world's record" for a jury to be sequestered. The financial burden and hardship it placed on his family and the "circus-like" conduct that went on during the trial caused him to feel this way. He commented on the slow unnecessary proceedings and improvements that should be made in the courts. The worst part of the entire trial, said Daut, was the overwhelming boredom and lack of physical activity and the isolation from the normal outside world.

Dorothy and Joseph Krenwinkel

Besides having to bear the censorship and constant chaperoning by deputies, "the juror's worst problem was simply killing time" said Daut. He said with all the sitting around he was tempted to take up knitting. To help pass the time, he learned to play cribbage and played 500 games, he read 18 novels, built a model airplane, fashioned beer bottles into mugs, painted number pictures, worked out at the gymnasium and swam.

"There was nothing to do but sit and sit. There were times that we didn't leave the sixth floor of the Ambassador Hotel for a week, except to stand on the fire escape and get a little sun. That just about drives you out of your mind." "Christmas Eve was the most miserable I ever had in my life."

To keep up one's humor, Daut said, he joined the group in playing a lot of practical jokes on the bailiffs, hiding keys and badges, decorating a room in toilet paper, stripping sheets and blankets off the beds and putting them in the shower. With a big sigh of relief, the juror admitted how nice it was getting back to normal with his family and back to home cooking.

On the weekend of January 30 and 31, the jurors visited with spouses and their families at the Ambassador Hotel.

The penalty phase of the trial resumed in the courtroom on Monday, February 1, 1971; prosecutor Vincent Bugliosi called his final witness to the stand, Corporal Thomas Drynan, an Oregon State Trooper from Salem.

Corporal Thomas Drynan testified that he arrested Miss Atkins and two men on Sept. 12, 1966, near Stayton, Oregon. He said he found a loaded gun in Miss Atkins coat pocket. On the way to jail, where she was charged with receiving stolen property, Corporal Drynan asked her what she had intended to do with the gun. "If I had the opportunity I would have shot and killed you."

The witness was cross-examined by defense attorneys Paul Fitzgerald, Daye Shinn, Irving Kanarek and Maxwell Keith, but the questioning seemed immaterial.

Defense attorney Paul Fitzgerald called the next witness (witness number 1), Joseph Krenwinkel, the father of the convicted defendant, Patricia Krenwinkel to the witness stand.

Mr. Krenwinkel, age 59, described his daughter's childhood as typically middle class; Sunday school attendance, she sang in the church choir, was taught the Bible, liked religion and was never hostile, violent or disrespectful. She participated in the usual girlhood organizations and was an average student in high school.

Joseph Krenwinkel said that his daughter was a good baby, never a behavior problem, was gentle and loved animals. As a child she never caused any trouble or grief. Her father said, "I couldn't have asked for a better one."

When asked by the defendant's attorney, Paul Fitzgerald, "Did you love your daughter?" the father looked at his daughter at the council table and became emotional as he answered. "Very much, and I still do."

Dorothy Krenwinkel was called to the witness stand and she was asked the same question by Fitzgerald. The red-haired Mrs. Krenwinkel sobbed and said "I did love my daughter. I do love my daughter. I will always love my daughter, and no one will ever tell me she did anything horrible." (witness number 2)

The parents, Joseph and Dorothy Krenwinkel were wed in Las Vegas in 1944 and 20 years later, when their daughter "Pat" was 16 or 17, they parted in a friendly divorce. Miss Krenwinkel went to live with her mother in Mobile, Alabama, but they returned to California and Pat attended university High School and graduated.

In 1967, Miss Krenwinkel went to work as a clerk for an insurance company and moved in with her half-sister, Charlene, 29, in an apartment in Manhattan Beach.

Later, Mr. Krenwinkel said he learned that his daughter had left with a man named Charles Manson, abandoning her car and leaving her job. It was 2 years later in 1969, about two months after the Tate La Bianca killings that Mr. Krenwinkel saw his daughter again.

Mrs. Krenwinkel's brief testimony on the witness stand related similar facts about her daughter's background. In December 1967 she picked up Pat in New Orleans, Louisiana; her daughter was accompanied by others and acted "kind of funny." It was two years later in 1969 that she saw Pat again.

Both parents of the convicted murderer, Patricia Krenwinkel, declared their support and their love for their daughter.

On Tuesday, February 2, 1971, the third witness, Mrs. Jane Van Houten took the witness stand in the penalty phase of the trial, on behalf of her daughter Leslie Van Houten. (witness number 3)

The well-groomed Mrs. Van Houten told attorney Maxwell Keith that "Les" was a frisky child, small for her age, always fun to be around. Her daughter attended church, she sang in the choir, she belonged to Fire Girls, she played the sousaphone, took piano lessons, loved camping and enjoyed elementary and junior high school. Then she attended Monrovia High School.

Van Houten's mother continued that "Les" had an unhappy high school romance and seemed to be "hurt very much" by her parents' divorce eight years later. In her junior and senior high school years at Monrovia, said Mrs. Van Houten, things did not go well for her daughter; her grades dropped, and she seemed "very unhappy."

Mrs. Van Houten, a teacher in the Los Angeles school system, said it came as a terrible shock when she learned her daughter was arrested on murder charges.

Defense attorney Maxwell Keith asked, "do you blame yourself for what has happened?"

"Any thinking person must consider that possibility," she replied. "You go over a hundred things in your mind and wish they were different. I would never have believed it, and I still don't believe it."

When questioned by Mr. Keith about how she feels about her daughter now Mrs. Van Houten said, "I love Leslie very much." Mr. Keith asked, "As much as you did before?"

"More," she replied.

Mrs. Van Houten said that her daughter completed a course as a legal secretary and went to live with friends for the summer at a ranch near Victorville and then had gone on to San Francisco. They always kept in touch, until one day "Les" called and said she was going to drop out and I wouldn't be hearing from her. "We argued and when we hung up, we were both angry."

Later when she heard from her daughter in April 1969, she learned that Les was in jail for hitchhiking in Reseda. Leslie stayed one night with her and left to see friends in Hollywood, ignoring her request that she leave a telephone number where she could be reached.

The next time she saw her daughter was at the Sybil Brand Institute for Women after Miss Van Houten had been arrested.

The next witness (number 4) to approach the stand was Mr. Samuel Barrett, probation and parole officer for Charles Manson.

Defense attorney Irving Kanarek questioned the witness, relating to Charles Manson's prison record and parole. The probation officer testified that he met Manson for the first time in 1956. The cult leader and ex-con served seven years in Federal prison; the last twenty-two intermittent years spent behind bars.

Samuel Barrett said the last time he spoke to Manson was at the Spahn Ranch in June 1969, and after that Manson's whereabouts were unknown. While Manson served time in federal prison, said Barrett, he attended school and received a fairly good education.

Another defense witness called to the stand was freckle faced Lynette (Squeaky) Fromme, the fifth witness in the penalty phase of the trial. (witness number 5)

The 22-year-old "family" member questioned by Paul Fitzgerald, began her testimony, telling about the lifestyle and philosophy of the Manson group.

Miss Fromme stated she was a student at El Camino Junior College when she left home and that her family came from an upper middle-class background. She said she grew up in the LA beach town area, was the daughter

Lynette "Squeaky" Fromme

of an aeronautical engineer in a middle-class home but fought with her family and was kicked out.

Miss Fromme related how she met Manson in 1967.

"I had been kicked out by my father," said the witness. "I hitchhiked from where I lived in Redondo Beach to Venice Beach. I was sitting there crying and this man (Manson) walked up and said, 'your father kicked you out of your house today.'" Manson offered to take her with him, she said "no one had treated me like that before, not pushing me around, so I picked up my stuff and went."

Lynette testified how she accompanied Manson and other "family" members to San Francisco and Sacramento before the group settled at the Spahn Ranch in the summer of 1968, where they lived into the next year. In San Francisco they picked up Mary Brunner, a University of California at Berkley librarian. Lynette gave them her paycheck and went with them in the school bus. They went to southern California and picked up Patricia Krenwinkel who disliked her office job.

"We were like the wind," she said, describing their travels on the West Coast. "We watched the hippie cult grow and die and watched it get dirty."

The witness stated that they went back to Haight-Ashbury where they met Susan Atkins who was living in a commune but wanted to come along.

She said the group grew to about 25, mostly women. They lived in a condemned house in Los Angeles for a while and Mary Brunner had a son from Charles Manson.

She said they moved to the Spahn Ranch where the women adjusted to Manson's philosophy of polygamous sex, but she said that didn't happen easily. "We were used to having a man all to ourselves, there was competition, fights but then we'd look in each other's eyes and realized we loved each other."

The witness described Manson as a father who knew that it was good to make love. She said she made love to Manson; it was guiltless, like being a baby.

On Wednesday, February 3, the penalty session resumed with Lynette Fromme recalled to the witness stand.

Defense attorney Fitzgerald asked the witness if Manson had ever hit her. "Yes, it was the most ferocious, frightful experience I ever had but I wasn't hurt at all."

The witness said that Charlie hit her so hard he knocked her across the room; she said it was what she needed. "it was because I had kicked a baby, because I wanted attention, he threw me across the room, but it was what I wanted him to do." She said that Manson had struck other girls also but didn't hurt them.

Fitzgerald asked if Manson had a power over his followers.

"He loves, that is the only power that doesn't look like power, and it is non-control."

Miss Fromme said that the other girls were fascinated with Manson's every move. "He'd go into the bathroom to comb his hair and beard; they'd follow him and watch him make faces at himself in the mirror. It's hard to conceive that man being much of a child and yet being that much of a man."

She was asked by defense attorney Fitzgerald if Manson gave orders on what to do and where to go. "No" replied Squeaky. "We were riding on the wind; Charlie was never our leader. He would follow us. All he had to do after getting out of prison," testified the witness, "was to see what we needed; he really cared about us."

Then she described Manson as "a man of a thousand faces." He was kind to dogs and animals. The members of the "family" looked to Charlie as "father," accepting his observations about the world along with physical punishments when he thought they needed it. "Manson was always very happy making a game out of everything," she said.

When questioned if she loved Manson, Miss Fromme replied, "Charlie is in love with love, and I'm in love with love, and so we are in love with each other."

Squeaky, prompted by defense attorney Paul Fitzgerald, said that Manson did not hate black people but predicted a revolution of a black white race war called Helter Skelter. The Beatles album record was a favorite and played often at the Spahn Ranch.

Miss Fromme was questioned by defense attorney Irving Kanarek. He asked, "Does Manson have any power?"

"He loves" she said. "That's the only power that doesn't look like power. He's the only person I ever knew who has real power. He sees things as they are and does not judge." When asked if she thought Manson was Jesus Christ, she gave no direct answer, and only replied "Jesus Christ is love."

On cross examination prosecutor Vincent Bugliosi asked Miss Fromme why she had cut an "X" in her forehead. She replied that it was a mark of loyalty; she cut the "X" and then burned it, four months ago, in November 1970, to show that the "family" members were "clearly marked."

"It's a fallen cross" she said. "It means the system as it now stands has fallen."

Nancy Pitman

The next witness (number 6), was another "family" member, Nancy Lora Pitman, 19, also known as Brenda McCann. Nancy Pitman testified that Manson was not the leader but the follower of others. "His love leads Charlie. The only thoughts Charlie has have been the thoughts that we gave him. Manson is right in all things," the young woman said, having the power to read the thoughts of other family members and know what a person was reading in a book without looking.

"Once he picked up a dead bird, he breathed on it a few times and it flew away," she said. "Charlie would sit in the desert and wild animals would gather around him, he once reached down and petted a rattlesnake and he would be friends with coyotes."

The witness said she ran away from her home in Malibu to join Manson. She was walking along a road with the daughter of Angela Lansbury and Manson came by with his bus and gave them a ride.

She was asked if she thought Manson was a deity. She said she never considered it until the police came asking "where's Jesus Christ? We want to crucify him." She said the police were always coming to the Spahn Ranch.

Nancy Pitman denied that Manson hated Blacks. "He loves the black people very much. He spent 23 years in prison with black people." She said that Manson said, "Black people are going to rise to the top and everyone who doesn't get down on their knees to these people will die."

The witness said he healed sores on horses by putting all his attention on them. She was asked how he did that. "It's just love; little kids believe that when you wish for something or concentrate on something it comes to you."

On the following day, Thursday, February 4, Nancy Pitman was recalled to the witness stand. Prompted by defense attorney Irving Kanarek, Miss Pitman testified that when Linda Kasabian came to the Spahn Ranch to live with the family in July 1969, she brought a "little bag of LSD" and $5,000. She said that Linda took the drug every day for a week. Mrs. Kasabian was hiding in a cave from her husband, said Miss Pitman, and took the drug every day for a week, neglecting her baby at the campsite.

Bugliosi asked on cross examination if Charles (Tex) Watson, another family member accused of the Tate La Bianca murders, was slavishly obedient to Charles Manson. Miss Pitman denied that it was so. "In all the time that I knew Tex, he did exactly what he wanted to."

Prosecutor Bugliosi asked Miss Pitman if she would die for Manson if the defendant asked her to. "Yes, I would," she replied, unequivocally.

"Would you get on the witness stand and lie for Charles Manson?" he asked.

"No, I would tell the truth on the witness stand, I don't need to lie," she responded.

On re-direct questioning by defense attorney Paul Fitzgerald he asked whether Manson had asked her to lie. "No" replied Miss Pitman, "I'm telling the truth. There is no reason to lie."

The next witness (number 7) for the defense was Sandra Good, age 27, who met Manson in 1969, and was a member of the "family" group since that time. She left home at the age of 17, traveled around the country alone before meeting Manson and the others.

The testimony of the blonde, blue eyed Miss Good followed the general pattern established by Lynette Fromme and Miss Pitman. Miss Good said

Sandra Good

Manson "could see every thought" that members of his family had, he loves everything and has the ability to "bring you into now."

"I believe his voice could shutter this building if he so desired."

The witness was asked about Linda Kasabian and she said she thought the former family member resented things because Manson did not pay enough attention to her. She said that Linda was aggressive and when someone would refuse to give her money Linda would yell "pig" or "fascist pig" at them.

Sandra Good said she did not believe that Manson was God, but that Linda Kasabian believed that. She also said Linda was infatuated with Tex Watson.

Sandra Good denied that Manson was the leader of the group, as did the others. She said that she was attracted to him because "he was always the happiest, always singing, and always loving."

Asked if she thought Manson was Jesus Christ, Miss Good replied "I never really thought about it. I saw him as a million things."

The witness testified that she gave her money to Manson and Charlie was freely giving a helping hand to others.

After examination by defense attorneys Shinn, Keith, Fitzgerald and Kanarek, Sandra Good was excused, and court was adjourned for the day.

On Friday, February 5, the honey blonde, Sandra Good was recalled to the witness stand. Charles Manson's attorney, Irving Kanarek, sought further questioning from the witness.

Sandra Good testified that the Manson family looked to their babies as leaders, not Manson.

Miss Good said the elderly, blind George Spahn was in charge at the Spahn Ranch, the family hangout in Chatsworth until after the seven Tate La Bianca murders.

When the witness was asked once again by Kanarek if Manson was the leader of the group, Miss Good replied, "No, we looked at the babies as our leaders, wherever they went, we followed them."

Sandra was asked to list the children born to family members and their mothers and their fathers. She said there were perhaps seven or eight children born to Manson family women.

Her child she called "Chosen."

Others were Pooh Bear, Sun Stone Hawk and Zee Zae.

The witness then said "what difference does it make who the fathers are? The baby is the father of themselves."

Sandra Good also denied that Manson hated Black people or that he planned to start a black-white race war. "Charlie is love," she said.

Miss Good described a music festival that was performed by the Manson group for Terry Melcher on several occasions when he visited the ranch.

The eighth witness called by the defense was Catherine (Gypsy) Share, another member of the Manson "family."

Miss Share said she was a French war orphan adopted by American parents. She had left home before she met Manson and then joined the "family."

Miss Share, 28 was jailed last December on a Los Angeles County Grand Jury indictment accusing her of conspiracy to murder Barbara Hoyt, a former member of the "family" and witness for the prosecution in the Tate La Bianca trial.

Catherine "Gypsy" Share

Miss Share said she met Linda Kasabian in July 1969. Share said she was out walking one day and met Mrs. Kasabian who was living in a truck with her husband and a friend. She (Kasabian) said she was unhappy and that she (Catherine) looked very happy. "It's because I live with some very beautiful people, I told her." Linda asked if she could come with me, and then she did. It was at the Spahn Ranch that Mrs. Kasabian became infatuated with Tex Watson.

Prompted by defense attorney Kanarek, Miss Share testified; "Linda didn't ask me to go to the Tate residence, but she asked me to go out and do some killings." She couldn't recall the exact date Mrs. Kasabian made this request, but she thought it was early August of 1969. The Tate La Bianca slayings occurred August 9 and 10, 1969.

The conversation took place at the Spahn Movie Ranch according to the witness, and at the time, Leslie Van Houten was present. Miss Share said that Linda and Leslie felt responsible for the arrest of Bobby Beausoleil because of a car they gave him; it was registered to Gary Hinman, and they had to do something to get him out.

Prosecutor Bugliosi cross-examined the witness and asked," Isn't it true that what you're trying to do here is clear Charles Manson at the expense of Susan Atkins and Leslie Van Houten?"

"No, it isn't true" replied Miss Share.

Bugliosi asked "If the Manson family committed murder, you'd still love then, wouldn't you?"

"Yes, I would," she said. "Yes, I do"

The prosecutor hammered away at the witness; his disgust quite evident.

 "How come, if they stabbed other human beings and butchered them, you would still love them?"

Miss Share replied, "It's for better or for worse."

Bugliosi asked why she didn't go to Manson and tell him what Mrs. Kasabian had told her about planning the murders.

"He probably would have been mad at us, but he wouldn't tell us what to do. He would say you do what you do."

Miss Share testified that she first heard about the seven slayings on the radio and "Linda, Leslie and Sadie came very much to her mind."

The witness stated that she was worried over losing her month-old son, Phoenix and that had prompted her action in making allegations against Mrs. Kasabian and the others.

Miss Share said that she always regarded Manson as being innocent of any involvement in the slayings.

As defense attorney Kanarek followed with further questioning of the witness, court was adjourned for the weekend.

CHAPTER TWENTY-EIGHT

THE GROUND SHOOK

As the penalty phase of the Tate La Bianca murder trial approached the third week, the jurors were in a high state of agitation and complaining bitterly about the length of the trial.

When my wife arrived at the Ambassador Hotel Saturday afternoon, February 6th, she immediately noticed the change among the jurors.

"Unbelievable" Helen commented, after an attempt to talk with a few of the jurors and their spouses. "They were ready to snap your head off, and one doesn't dare to be cheerful or optimistic. I can see that even the deputies were worried."

It was true; the atmosphere on the 6th floor was penetrated with tension and emotional distress. I made a strong effort to discourage any rash movements by some of the jurors, urging patience and good cheer, but my efforts flattened out. I too was worried and concerned; the uncertainty kept gnawing at me; "will the jury stick it out?"

On Monday February 8th, the dispirited panelists were back in the courtroom. The penalty phase of the trial resumed.

Defense attorney Irving Kanarek recalled Catherine Share to the witness stand. Miss Share testified that Charles Manson talked about a revolution but had no intention of trying to trigger a race war. "It was crazy," she said, of the prosecution theory that Manson ordered the slayings of Miss Tate and six others for the purpose of touching off a black versus white race war.

Miss Share declared it was not true that Manson was prejudiced against

Negroes. Pointing out that he had been close to many black people during his 23 years in institutions. And they, the blacks, like a father, taught him many things.

According to the raven-haired "Gypsy," she never heard Manson use the term *Helter Skelter* except in singing the Beatles song with that title with the rest of the "family" members at the Spahn Ranch.

Miss Share denied that she thought Manson was Jesus Christ. When asked if it was against the law to disagree with Mr. Manson, she replied "no, he agreed with everyone, he had no opinions."

The witness was further examined by defense attorneys Daye Shinn and Paul Fitzgerald, with questions related to her background and education. Miss Share said she had three years of college and was born in Paris, France.

Under cross-examination by prosecutor Vincent Bugliosi, the witness admitted to stealing money, clothes and jewelry, and serving time in jail.

Under redirect questioning by the defense, Miss Share admitted taking LSD many times, using the drug for about four years. The witness was excused, and court was adjourned for the day.

Catharine Share testified that Manson had nothing to do with the Tate La Bianca killings, but that Linda Kasabian was the mastermind. She stated that Leslie Van Houten and Susan Atkins were at the massacre planning session.

The witness said that about two weeks before the August 1969 raid at the Spahn Ranch, about a week before the murders, she said Miss Van Houten, Atkins and Kasabian were sitting on a couch in front of the boardwalk at the Spahn Ranch.

The witness testified that Linda Kasabian asked her to go out on some killings. Catharine said, she didn't want to do it and wanted to go away. She said she just walked off, went into the hills and tried to understand. She said she didn't have anywhere to go but she loved everyone at the Ranch. She stayed a couple of weeks in the mountains and when she came back Linda Kasabian was gone. Catharine talked about when Leslie, Susan and Linda went out to houses and stole things like money, clothes and jewelry.

She said the motive for the killings was centered on the murder of Gary Hinman and the arrest of Bobby Beausoleil for the murder.

Leslie, Linda and Susan were there talking about Robert getting arrested and said they had had to get him out of jail because they had put him there. Catharine stated that Linda Kasabian didn't say who they were going to kill but she used the word "pigs."

Under questioning by Paul Fitzgerald Catharine Share said she never wanted to "snitch," she didn't want to implicate anyone and didn't want to be involved. She was worried about her baby that they were trying to take him away from her.

She looked at prosecutor Bugliosi and said, "You said I'd go to jail if I didn't tell the truth. I just want to get out of jail; I don't want to be on the witness stand. I want to get out of jail and get my baby."

On the following morning, Tuesday, February 9, 1971 the dawn had just broken and at 6:02 a.m. for one long violent minute, Southern California rocked and rolled in the clutches of a jolting and terrifying earthquake. The quake was in the foothills of the San Gabriel Mountains and we found out later had the extreme magnitude of 6.5.

I was awake at that hour and was preparing for my morning shower when the first severe jolt struck with its maximum force. The Ambassador Hotel swayed and rocked like a puppet on a string, the loud sounds of doors flying open, the buckling and cracking of the ceiling, bits of plaster and dust falling onto the floor. As I looked towards the shade drawn windows, flashes of lightning in brilliant reds, yellows, greens and blues flooded the room as power transformers popped like firecrackers and high voltage lines snapped. For a moment, terror seized me; "this must be the all Hell broke loose!" The thought flashed through my mind that "any second now we would crash down to the bottom." There was no place and no time to run to safety. I began to pray, asking God to have mercy and spare us. That one long, terrifying minute seemed like an hour. The earth's movements finally began to taper off in a slow series of shocks and tremors.

I gathered my wits about me and started dressing when a deputy knocked on my door checking if all was well. I walked out into the hallway and was surprised to see fellow jurors carrying out Mrs. Kampman's belongings and placing them in another vacant room. The woman, an alternate juror, was very upset and distraught by the incident. A water pipe had ruptured above and flooded her room. We all knew that it could have been worse, but we also knew that for her it must have been frightening.

The terrifying morning with all its distressing moments, and the menacing turbulence had brought enough anxiety to the jurors without the added agony of uncertainty, the welfare of the families at home and what damage was done by the tremor. There was no means of communication to the outside. The telephone lines were not in service because of the quake.

The jurors gathered in the recreation room; the deputies had the television news on. Everyone was anxious to learn the extent of the casualties and damage from the earthquake. Saugus-Newhall was hit the hardest, with several deaths reported. The giant tremor collapsed buildings, triggering fires and rupturing gas and water lines. Several buildings in the downtown Los Angeles area collapsed, many others sustained heavy damage, glass windows were shattered everywhere. Highways cracked and buckled, power and phone service were knocked out throughout a wide area.

[EDITOR'S NOTE: There were 58 known casualties related to the earthquake. They were mostly due to highway overpass collapses, some hospitals and a ceiling collapse at a homeless shelter called the Midnight Mission, in downtown, Los Angeles. Steinbrugge, K. V.; Schader, E. E.; Moran, D. F. (1975), "Building damage in the San Fernando Valley", San Fernando, California, earthquake of 9 February 1971, Bulletin 196, *California Division of Mines and Geology*, pp. 323–353.]

❖ ❖ ❖

On that predestined morning, in the emotion charged atmosphere of the 6th floor of the Ambassador, the distressed jurors walked down six flights of stairs to the lobby, through the dining area and on to the coffee shop cafe. The place was deserted; there wasn't a soul in sight, except for a couple of waitresses and kitchen help. As we sat waiting for breakfast to be served, I don't think anyone had a taste for food. It all felt very weird and and we were still having earth tremors. I know I was consumed with a sense of profound uneasiness.

As we drove in the sheriff's bus to the hall of Justice that morning, we couldn't see much through the smeared windows, but we noticed the deserted streets in downtown Los Angeles and the lack of normal traffic. Once we disembarked at the back entrance of the courthouse, we could see the glitter of broken glass and bits of masonry scattered everywhere.

Before the court was called into session, the deputies reassured the anxious jurors that they would phone the families, confirming that everyone was well and safe, and make inquiry about conditions on the home front.

The penalty phase of the murder trial proceeded as planned with the first witness of the day, Pete Miller, an investigator for Channel 11 TV news. He was briefly questioned by the defense relating to the television news coverage of Susan Atkins, the convicted defendant and member of Charlie's "family." (9th witness)

Susan (Sadie) Atkins, the 22-year-old convicted defendant was the 10th witness called by the defense in the penalty phase to take the stand. Miss Atkins gave a brief outline of her early background; her mother died when she was 14 years old, her father was a carpenter by trade and a real estate broker. Childhood and family life were normal; she quit school in the 11th grade and left home at the age of 18. Pale, dark haired "Sexy Sadie" as she was nicknamed by the "family" said she worked as a waitress and gained worldly experience from older men.

She later worked as a "Go-Go" dancer, smoked marijuana and used the drug LSD. Susan Atkins admitted killing actress Sharon Tate and musician Gary Hinman. The witness said she had to kill Hinman when he came after Manson with a gun. "I had to protect my love."

Susan Atkins confessed to the killings of Sharon Tate and Gary Hinman. She said Charlie had nothing to do with the seven murders and he wasn't there the second night at the La Bianca residence. She said that Linda Kasabian had the motive for the murders, she picked the victims and directed the killers to the scene.

She implicated herself in the murders and also placed Patricia Krenwinkel and Leslie Van Houten at the murder scenes.

She stated that Bobby Beausoleil went to Gary Hinman's house to get back $100 or the pink slip of a car which the musician had sold him. Hinman resisted and so she (Susan) and Beausoleil came back the next day to make the same demands. The two men fought, so she called Manson at the Spahn Ranch to settle the dispute. Manson came and got the car pink slip but after arguing with Hinman, the latter pulled a gun and shot at Manson who then hit Hinman with something.

She said that Manson was leaving but Hinman went after him with a gun and it appeared like he was going to shoot Manson. The witness said she didn't know what Hinman was going to do. "I had my knife and I ran at him and killed him."

She said she didn't remember the details but said "All I know is Bobby was taken to jail for something that I did, and he was found guilty for something that I did and I cannot let him go to the gas chamber or sit on death row for something that I did."

"You can all judge me accordingly, but you've got an innocent man on death row and you've got an innocent man sitting in here."

The witness said that she (Susan), Linda Kasabian and Leslie Van Houten talked at the Spahn ranch about how they could free Bobby Beausoleil of murder charges. Linda Kasabian suggested they could hire an attorney for Beausoleil, or they could commit copy-cat murders. The witness said Linda Kasabian said if we make lots of them, they will cut Bobby loose and everyone will go free.

The witness said that on the night of the murders "we dropped acid, I couldn't accept it until we did, she (Linda) said get a knife and some clothes."

She testified that on the night of August 8, 1969 Linda gave Tex the drug STP and LSD and also gave them to her (Susan) and said the three girls and Tex drove to a house that she later learned was 10050 Cielo Drive, the home of Sharon Tate.

Susan said Linda might have picked this house because her husband had been "burned" in a $1000 drug deal with someone in Beverly Hills. She said that Watson killed Stephen Parent in the driveway, and they all entered the house.

Susan told of "herding" Tate, Sebring and Folger into the living room, Frykowski was already there with his hands tied. She said that the four of them (Linda, Susan, Tex and Patricia) were all in the living room when the smaller man started walking towards Tex and Tex shot him. The two women screamed, the man on the couch said something, I said "Shut up."

She told Defense Attorney Shinn; "The rope went around; Tex tied it around the people's necks and threw it over the beam. Tex said turn out the lights and told the people to get on the floor; they were crying and saying, 'please don't hurt me.'"

Defense attorney Shinn asked Susan what happened after that. "The man got up, I tried to stop him, we were fighting, I just kept swinging my knife. I could feel the knife going into something; he had a hold of my hair. I yelled 'Tex, help me.' The man let go and started to run, I ran after him and then I saw Katie calling for help.

She was fighting with two women, the dark-haired woman (Folger) had a hold of Katie's hair and was pulling on it. Katie called for Linda who came in and I ran to the pregnant woman (Tate), she was starting to take the rope off her neck.

I put my arms around her neck and had her head in my arms. Tex came back to the man on the floor and started stabbing him."

Susan said she dropped her knife and Linda gave her the one that she had. She was then alone in the living room with the pregnant woman (Tate). She kept pleading "please don't kill me. I'm not going to say anything."

Susan said she told her to "Shut up, I don't want to hear it. I threw her down and held my knife over her and said, 'don't move.'"

"Sharon Tate said, 'please, all I want to do is have my baby.' I said, "Don't move, don't talk to me, don't say anything to me, I don't want to hear it." Tex came in and stood over her and said, "kill her." Susan said she stabbed her, and she fell, and she stabbed her again. She put up her arms and then her arms fell. "I don't know how many times I stabbed her; I don't know why I stabbed her."

Susan said she remembered seeing Tex hitting a big man on the top of his head in the doorway. She said she ran outside, and Katie was just getting up from in front of the woman on the grass (Folger). Susan said that before she left, she took a towel, touched Sharon Tate's stomach with it and wrote "PIG" on the front door. Then we walked away from the house. Susan said she was now telling the truth and that she had lied to the Los Angeles Grand Jury. The witness was excused, and court was recessed for lunch.

The concern over the earthquake was not over. During lunch we were escorted by deputies through spacious air raid shelters underground and minutes later we reached the Municipal Court restaurant. The sheriff's bus was being put to good use making emergency runs to the disaster earthquake areas.

After a very tasty cafeteria lunch, the jurors went back into the courtroom, to listen to the obviously remorseless Susan Atkins, repeating her tale about the Tate residence. She claimed the killings were not out of anger or hate, but out of love for the victims.

Under questioning by defense attorney Paul Fitzgerald, the convicted murderer said she didn't know any of the people at the Tate residence. When asked about remorse, Miss Atkins replied, "I have no remorse; I did what was right to me. I feel no guilt for what I have done." The witness said Manson is innocent; that it was her idea and the idea of the State's key witness Linda Kasabian to commit the "copycat" killings to free Beausoleil. Court was adjourned for the day.

For the next two days, Wednesday the 10th and Thursday the 11th, Susan Atkins was on the witness stand and repeated her testimony about the motive.

Defense attorney Fitzgerald asked the witness, "Did you kill them out of passion?"

"Passion? Hatred? No!" she replied.

"Did you have any feelings towards them?"

"No, I didn't know any of them, how could I have felt emotion without knowing them, I just loved them."

Fitzgerald asked what she was feeling at the time of the killings.

"I was at the height of my fear; I was aware of everything that was going on and at the height of my fear what I was doing was right when I was doing it. I felt no hatred, I felt no malice, I was at the height of my love." She said that when she stabbed it was like she was stabbing herself; it was like death and life all in one motion.

Fitzgerald asked her, "How could it be right to kill?"

"How can it not be right when it is done with love, I feel no guilt for what I have done."

"Did you feel any remorse?"

"Remorse, for doing what was right to me?'

Fitzgerald pointed out that the Tate victims had nothing to do with the arrest of Beausoleil.

"They are part of the system, the system had my brother for something that I did, and I was going back on the system, I have no guilt in me."

The witness said she lied when she implicated Manson before the Grand Jury.

"Why did you lie?" Fitzgerald asked.

"He represents and has always represented strength to me. At the time I was telling the story to the two girls it was all fun and imagination. I told the Grand Jury the story because I was pressured and threatened and offered a life sentence. It was suggested that I might get immunity if I became a State's witness, but I snubbed the immunity offer because it didn't make any sense."

Under cross-examination and redirect questioning by the defense and prosecutor, the witness explained events leading up to her appearance before the Grand Jury.

From Defense attorney Shinn; the witness explained events leading up to her appearance before the Grand Jury and the details of a contract for a book. She visited with Richard Caballero, her original attorney twice. DA Vincent Bugliosi was there the second time to go over testimony that she was going to give on December 5, 1969 to the Grand Jury.

The witness said she didn't want to testify but finally did because of pressure. Shinn asked her about threats. She said that Bugliosi said, "If you don't testify to the Grand Jury, you'll probably get the gas chamber and so will everyone else."

She said her account of the murders was tape recorded by Caballero at the first visit to the office. He promised to destroy the tape but didn't and sold it.

Shinn asked her if she had signed a contract for her story. The witness said she had, but said the words permitting the use of the tape recordings had been written in after she signed the contract. She said the story was supposed to be about her life from childhood to her arrest in Inyo County in October 1969, not about any murders.

[EDITOR'S NOTE: Attorney Caballero had worked out a plea deal for Susan Atkins that according to later testimony by Bugliosi would remove the death penalty from the table if she would testify and tell the truth. She testified at the Grand Jury. After the indictments Manson seemed to exert his control by gathering the defendants together. Under what is called the Aranda-Bruton Rule if part of a defendant's statement incriminates his codefendant, it is not usable by the prosecution against either one. With all of them together they would not testify against each other. At this time Leslie Van Houten dismissed her court appointed attorney and hired one of Manson's choosing. Patricia Krenwinkel decided not to fight extradition and agreed to come to Los Angeles to stand trial. In addition, after meeting with Manson, Susan Atkins fired Caballero and repudiated her Grand Jury testimony. She gave up immunity from the death penalty. Linda Kasabian who agreed to testify was given immunity from prosecution. Family members tried to see her attorneys and Manson asked to see her but that did not happen.]

❖   ❖   ❖

Prosecutor Vincent Bugliosi cross examined Sadie Atkins and asked her several times if she believed that Charlie was the second coming of Christ. Her answer was always evasive and finally the question was dropped.

Bugliosi also asked, "Killing eight people is just business as usual, right Sadie? Eight bodies were no big thing for you?"

Sadie replied "Well, are they? Are one million dead because of napalm, because of your justice a big thing? It doesn't seem to be to you at all."

The prosecutor asked again, "Do you think Charles Manson is a second coming of Christ?"

The witness replied, "Maybe yes, maybe no. To me Manson was God."

Bugliosi stated, "You would kill for God, wouldn't you?"

"I would commit anything for my God."

Bugliosi asked why she had waited until Tuesday to relate the supposed account of Linda Kasabian's role in the murders.

"I didn't because I didn't."

Prosecutor Bugliosi asked if she, Susan Atkins loved her brother Bobby Beausoleil and wanted to free him for a crime she had committed why did she wait until this week when Beausoleil has been convicted and is on death row?

Susan Atkins replied, "Because I didn't see any wrong in what I did."

"Why did you do it?"

"That's what I did."

"And you did it because you did it because you did it." Bugliosi seemed visibly frustrated but he may have been simply making a point.

Sadie gave further details of the plotting related to what she and Linda did to get Bobby Beausoleil freed. After more probing of her story to the Grand Jury and admitted lies under questioning by the prosecutor, the witness was excused.

Judge Older called for an adjournment for the day. The jury was instructed to return to court on Tuesday, February 16th. Upon these instructions, the jurors were assuming that for the next few days there would be a private conference with the attorneys in the Judge's chambers.

On this lengthy weekend of three days, the deputies tried to relieve some of the tension and pressure among the jurors by planning an outing and dinner out on Sunday. I didn't participate in the excursion. I was still battling a hacking cough and a loss of appetite. A few of the jurors stayed behind, and one-woman Mrs. Kampman showed signs of being quite ill. My wife arrived for our usually visit of togetherness. We didn't know at the time, but this would be our last weekend for the jury and spouses at the famous Ambassador Hotel on the Wilshire strip.

On Tuesday morning, February 16th, 1971, the sheriff's bus transported the jurors to the Hall of Justice and the group gathered in the jury room. This was the usual procedure before the panelists entered the courtroom; this morning however, the regular course of action was changed.

One of the regular jurors, Larry D. Sheely, approached me and asked permission to see Judge Older in his chambers.

I relayed the message to Bailiff William Murray, who in turn, asked for a written request from the juror before permission was granted.

The jury entered the courtroom taking their seats in the panel section. Minutes later Judge Older entered with the counsel and Mr. Sheely and announced that Mr. Sheely was excused.

Superior court Judge Charles H. Older did not comment on why Sheely was excused but the jurors were aware that Larry's wife was under a doctor's care and they had two pre-school children.

Mrs. Victoria Kampman, an alternate juror was chosen by lot and sworn in to replace Sheely. Mrs. Kampman was not only surprised to be chosen and sworn in to take her place among the regular jurors, but she was too ill to go on. When she asked to speak to the Judge, and was told she could not, the shock was more than she could take. She complained of feeling dizzy, then sat down, slumped over in her chair and fainted.

Bailiffs Elaine Slagle and Odon Skupen rushed to her aid and Mrs. Slagle revived her with smelling salts and a fellow juror applied cold compresses to the back of her neck. Judge Older ordered the noon recess.

When the jurors returned from lunch and assembled in the courtroom we were in for a surprise. Judge Older announced, "I have good news for you." The panelists listened without showing any visible signs of emotion, but I'm certain many heart beats quickened as the Judge explained that after conferring with counsel, he had decided to vacate his sequestration order.

The Judge admonished the jurors not to talk or discuss the case or their early deliberations in the guilt or innocence phase with anyone, families, relatives, well-meaning friends or members of the press. The Judge announced that Larry Sheely was reinstated as juror number 11 and that Mrs. Kampman would remain an alternate.

The jurors were told that we would spend one more night at the hotel to collect our belongings and that we could go home in the morning. The trial would be recessed for the day while the jurors prepared to move. Superior Court Judge Older concluded, "I know you will be glad to get back to your families."

How do we explain the earthquake of February 9, 1971, which struck during the crisis of stress and dissension among the jury panel? After the devastating quake, and a week later, whereupon Judge Older, after receiving several letters of protest from the jurors and spouses, made his decision to release the jurors to go home. Was its mere coincidence, or did God in his good way, graciously arrange everything to eliminate further confusion, uncertainty and rebellion and brought about an end to the incarceration of the jury members?

Once again here is a written message from my wife Helen.

Homecoming! The day, long waited, was finally here! How well I recall that day. Particularly poignant is the memory of the emotional joy and happy anticipation of getting back to normal. The family at home heard the good news on Tuesday, in the late afternoon, shortly after Judge Older made the announcement in the courtroom that the jurors were to be released from sequestration and allowed to go home. With the news media covering the Manson murder trial so closely, the public on the outside was well informed; one only needed to keep tuned to the radio news on the hour to know what was happening.

Upon hearing the glad tidings, I went around the rest of the day sky-high! Hurriedly I made out my grocery list and went off shopping, stocking the refrigerator with delicacies, in readiness for that first dinner at home.

That evening the jurors went down to dinner in the Ambassador Cafe, my husband called me and said, "I'm all packed Sweetheart, ready to go; pick me up in the morning."

On Wednesday, February 17, 1971, it was moving day for the Tate La Bianca jurors after an "imprisonment" at the Ambassador Hotel for seven months.

The morning was full of activity and joyous exuberance, not only for the jurors and their families, but it was evident that the jubilant and sentimental spirit of the homecoming was shared by the reporters and the news media as well.

The Ambassador staff joined the happy celebration by treating the panelists and their families to a special gourmet buffet breakfast.

To my regret, I arrived at the hotel too late to participate with the group in their last farewell breakfast.

I had to eat breakfast at home, the excitement of my husband's homecoming caused "butterflies' on an empty stomach. It may seem foolish, but I was feeling so happy and excited, like a young bride preparing to pick up her spouse after a long absence.

The drive to the Ambassador hotel by miles is not far, but somehow this morning the distance seemed twice as long. Arriving at the Hotel I parked close to the main entrance in the parking lot, walking swiftly into the lobby and up on the elevators, up to the 6th floor. I flew up the short flight of stairs and on to the corridor and reached Herman's room 639, all out of breath, all a flutter and feeling exuberant as I knocked and entered.

Looking around I could see his suitcases were packed and ready, several boxes and paper bags were stacked up neatly. My husband walked up to me, gave me a funny little smile, not saying a word. I was startled and alarmed when I saw his face; he looked so weary and fatigued. He took me into his *arms, embraced me and wept openly. I embraced my husband tenderly, "thank God, I said, the ordeal is over."*

We had both felt frustration and anguish and had kept these deep emotional feelings pent up. Now we felt great relief, to realize that finally it was all coming to an end.

We waited until all was quiet and everyone had gone before leaving the room, we were in no mood to face the hubbub outside, the news reporters, nor the camera men. We hoped that the news media would understand, for it was not our intention to be rude or ungracious. Moreover, Herman felt, since he was foreman of the jury that it was best to avoid publicity and abide strictly to the court's admonishment. I drove the car home, something I never do when we go out driving together, but this time, I was delighted to take the wheel and give my husband a chance to relax, to sit back and enjoy the scenery. Driving along, we talked very little, there was a glow of happiness we shared in the thought of going home.

Herman commented how strange it felt sitting once again in his car. I glanced away, he looked so aged, so tired and fatigued, tears welled up in my eyes and my heart ached, as I suddenly realized that he had endured an ordeal so much greater than mine.

Arriving home, we saw a man standing in front of the apartment. He greeted us very courteously and said that he was a representative from "Life Magazine." After showing us his business card, he went on to explain that he was aware of the courts gag order to the released jurors. All he wanted was our permission to take a couple of pictures as we entered through the front door. We were happy to oblige.

As soon as we entered our apartment the phone rang. A newscaster from a television channel asked if my husband would appear on a personal interview as soon as the trial was over. I made some offhand comment and said that Herman would have to decide after an adjustment with his work schedule.

There were more calls from TV commentators, all asked for personal interviews after the trials end. I tried to jot down the different channels, but after the third call I gave up. Then a couple of news reporters from the Los Angeles Times newspaper phoned and asked if we would grant an at home interview for a news write up after it was all over.

Homecoming; the day was explosive; as the phone continued to ring, calls from friends and relatives, congratulating Herman on his release from isolation. Meanwhile, I ran wildly about in a state of frenzy, cooking a special

dinner and trying to silence the ringing of the telephone. Our first day at home
was a far cry from that peaceful and restful interlude that we had anticipated
and hoped for.

On Thursday, February 18, the jury was back in the courtroom. The penalty phase of the Tate trial reconvened with Larry Sheely reinstated as jury number 11 and with Mrs. Victoria Kampman excused. She had actually suffered a heart attack.

The first witness recalled to the stand was Susan Atkins, with examination by the defense and cross examination by the prosecutor, the testimony focused on the use and type of drugs used in the Manson "family." Miss Atkins testified that under the influence of LSD, one has a sharper mental awareness.

The next witness (number 11 for the Defense) was Patricia Krenwinkel, age 23. In a calm and friendly voice Miss Krenwinkel talked about life with Charles Manson and assured the court that the 36-year-old Manson was not a leader of the "family" and had nothing to do with the murders. The pale, brown-haired young women testified that she ran after and killed Abigail Folger on the lawn of the Tate residence and that she killed Rosemary La Bianca and then carved the word "war' on the stomach of Leno La Bianca. She then used his blood to write "Rise" and "Helter Skelter" and "Death to Pigs" on the walls. She denied that Manson influenced her to commit the murders.

When questioned by prosecutor Bugliosi if there was any remorse for these murders, Miss Krenwinkel said, "I don't know what that word means."

"Do you have any sorrow for having murdered these people?"

"No," she replied. "It was the right thing to do." She claimed she was in an LSD fog at the time of the killings.

Miss Krenwinkel maintained that the seven August 1969 slayings were committed in a similar fashion to the murder of Gary Hinman to "side-track" the police from Bobby Beausoleil, another Manson "family" member arrested for that killing.

Defense attorney Fitzgerald asked the witness what she did the day of the killings, but she couldn't remember because she was on LSD. She said some people were getting in a car and she said she got in also. She thought Susan Atkins said something like "we are going for a ride."

"We wound up on Cielo Drive, I remember Tex getting out and he cut some wires we took the car back down the street and climbed over a fence. I then heard gunshots. Tex went through a window and then I walked in the front door. One man was there and then a gun went off. I remember tying somebody's hands."

The witness said that Sadie walked in with some people. Linda Kasabian was still in the house. Sadie was then fighting with the two women. "I got up and started fighting with another woman who ran through the back door. We started fighting and I stabbed her and kept stabbing her (Abigail Folger)."

She responded to prosecutor Bugliosi's question telling him she wasn't sure how she caught up with Miss Folger. "She turned, they were standing, fighting and then she fell to the ground."

The witness said she didn't know how many times she had stabbed her.

"But you were sticking the knife in her as far as it would go?" Bugliosi asked.

She replied "yes."

The witness said that Miss Folger didn't scream, she just kept fighting me until she fell. She further testified that the next night, some family members went out on another ride and they went to the home of Leno La Bianca. They had taken LSD before they left.

The witness testified that Tex Watson and Linda Kasabian got out of the car, going somewhere, Linda came back and said Tex is staying and then Leslie Van Houten and I also got out of the car.

"They went to the front door, which was open, Tex was there, two people were on the couch, the man's hands were tied. The woman said, "I'll give you anything and won't call the police." Leslie and I took the woman into the bedroom, then the woman grabbed a lamp, Leslie pushed her away and I ran into the kitchen grabbing utensils and a knife. I went back and Leslie had put a pillow over her head. The woman kept saying, 'I won't call police, just leave.' I started stabbing her and I think Leslie did also."

The witness said she walked out of the bedroom and into the living room where the man was lying on the floor and then she thought "you won't be sending your son off to war so I carved "war" on the man's chest and I put a fork in his stomach. I wrote on the walls." The witness said they all then hitchhiked back to the Spahn ranch and she found Manson with Stephanie Schram in Devil's Canyon.

The following day, Friday, February 19, Patricia (Katie) Krenwinkel was recalled to the witness stand. Charles Manson and the three girls silently demonstrated their oneness in the penalty phase by an extended left arm above the head and pointed left index finger toward the ceiling. Katie

Krenwinkel appeared to be distracted at first when Manson raised his arm, but she adapted quickly, pointing her left index finger upward as she testified.

Defense attorney Kanarek asked why she had taken LSD.

"I do it because it's there and I like it. It's just good to me. I like and enjoy it." When questioned about her reasons for committing murder and if there was hatred for the victims, the witness explained, "It was there to do; there was no reason and there was no feeling of remorse."

Katie quoted, "To kill someone is to kill your own self because we are all one with ourselves."

Prosecutor Bugliosi asked Patricia Krenwinkel if she loved children and the witness replied, "yes, very much."

Bugliosi asked her if she knew that Sharon Tate was pregnant, she answered "yes," and he asked her if it bothered here that she had a baby in her womb.

"No, I didn't think about it."

The witness was asked by Bugliosi if she was willing to suffer the death penalty for the murders that she committed"

"Yes," she replied.

The next witness, the twelfth in the penalty phase was Leslie Van Houten, age 21. Questioned by her attorney Maxwell Keith, the tall dark-haired young woman said she loved her parents and did well in school in Monrovia until about her junior year in high school. She added emphasis to every answer, sometimes with a laugh, a frown, waving hands when Keith questioned her.

She said she enjoyed her childhood; she said her parents' divorce shattered her at first. But when she talked to her parents about it and they said they'd be happier, she told them to go ahead with it. She said she didn't care one way or another that she'd been chosen homecoming princess in her freshman and sophomore years in Monrovia.

Then she was introduced to marijuana and LSD by a young man that she met, Bobby Mackey.

"It wasn't escape." she said, "it was complete curiosity."

It was at that time that she lost interest in school and her grades went down. She said when she took acid, she was happy with herself. Bobby was thrown out of school. She said there were three kinds of kids at school; those who studied all the time, those who drank and smoked cigarettes and those who dropped acid. That was me, she said.

She said Bobby wanted to become a Monk, so she joined him at the Self

Realization Fellowship. She thought she would become a nun or something like that. So, she studied for it also because she wanted to be with Bobby. She was good at what she did, she said. She studied at Sawyers Business School. She could type 65 words per minute without mistakes.

But she said she found that a church can be hypocritical. She called Bobby and said she was leaving the Fellowship. Bobby left eventually also, but they never reunited.

She said she eventually started using drugs again, she went with a friend to the Haight-Ashbury district where she said it was frightening, and there was no love on the streets anymore. It had changed from what she had heard about it.

But she met Bobby Beausoleil who was with two girls and she became the third girl. She said she had a good feeling being around them, that they lived for the moment.

On Monday, February 22, Miss Van Houten was recalled to the stand. The witness described her life as dull until meeting Bobby Beausoleil in San Francisco in 1968 and (Gypsy) Catherine Share. Later she met Manson and his "family" members at the Spahn Ranch. Like the others, Susan Atkins and Patricia Krenwinkel, Miss Van Houten told her story in a matter-of-fact way, without remorse, and like the others, she tried to clear Charles Manson of taking any part on the evening of August 9, 1969.

She said that she and five other family members set off from the Spahn Ranch "just for a drive" that took them to the La Bianca's home.

Miss Van Houten said she never asked where they were going or why they eventually stopped at a house. The witness described the scene about how Charles (Tex) Watson and Linda Kasabian got out of the car and went into the house. She said Linda came back but that Tex was staying. She and Katie Krenwinkel followed a few minutes later up the driveway.

Defense attorney Keith asked her if she had murder in mind as she walked up the driveway. Leslie answered, "No, she didn't intend to harm anyone inside or to rob either."

The witness said, "The front door was open, so we walked in. Tex was standing and a man and woman were sitting, the man's hands were tied. The woman said, 'I'll give you anything.' She said she and Miss Krenwinkel took the lady into the bedroom."

Under questioning from Maxwell Keith, Leslie Van Houten said she fought with Mrs. La Bianca while her companion Miss Krenwinkel returned from the kitchen with kitchen utensils and knives. Then Miss Van Houten said she (Mrs. La Bianca) picked up the lamp and took one of the knives and they both started stabbing and cutting up Mrs. La Bianca.

When asked by the defense, "Do you feel sorrow or guilt in participating in the death of Mrs. La Bianca?" The witness said, "I have no feeling, it can't bring anything back." Under further questioning, Miss Van Houten denied that she knew anything about the five Tate killings on the late evening of August 8, 1969.

But she did implicate herself in another murder, the death of musician Gary Hinman in late July 1969 for which her former boyfriend, Bobby Beausoleil was convicted and sentenced to death. She was present when Manson severed Hinman's ear with a sword, said Miss Van Houten, and Sadie stabbed Gary Hinman in the living room to protect Charles Manson.

On the following day, Tuesday, February 23, Leslie Van Houten was back on the witness stand.

Examination by the defense and cross examination by the prosecutor focused upon questions regarding conflicting statements the co-defendant Leslie Van Houten admitted in telling her court appointed attorney that Manson was involved in the Tate La Bianca murders. But the young woman insisted she only had said what her lawyer, Marvin Part, told her to say so that he could support a plea of insanity by having a psychiatrist listen to her recorded statements. Miss Van Houten said she later fired Marvin Part, her attorney.

[EDITOR'S NOTE: Marvin Part was a court appointed attorney who prior to going into private practice was deputy state attorney general for a year and a deputy district attorney for Los Angeles County from 1960 to 1966. Marvin Part had her evaluated by a psychiatrist. He wanted to have her tried separately. At Manson's urging she fired Part and hired Ronald Hughes who eventually disappeared.]

◆   ◆   ◆

She also testified that she was obsessed with the knife in her hand and she continued to stab Mrs. La Bianca over and over again. She said it was "a whole lot, I didn't count."

She again said she had no sorrow for what she had done. "Sorry is something you say that doesn't mean anything, what good does it do. It's something you say when you don't want to look at what you've done." She also said during her testimony that she had thought about the death penalty but ignored it because she said there is nothing that I can do about it.

Defense attorney Kanarek questioned her and she said she was taking the witness stand because she was willing to carry the weight of the fact that she was in the house with that woman, a knife in hand and said she was ready to be done with it. The reason she killed Mrs. La Bianca was because "it just happened."

Under cross examination by prosecutor Bugliosi she admitted telling a court appointed attorney that Manson had ordered the murders. But she absolved Manson of any guilt in the crimes as Susan Atkins and Patricia Krenwinkel did.

Prosecutor Bugliosi was called to testify by Daye Shinn, Miss Atkins attorney, for details of the arrangement on a deal made for testimony on the killings (witness number 13).

Bugliosi explained that with the arrangement the prosecution made was that they would not seek the death penalty for her if she told the complete truth about the killings to the Los Angeles Grand Jury.

But he added the prosecution would now seek the death penalty because she admitted in Superior Court that she lied to the Grand Jury.

The prosecutor said he, Aaron Stovitz and then District Attorney Evelle Younger met on December 4, 1969 with Susan Atkins' attorneys Richard Caballero and Paul Caruso. He said an oral agreement was reached on the terms of Susan Atkins testimony to the Grand Jury the next day. He then went to Caballero's office to talk to the defendant.

Bugliosi said Richard Caballero, Miss Atkins' court appointed attorney, initiated the arrangement on behalf of his client and had recorded a statement that Miss Atkins had made about the seven murders.

To his knowledge, said Bugliosi "complete immunity" had never been offered in exchange for Miss Atkins testimony, as she testified in the trial.

The prosecution never promised not to seek the death sentences for any of the four defendants if Sadie testified before the Grand Jury. Bugliosi thought that Miss Atkins had substantially told the truth to the grand jury but had lied about who killed Sharon Tate.

On Wednesday, February 24, Samuel Barrett was recalled to the stand for brief questioning. The probation officer for Charles Manson presented documents and records from the Federal Court showing Manson served seven years in Federal prison for violation of parole.

The next witness (number 14 called by the Defense) was Linda Kasabian, the fourteenth witness in the penalty phase trial. Linda was interrupted right away while being questioned by Attorney Kanarek by Susan Atkins who yelled "you only got off by putting it on Manson, admit it, why don't you tell your part."

The witness snapped back "I have, why don't you tell your part," and then she turned to Manson and said, "why don't you tell your part." Manson yelled back, "Live with it, it's on your face."

Judge Older restored order and told the jurors to disregard the statements.

Mrs. Kasabian then said that since returning to court, "the whole thing seems to her insane." Attorney Kanarek asked why? Some of her answers were (the words came fast); it's almost like it is unreal. I know that it happened; it's hard after being away from it for a while. Kanarek asked what's unreal about the case.

Linda stated she didn't know. "Those words just came to my mind. I don't know what I meant. Now being back in the courtroom, it's strange, it doesn't seem real and it's like a dream."

The young mother of two children appeared calm and composed under questioning by the defense. Mrs. Kasabian assured the court that the story she told about the seven Tate La Bianca murders was the truth, and not from any LSD induced dreams. The witness said she never discussed any "copy-cat killings" as a way to free Bobby Beausoleil from charges of murdering Gary Hinman. Mrs. Kasabian admitted that she knew Hinman had been killed but did not remember when or from whom she learned it. Under questioning by the defense, Linda Kasabian denied that she or the others in the group were under the influence of LSD on the nights of August 8 and 9, 1969, but she thought that Charles Tex Watson might have taken a drug called speed on the second night. The witness was excused after about three hours on the witness stand.

After the noon recess, Court was called to order and Deputy District Attorney Aaron Stovitz took the witness stand. Mr. Stovitz testified to the presentation of an agreement made in December 1969 regarding Miss Atkins testimony to the Grand Jury; that the State would not seek the death penalty for her if she told the truth to the Grand Jury. However, he said, she lied when she testified. Stovitz confirmed the testimony of prosecutor Bugliosi (witness number 15).

On Thursday, February 25, Paul Caruso, the court appointed lawyer for Susan Atkins, and an associate of Attorney Caballero, took the witness stand. He said he met Miss Atkins on December 1, 1969 and she told him of her part in the killings. The witness testified about the deal made December

4, 1969 when the prosecution agreed not to seek the death penalty for Susan Atkins if she testified truthfully before the Grand Jury, which he felt she did.

He said that neither he nor his associate Richard Caballero knew that a newspaper was going to publish Miss Atkins' confession on December 14, 1969 four days after a gag order was issued. Mr. Caruso testified to tape recordings of Susan Atkins confession to the Grand Jury and the agreement and contract of Susan Atkins book "How I Killed Sharon Tate." (witness number 16)

The following day, Friday February 26, the 17th witness in the penalty phase was Steven Grogan, age 19, a member of the Manson "family."

Grogan testified to the lifestyle at the Spahn Ranch. He said he went to the Spahn Ranch when he was 15 years old and lived there about a year before Charles Manson and family came there. He said that Manson never gave orders, and everyone did what they wished. Daye Shinn asked him who the leader was. The witness answered, "Pooh Bear." He described the ample use of acid and drugs among all the "family" members. Like the others, Grogan said that Manson had nothing to do with the killings. (witness number 17)

The next witness (number 18) was Lawrence J. Schiller, a photographer and journalist, and an agent for Susan Atkins' book. Mr. Schiller testified and gave details of directing and publishing Atkins' book, the distribution and the share of profits.

Schiller obtained the rights to publish the confession of Susan Atkins stating he reached an agreement to sell the story (in Europe) from Miss Atkins' former attorneys Richard Caballero and Paul Caruso.

The witness also stated that Caballero gave him a tape recording of the conversation that he had with Miss Atkins on December 1, 1969 in his office where she made the admissions. The book was titled "The Killing of Sharon Tate." He said the book grossed more than $100,000.

On Saturday and Sunday, February 27 and 28, the jurors had their first weekend at home.

Court was in session on Monday March 1, 1971. Dr. Andre R. Tweed, a psychiatrist was called by the defense (number 19) in the penalty phase of the Tate La Bianca murder trial.

Dr. Tweed testified that he did not believe that Patricia Krenwinkel is "acutely psychotic." However, he said her behavior which he observed in a recent interview; leads to the conclusion that she is suffering from "residual schizophrenia." The psychiatrist said he had examined more than

12,000 drug users for Los Angeles County in the last eight years to determine whether they were addicts or were about to become addicts. In Miss Krenwinkel's case, Tweed said LSD may have helped disturb and distort her mental state so that she believes what she did was out of love, was not wrong and therefore there is no reason for remorse.

Dr. Tweed based his diagnosis on the girl's responses, that she had lack of concern about things that were happening now and her bizarre ideas about love. He said Miss Krenwinkel didn't feel she had killed anyone because she thought it's impossible to take a life because life and death are one.

Dr Tweed, questioned by Defense attorney Fitzgerald, stated that a person is much more suggestible while under the influence of LSD, that there is a certain feeling of solidarity among drug users, that there is oneness.

Fitzgerald asked if "oneness' could bring about brotherhood and love; the answer was "yes." Fitzgerald asked if that could bring on brotherhood and love and is it legitimate?

The witness testified that "It's a genuine feeling that they have something that others don't, that others have to learn."

On Tuesday, March 2, prosecutor Bugliosi cross-examined Dr. Tweed, the psychiatrist. Tweed said he based his opinions on Miss Krenwinkel and her parent's testimony at the trial and an examination by Dr, Claude L. Brown of Mobile, Alabama on December 24, 1969.

Defense attorney Maxwell Keith asked whether Miss Krenwinkel had told Brown she was afraid of Manson. The witness said, "she had" and quoted from the Brown letter

"She said that after she was released from jail that she came to Mobile to live with her mother and other relatives, primarily because she was more and more afraid of Manson finding her and killing her."

Patricia Krenwinkel and Steve Grogan were recalled to the witness stand and examined and cross-examined by the defense and prosecution attorneys.

Patricia Krenwinkel denied a psychiatrist's report that she killed on the orders of Charles Manson and then fled in fear of the leader.

"I fear him (Manson) as much as I love him."

Miss Krenwinkel denied taking orders from Manson. "Your fear is your love, anything more powerful than you, you fear," she said.

But in a report from Dr. Andre Tweed she was quoted as saying that "after a year or so her feeling for Manson changed. She said she became fearful of him because he became cruel." Later she said, "He became the Devil and threatened them with harm if they didn't do as they were told."

She was asked why she implicated Manson while in Mobile, Alabama after her arrest. "I was just following what my lawyer told me to do, my lawyer told me all kinds of crazy things. He said I should go talk to this man and act crazy, so I did that."

Steven Grogan said that he remembered going on a drive with Linda Kasabian and Susan Atkins in the summer of 1969.

He said he couldn't remember much as he said he was loaded on LSD and thinking about the sun burning. He remembered others going along also but couldn't remember who they were, saying some were dropped off before he, Linda and Susan drove to the beach.

On Wednesday, March 3, Dr. Keith S. Ditman, a specialist in the study of alcoholism and drug abuse offered his opinions as a witness (Number 20).

Dr. Ditman testified that LSD can so affect the mind, that a chronic user could conceivably be influenced to commit murder. Under further questioning by defense attorney Maxwell Keith on behalf of defendant Leslie Van Houten, the psychiatrist said that his experience with chronic LSD users convinced him that one's personality and mind could be affected, and change value standards, particularly in immature, poorly identified young people. It could alter judgment and goals, cause an "unreality" viewpoint, and lead to bizarre behavior and psychosis.

During the questioning Miss Van Houten spoke out and said, "That's not me" and "It's obvious who he's dumping on." She was referring to Maxwell Keith's opinion that Charles Manson influenced her.

Dr. Ditman was asked whether chronic LSD use alone could have led Miss Van Houten to participate in the La Bianca murders. The psychiatrist did not give a definitive answer of "yes" or "no," but said LSD interferes with the brain, usually is a stimulus that can lead someone to act against another person. It also leaves them open to suggestions.

On Thursday, March 4, Dr. Keith Ditman was recalled to the witness stand.

The witness testified that he did not know if LSD caused permanent brain damage, but he said the drug, given to a cat changed the cat's brain wave patterns for six weeks. When Kanarek questioned him he said, "The thinking process, ability, perceptions, moods and behavior control can be disrupted in a group that has taken a large amount of LSD."

The witness said that under that kind of influence they are suggestible, impressionable and less than normal human beings.

The next witness (Number 21) was Dr. Joel Forte, a psychiatrist and founder of a free clinic in San Francisco's Haight-Ashbury District. The noted psychiatrist said that members of the Manson "family" were in effect brainwashed to produce new patterns of thinking and behavior. He said it was possible to program chronic drug users under certain conditions, to commit murder.

Dr. Forte maintained that Miss Van Houten's personality had been adversely affected by the chronic use of LSD and the drug could have been a factor when she helped murder Mrs. La Bianca.

The psychiatrist said, in response to questioning from prosecutor Bugliosi, that Manson's influence was a very significant factor in the Tate La Bianca murders.

Dr. Forte explained after being questioned by Maxwell Keith, that the LSD drug had been used in the Manson "family" to create a "total neutral system." It was used to brainwash or produce a new form of thinking, a new pattern of behavior for the girls living with Manson.

Kanarek told the psychiatrist to assume that someone with his knowledge could influence LSD users under proper conditions and then asked if "subjects" could be programmed to commit crimes, like murder in a "school for crime."

The witness replied yes. Forte said LSD used in conjunction with other factors can change a person's values and behavior and basically brainwash them. The witness was excused after further questioning.

On Friday, March 5, the 22nd witness for the Defense to take the stand in the penalty phase of the murder trial was Richard Caballero, a former attorney for Susan Atkins. Caballero testified that he made a deal with the District Attorney's office for Susan Atkins testimony relating to the Tate La Bianca murder trial in order to save his client's life. The prosecution had promised not to seek the death penalty if she testified truthfully before the Grand Jury.

However, in November and December 1969 Caballero said that he became convinced that Miss Atkins would be convicted and sentenced to death. His client had confessed to the Hinman killing to two Police officers and had told cellmates at Sybil Brand Institute details about the Tate and La Bianca murders.

Mr. Caballero said he learned for the first time that his former client had filed a Superior Court declaration that she had lied to the Grand Jury. Under further questioning by the defense, Caballero testified to details of a contract approved by Miss Atkins for the sale of her book to be published overseas.

He said that he had made an arrangement with the District Attorney's office that he could enter a plea of insanity on Susan Atkins' behalf, anytime during the trial but said he was fired by Miss Atkins because he wanted to have her examined by a psychiatrist and she disagreed. Court was adjourned for the weekend.

The Tate La Bianca jury was now approaching the ninth month of court testimony, now listening to testimony before making a recommendation for life in prison or death in the gas chamber for Manson and his three women followers.

On Monday, March 8th, 1971, the jurors assembled in Department 104, taking their familiar seats in the jury section. Attorney Richard Caballero was recalled to the witness stand.

Caballero denied that he made a deal with the District Attorney's office to "get Mr. Manson" for the Sharon Tate La Bianca murders in exchange for his client's life." The witness testified that he had three tape recordings which he made where Susan Atkins told of the seven brutal slayings in August 1969, of which she had been found guilty. Caballero refused to surrender the tapes to defense attorneys.

Whereupon Miss Atkins rose from her seat at the defense table and said, "I want them destroyed." Miss Atkins appealed to the Judge to force Caballero to give her the tapes but Judge Older refused her request.

Caballero testified that Miss Atkins had told him in "many conversations," some of which were taped, that Manson wanted to bring "Helter Skelter" and "it wasn't happening fast enough," so the murders were ordered by him. The witness stated also that Susan Atkins told him that Manson had ordered the murders at the home of actress Sharon Tate and had personally directed the slayings of the La Bianca's with instructions to "kill them, but not get them upset."

Mr. Caballero stated that he rushed Miss Atkins into the Grand Jury because he thought that the longer he waited, Manson might somehow convince her not to testify. He also said that Miss Atkins told him that others wanted to go along the night of the La Bianca murders but there wasn't enough room in the car.

On Tuesday March 9, Mr. Caballero was back on the witness stand. He said that his former client Susan Atkins said that she never questioned what Charlie did. Under cross-examination by Prosecutor Bugliosi the witness said his client never told him that the murders were committed to free Bobby Beausoleil. He said Miss Atkins told him that the motive was to begin a black-white war.

Susan Atkins said the reason Manson picked the Tate house was to scare Terry Melcher. Manson had also told the murderers to go to the next-door neighbor's house and to do the same thing. Mr. Caballero also said that Susan Atkins did not admit to him that she killed anyone. She said she was holding Sharon Tate down when Tex Watson said "kill her." She said she couldn't do it, so she held her down while Tex killed her.

The day's final witness (Number 23) was Dr. Joel Hochman, a UCLA psychiatrist, cross-examined by prosecutor Vincent Bugliosi. The deputy district attorney asked Hochman, the only psychiatrist to examine all three women defendants in the case whether he thought any of them was psychotic.

Hochman testified that he did not think any of them was psychotic nor had they been psychotic in the past except temporarily while under the influence of drugs.

He said the killings would not have been committed without the use of LSD. He said if the girl was on LSD at the time of the murders, it facilitated the act. He added that he felt that she would not have killed without LSD. He was referring to Leslie Van Houten who he interviewed last week.

The witness said that Leslie went into drugs with a vengeance and said he had seen only one other case where another patient did the same thing. She loved Manson but her feelings toward Bobby Beausoleil were much stronger sexually because he was physically attractive.

Dr. Hochman said that Miss Van Houten was a chronic user of psychedelic drugs who didn't trust anyone now, mainly because of the confession of Susan Atkins. He said that Leslie didn't feel anything when stabbing Mrs. La Bianca; it was like an animal thing. At the time, it horrified Leslie that murder was part of her, but now she accepts it. On Wednesday, March 10, Dr. Joel Hochman was back on the witness stand.

A special consultant on drug use, the psychiatrist said Manson was a "core figure" in the thinking of the three girl defendants and that in his opinion Manson's influence was "great" because he seemed to them like a substitute father, satisfying their needs more than anyone else.

The witness said that the three women defendants are mentally ill and that their problems are an unsatisfied yearning for love. He stated that Patricia Krenwinkel was so disturbed, that she could become psychotic if not given treatment. The need for love was apparently fulfilled by Charles Manson. He said each of the three girls was "lost" when they arrived at the Manson's place at the Spahn Ranch.

Miss Krenwinkel's personality disturbance was the most severe, he said, "she described never accepting herself, feeling she was ugly, she talked about being too hairy and being obese in her teens."

Leslie Van Houten was deeply affected by her parent's divorce and was confused with her father who she idolized. At age 14 she had a love affair with a boy and used LSD for the first time. She became pregnant and had an abortion and that she had trouble forgiving her mother who arranged it, but realized it was the best thing to do at the time.

Susan Atkins told him that she had a deprived childhood, her father was an alcoholic and that her mother died of Leukemia at age 12, but never really liked her. She was taking LSD every other day and had tried to commit suicide twice before she met Manson. She said in a years' time she'd been through a lot. "I'd been a gangster, a gangster's woman, a prostitute and a dancer. I was proposed to and done it all with a man. That's when I met Charlie. I wanted to be happy and Charlie told me what to do."

On Thursday March 11, Dr. Hochman was back on the witness stand for a short time.

The psychiatrist said that each of the three girls demonstrated mental disorders but none of them was insane or had been insane.

State Attorney General Evelle J. Younger took the witness stand (Number 24). Mr. Younger testified that he had approved a deal to keep Miss Atkins from the gas chamber in return for her truthful testimony to the Grand jury, but the arrangement was cancelled, and he personally approved the death penalty in her case because she had lied to the Grand Jury. He said he couldn't remember when he made the life or death decision. During Younger's testimony Charles Manson and Susan Atkins interrupted the courtroom with outbursts, whereupon Judge Older warned them to be silent.

State Attorney General Younger was excused and Dr. Joel Hochman, the psychiatrist once again took the witness stand.

Dr. Hochman was questioned briefly by prosecutor Vincent Bugliosi, regarding the mental disorder of the three women defendants, confirming once again that they were sane.

The following day, Friday, March 12 Court was called to order and the first witness of the day was Canella Ambrosini, a reporter and stenotype secretary. The witness (Number 25) testified to typing (shorthand tape) the confession testimony of Susan Atkins at the Sybil Brand Institute in December 1969 for journalist Lawrence J. Schiller. Charles Manson interrupted her testimony and was warned by Judge Older he would be locked up if he persisted.

The next witness, Pete Miller, reporter and investigator for KTTV, channel 11, was recalled to the witness stand. Mr. Miller testified briefly regarding the publication of Susan Atkins story in the Los Angeles Times, December 14, 1969.

After the noon recess, the final witness of the day, Steven (Clem) Grogan was recalled to the witness stand. Grogan, a Manson "family" member testified under questioning by Kanarek that Manson didn't go with Susan Atkins and Linda Kasabian for a ride on the night of August 9, 1969, when Leno and Rosemary La Bianca were murdered.

During Grogan's testimony, Manson disrupted the courtroom with loud comments, finally after repeated interruptions Manson was removed from the courtroom.

Catherine Gillies

Grogan, like the other "family" members that were questioned on the witness stand, tried to clear the cult leader, claiming he couldn't remember what happened the night of the killings because he was under the influence of LSD, but was almost positive Charles Manson was not there.

The three women defendants disrupted prosecutor Bugliosi's cross-examination of Grogan and were removed moments before the end of the day's session.

This day, Monday March 15, 1971 marked month number nine of the Tate La Bianca murder trial. The penalty phase proceedings resumed with the 26th witness, Catherine Gillies, age 21, one of Manson's "family" members.

The witness testified that on the night of the Tate murders she was awakened by Miss Krenwinkel who asked for some leather strips. She said she followed her to the car and asked if she could go along. But they had plenty of people to do what they had to do. She said she didn't know what they were going to do and doubted they knew either. The young woman testified that on the night of the La Bianca murders, "I would be willing to kill had I gone along, but they didn't need me."

The witness said Miss Krenwinkel told her about the murders early one morning in Devil's Canyon near the Spahn Ranch. "It was evident to me" said Miss Gillies, "why they took place, it was to free bobby Beausoleil," a family member who had been arrested on a charge of murdering musician Gary Hinman in late July 1969. She said she didn't ask her any questions because she wasn't interested and didn't want to know. Miss Gillies, like the others, tried to set up an alibi for Manson on the night of the La Bianca murders; she said he was in Devil's Canyon with a girl named Stephanie Schram the morning Katie arrived and told her about the two nights of murder.

The witness denied that Charles Manson was the leader. Under cross-examination, Miss Gillies was asked if she would lie for the defendants. "No, I would not, there's no need for me to lie," she said.

The next witness (Number 27) was Mary Brunner, age 27, another one of "Charlie's girls." Miss Brunner, a librarian at UC Berkeley said she met Manson in April 1967 and bore his child Michael (Pooh Bear). She said she had lived with him and the others until her arrest for credit card fraud, a day before the Tate murders.

Miss Brunner, like the others, trying to protect Manson, testified that Manson and Stephanie Schram arrived at the Spahn Ranch August 8, 1969, in the afternoon in a milk truck. Under further questioning by the defense, the witness said Susan Atkins admitted to her that she stabbed Gary Hinman.

Mary Brunner

She said she first learned Bobby Beausoleil was arrested when he called the Spahn Ranch after his arrest. The witness said she and Susan Atkins discussed going into the jail to get him out.

The following day the weary jurors were back in the courtroom hearing final testimony in the penalty phase. Mary Brunner was recalled for a brief cross-examination and the final witness recalled was Nancy Pitman, also known as Brenda McCann.

Mary Brunner said she and Charles Manson had been issued a marriage license in 1967 but they never married because they thought he was going back to jail and it was better if he didn't have a wife. But she also said Manson was the father of her son. The son's name was Michael or "Pooh Bear." She said on Tuesday that she was not at the Gary Hinman home when he was murdered (as she had previously said) and was told about his killing by Miss Atkins and Miss Krenwinkel.

Miss Pitman, age 19, a member of the cult family testified that on the night of the Sharon Tate killings, Charles Manson was about 3 miles from the Spahn Ranch in Devils' Canyon. She said she knew he was there because she was making a pair of leather pants for him and had to take them out there for fitting.

Miss Pitman said she first heard about the murders when the girls came back but didn't know who was killed until the next night when they saw it on television.

The witness also said the motive for the murders was not to incite a race war, but rather to get our brother Bobby Beausoleil out of jail who was arrested for the Gary Hinman murder but was innocent according to her.

According to the witness, on the first night of the murders, Linda Kasabian drove the car and Sadie Atkins and Katie Krenwinkel went with her. After further cross-examination by the prosecutor, the witness was excused.

The prosecution and defense rested their cases Tuesday, March 16, 1971. The jurors were Superior Court Judge Older to return to court on Thursday, March 18th.

Chapter Twenty-Nine

Unanimous for Death

The jury reassembled in the courtroom, Thursday, March 18, 1971, prepared to hear the final arguments in the penalty phase of the Tate La Bianca murder trial.

Prosecutor Vincent Bugliosi stood at the lectern facing the jury and began with a potent description of Charles Manson and the three female followers. He labeled the leader, Charles Manson as "indescribably vicious and evil."

"These defendants aren't human beings, ladies and gentlemen. Human beings have hearts and souls. No one with a heart or soul could have done what these defendants did to those seven innocent victims. These defendants aren't even animals. Animals kill only for food or to survive. These defendants are human monsters, human mutations."

Bugliosi said that the three female defendants not only confessed to the crimes, but they tried to make it look like Charles Manson was not connected with the murders and called it a disgraceful spectacle.

With rapid forcefulness, Bugliosi told the jurors that the murders were "so incredibly savage, ghastly and bizarre, that a death verdict is the "only proper ending" for the Tate La Bianca slayings.

"Voting for the death penalty will not be pleasant," he continued, "but under the circumstances, it is the only reasonable decision."

He turned to the jury and paused. He then said, "The eyes of Los Angeles and the entire world are focused on you people and there is only one ending to the Tate La Bianca murders; that is a verdict of death for all four defendants."

In conclusion, Mr. Bugliosi reminded the jury that it was plain to see that the three "girls" were lying on the witness stand to protect and to "do what they could for this god, Charles Manson."

The prosecutor's argument was precise and thorough and was brought to a finish in 10 minutes.

Charles Manson's attorney, Irving A. Kanarek, carried an armload of transcripts to the lectern, adjusted the blackboard into position and opened arguments on behalf of his client.

Mr. Kanarek argued that his client is "society's victim, not a "Svengali." He declared that the public mind had been prejudiced against Manson because of politics, publicity and the desire to make money from Miss Atkins' confession.

Kanarek called for the jury to perform a public service by giving these people life. He denied that Manson was the leader who ordered the killings and said that a person can't be forced to pull a trigger or use a knife. The killers were under the influence of LSD. Mr. Manson was not involved.

Kanarek charged that the former Los Angeles County District Attorney Evelle Younger used the case to gain publicity in his race for State Attorney General. He accused the newsmen of turning the trial into "entertainment" while protecting political figures and suppressing information.

Defense attorney Kanarek argued for over two days trying in his final plea to save Charles Manson's life.

"There is no reason to believe he is anything more than a 140-pound guy who likes girls," Kanarek argued. "That's probably where his troubles stem from."

He described Manson as a very poor Mafia head, stating that Manson was charged with going to the home of Leno La Bianca to show his family members how to murder. But they didn't even have their own weapons using utensils from the kitchen.

Mr. Kanarek reminded the jurors that Manson had spent 23 years in prison, had only a fifth-grade education, no parents and considered penitentiaries his home. The attorney read back into the record long passages of the courtroom confessions of defendants Leslie Van Houten and Patricia Krenwinkel and argued their answers showed they were telling the truth. Finally, on Monday, March 22, in the late afternoon, Kanarek ended his plea.

Defense attorney Daye Shinn took the floor for a brief argument on behalf of his client, Susan Atkins.

Mr. Shinn based his plea on the agreement made between Attorneys Caballero and Caruso, and the District Attorney's Office, regarding his client's confession to the Grand Jury in December 1969. He called it a conspiracy and said the girl had been promised a term of life imprisonment if she testified against the other family members before the Grand Jury.

She did that, but the District Attorney Evelle Younger reneged on the promise. The attorney cautioned the jury to decide if Susan Atkins lived up to her agreement. He said she was still young and there was hope for her. He said he didn't see the necessity for sending her to die and that if she spends the rest of her life in prison maybe she'll realize what she had done.

On Tuesday, March 23, Defense Attorney Maxwell Keith began his final argument on behalf of defendant Leslie Van Houten. Keith did not mention Manson by name, but he hinted at a fearful, frightening, evil force that had produced the murders.

"I think you all know, ladies and gentlemen," the attorney told the jurors, "you have insight, I think you know." He continued to speak about the life at the Spahn Ranch, of Manson's "family" members describing as "idyllic an existence of complete freedom from rules, no order and no government." But Keith reminded the jurors that in order for the "family" to have existed as a cohesive unit for more than two years there had to be a leader. An environment existed where total evil and hate were disguised as love. Arrogance masqueraded as non-violence and total immorality was fobbed off as total freedom.

The attorney argued that when Leslie Van Houten came into the Manson subculture at age 19, she didn't have a chance because of her chronic use of LSD. When Leslie arrived at the Spahn Ranch, her mind was a vacuum, a vacuum for the intrusion of the devil. Mr. Keith described his client as "malleable, impressionable cannon fodder" and totally unprepared to cope with what she found there.

The Attorney made a final plea to the jury and said that Leslie's mental and emotional development was stopped by LSD, but her mental state had been turned back by the drug to the point that she is now a "sick child." Keith pleaded for intensive help and intensive treatment for Leslie Van Houten, attacking the death penalty.

The last of the four defense attorneys to offer final argument was Paul Fitzgerald, on behalf of his client Patricia Krenwinkel. The attorney joined Keith in attacking the eye-for-an-eye philosophy of the death penalty.

Fitzgerald centered his argument on LSD and its effects and said, "This case may be the first of the LSD murders." Mr. Fitzgerald argued that the savagery of the crimes themselves and Patricia Krenwinkel's lack of remorse and lack of concern for herself are signs of mental illness. In his final plea, the Attorney petitioned the jurors to consider life imprisonment but not the death penalty.

Prosecutor Bugliosi began his final summation and told the jury that a vote of the death penalty should be automatic. The prosecutor argued that Manson's "slaves" were so dominated by "their god" that he wouldn't be surprised if they followed Manson to San Quentin and offered to take his place in the gas chamber.

Court was adjourned for the day. The jurors brought suitcases along and were prepared to retire to deliberate if and when the Judge ordered a lock-up for the penalty phase of the trial. And as the day's session ended in the courtroom on Tuesday, March 23, the Judge informed the jury that they would indeed be sequestered for the remainder of the penalty phase. The jurors had no idea where the lock-up would be, however, the group soon learned where it was when the sheriff's bus drove up to the Alexandria Hotel in downtown Los Angeles.

We had been moved to a different hotel because Manson had made death threats against the jury.

[EDITOR'S NOTE: Bill McBride, a juror during the trial, remembered the heavy security surrounding the jurors, especially during the penalty phase and the deliberations. They were guarded by two cop cars in front and two behind and there were four or six policemen with rifles on the bus. We were told not to walk into the door at the side of the new hotel, but to run.]

For the next three days March 24, 25 and 26th the prosecutor and defense attorneys submitted their final rebuttal arguments to the jury in the penalty phase of the Tate La Bianca trial.

Prosecutor Vincent Bugliosi described Charles Manson as the most "evil satanic man that ever walked the face of the earth." He called the co-defendants "bloodthirsty." He said, "These people can't be rehabilitated."

"Should they be permitted to live?" He said as he pointed to the three girls. "They saw to it that Sharon Tate, Jan Sebring, Wojciech Frykowski,

Abigail Folger, Leno La Bianca and Rosemary La Bianca, all of who wanted to live just like you and me, would never savor another dinner, hear music, meet other friends or see another sunrise. They all had full lives in front of them until these savages brutally snuffed out their lives." He said the defense attorneys want you to give them a break, a chance, but they didn't give their victims a chance.

He pointed out that Miss Krenwinkel participated in all seven murders and she laughed about the fact that she committed them.

He said Miss Atkins was not only a murderess, but a vampire as she tasted Sharon Tate's blood. She stabbed Sharon Tate until her heart stopped and a few minutes later her baby's heart stopped.

He called Leslie Van Houten a vicious cold-blooded premeditated murderess in her own right.

Defense attorney Irving Kanarek began his final summation and said he wasn't begging for his client's life.

Kanarek said that one can't substitute prejudice, passion, hatred and complacency for evidence. He said something good should come out of this trial, stating that a study of the defendants alive would be better than killing them. His said that this trial showed one thing, "that we have a drug problem."

Defense Attorney Paul Fitzgerald depicted Prosecutor Vincent Bugliosi as representing death and "a sword rattling harbinger of death." He said he used the word murder 234 times in his final summation. He said he was shocked and embarrassed that somebody would demonstrate such relish for the death of others.

Attorney Fitzgerald asked the jury to ask themselves if Jesus Christ was a fellow juror how would he vote.

He told the jury not to react out of condemnation, vengeance and retaliation. In his summation Mr. Fitzgerald described the gas chamber, the preparation of the cyanide, the ready room for prisoners and the procedure where the prisoner is strapped into the metal chair.

Defense Attorney Daye Shinn, Susan Atkins attorney pointed out again that his client was promised "life" if she testified for the prosecution before the County Grand Jury. She has done that, but the prosecution has reneged on its part of the bargain.

Defense attorney Maxwell Keith claimed prosecutor Bugliosi demanded death, revenge and more blood. He asked if the State of California was more reasonable, more merciful than these three girls and their master, Mr.

Manson. He stated that Manson had influenced these girls, or they wouldn't have committed murder. He said someone had to control their thoughts, but he said that all of the defendants were entitled to live.

Mr. Keith said he thought Charles Manson was legally insane and the evidence showed that his mind is disordered and sick. From this mental illness Manson was under the delusion that killing members of the establishment was beautiful and not morally wrong. He said it was simple and easy to control the minds of these girls, they were empty when he, Manson, got them.

Without Charles Manson and LSD these murders would have never happened, he said. He said the girls were the extension of someone else, their will was his will.

"Manson was their father figure and their god, and they couldn't say no to him."

He said that his client, Leslie Van Houten was not a born killer and the murder does not run in her blood.

Finally, on Friday, March 26, 1971, at 4:40 in the afternoon, Superior Court Judge Charles H. Older instructed the jury on the law for 45 minutes and submitted the case to panelists at the end of one of the longest sessions since the trial began last June 15. The question of life or death for Charles Manson and the three women defendants was now for the jury to decide.

On Saturday, March 27, the jurors arrived at the Hall of Justice at 9:00 a.m. and assembled in the jury room in Department 104 to start deliberations. It had taken nine weeks to hear all of the testimony in the penalty phase of the bifurcated trial. The panelists followed the same method as in the guilt phase, by general discussion with each juror and allowing as much time as one desired to consider every aspect of the case. The procedure in deliberating as before would begin with a silent prayer for guidance and would end with a prayer of thanks.

On Sunday morning, a priest came to the Alexandria Hotel and celebrated Mass in the recreation room for the few Catholic jurors who were privileged to receive Holy Communion. Later in the afternoon, a minister arrived and conducted services for the Protestant group.

The remainder of the day went by quickly for the jurors, some read, some worked jig-saw puzzles, and others played table tennis or just watched television in the recreation room.

In the evening the group was escorted by the deputies to the Casa Vega restaurant for a Mexican meal. This was our last dinner shared together with the Tate and La Bianca jurors and the faithful deputies. In the afternoon at 2:50 p.m. on Monday, March 29, 1971, the Tate La Bianca jurors decreed the death penalty for Charles Manson, Susan Atkins, Patricia Krenwinkel and Leslie Van Houten. The jury deliberated 10 hours. The decision was unanimous. They were all sentenced to death.

[EDITOR'S NOTE: Juror Bill McBride remembered being very aware of how the women defendants slanted their penalty phase testimony towards a lack of culpability on the part of Manson. They didn't seem to care about their personal fates at all. "On the one hand, it was honest that they said they had no remorse or regret. But it was kind of nuts not to be sorry to have killed people they did not know. They each admitted guilt while trying to clear Manson.

None of the jurors was against the death penalty. When we went through jury selection, we were all asked the question if the proper penalty was death could we vote for it and we all answered affirmatively. I think the grisly nature of the crimes and the facts of the case coupled with Bugliosi's statement that if this case is not a case for the death penalty, what would be, was very influential in our decision."]

❖   ❖   ❖

As the court clerk, Gene Darrow started to read each verdict Manson and his three women defendants screamed defiance and threats at the Judge and the jury.

Manson shouted at the Judge, "Half of you here aren't half as good as I am to begin with; it's not a people's court!"

Manson continued, "You don't have any authority over me." The Judge had him removed from the courtroom.

"It's gonna come down hard," Miss Atkins warned the seven men and five women on the jury as she was led past them. "Lock your doors and protect your kids." All three girls were removed after screaming death threats at the jurors.

After the death verdicts on each of the 27 counts against the four defendants had been read, Judge Older thanked the jurors exuberantly and told them, "No jury in history has been sequestered for so long a period or subjected to such an ordeal." Then Judge Older rose from the bench and in his black robe walked along the jury box, shaking hands with and personally thanking each of the seven men and five women for "their devotion to duty." The Judge then told the jurors that he would bestow "a medal of honor" upon them if he could.

It was all over, after 158 days in court the longest murder trial in California history finally came to an end. Later, as the jury members prepared to leave the Alexandria Hotel, a few in the group talked with the news media in the lobby and told some of the main reasons for reaching the death vote.

One juror commented, "We couldn't argue against it because of the weight of the evidence." Several other reasons were mentioned, such as "defendants know right from wrong and they were not insane when they committed the savage killings."

There were three jurors who at first were undecided about the death penalty for Leslie Van Houten, but upon further deliberation and reviewing all of the evidence, they finally agreed on the decree of death.

In view of the orgy and incredible brutality of these murders I felt that the death penalty was the only just one, that belief was also shared by all of the panelists.

There was sorrow in my heart for all four defendants, especially for the women. There were moments in the courtroom, as I reflected on the wasted lives of these young girls, the thought crossed my mind; by the grace of God they could be my daughters. There is no jubilation in something like this, no sense of satisfaction; it was a task that I did not relish. The issue was not how I felt, but that it was a job that had to be done. And in a crime of this nature, the defendants were seemingly unrepentant killers. I could not let my heart rule my head.

The Tate La Bianca murder trial dragged on for too long; to put it even more bluntly than that, all of us on the jury panel felt that the trial should have been over in half the time. It is truly amazing how the jurors withstood their ground through the long ordeal, despite the many hardships and problems we had to face. Despite the girding efforts of the defense attorneys to prolong the trial; the many legal tactics in their stalling devices and the purposeful addition of a "loner" on the jury to potentially create confusion and disharmony, none of their maneuvers worked in the end. We suspected our contrarian juror was chosen to contradict the majority and thereby hang the jury, but even he became a compatible member of our unit. We were all certain that the verdict of death was the right decision.

I withstood the strain and stress of the long confinement by daily prayer and the love and support of my wife and daughters. As was my practice at home, I would begin and end each day with prayer of dedication to the Sacred Heart of Jesus, offering my works, joys and sorrows.

This gave me my source of strength and great emotional stability to endure. In addition, there was no question that I was given the patience and understanding to offer help and encouragement to some of the jurors when they came to me during their most frustrating moments. During the lengthy trial there were many prayers that were said for our support.

As to my relationship with the jury members and the deputies, I had no difficulty getting along with everyone. With the fellow "loner" (William Zamora) in the group, I had no serious problems, our relationship was not, what you would call, a close friendship, but we understood each other and got along quite well. During our isolation we occasionally traded a few sharp words but that was all it amounted to. It is understandable, that the jurors were bound to rub one another the wrong way from time to time during the long ordeal, but other than that I thought we reached an understanding.

However, I have been deeply saddened by the unfounded accusations of promiscuous behavior also made by that juror (William Zamora). Unfortunately, it reflected a bad image on the good work and the dedication of all of the jury members. I can honestly confirm to the good moral conduct of the jurors. I came to know them so well in those many months under one roof; and in my opinion, the rash insinuation was pure nonsense, and an outburst of personal defiance. In those last few weeks of isolation our "agitated juror" made no attempt to disguise his hostility toward some of the members of the panel.

After the reading of the death sentences in the courtroom, the Judge dismissed the jurors, we were escorted up to the jury room and prepared to return to the Alexandria Hotel and pack our belongings. It was then that one juror (Larry Sheely) announced that $200,000 was to be made from an exclusive sale of our story to Life Magazine, if we all agreed and stuck together. The amount of $10,000 each was to be paid, after payment to the attorney.

[EDITOR'S NOTE: $10,000 in today's money would be the equivalent of approximately $60,000. This was a substantial offer.]

❖   ❖   ❖

It took me and the majority of the panel by surprise. Some members in the group were amazed and against the idea in selling a story of their personal trial experiences and I echoed their sentiment at that time.

It was late in the evening, when I returned home from the Alexandria Hotel. It was all over, or so I thought, as I experienced a feeling of great relief and a wave of weariness came over me. The ordeal took its toll. I lost 20 pounds, I felt considerably weaker, tired and more fatigued than I had ever been in my life. I was still plagued with an irritable cough. I also discovered however, that I also became irritable more quickly and had less patience with people around me. I found that my tolerance for upsetting news had gone way down. I didn't much like the change in my character.

The following day, Tuesday, March 30, we were awakened by the shrill ringing of the telephone at 6:30 a.m. in the morning. My wife answered the phone, a news reporter asked to speak to Mr. Tubick. My wife brushed him off and said that I was still asleep and resting, and to call back later.

That was a big mistake; we were besieged with phone calls from newspaper reporters and television newsman. The explosive news had reached the press "Tate La Bianca jurors became promiscuous during the long sequestration" and "a juror urged the others to join him in a package deal to sell their story for $200,000 to Life Magazine."

The next few days were disastrous; our home was no longer a place of peaceful refuge. I kept away from the phone, desperately wanting a little time to relax and unwind before making any attempts for personal interviews and answering questions. As it turned out however, I didn't have much choice in the matter. Perhaps this was a way out of the dilemma. A call came in from the District Attorney's Office from Mr. William Farr, who at the time was a public relations man on the staff.

He spoke to me and informed me that a press conference was set up at the Ambassador Hotel on April 1, 1971. The news media wanted the Jury Foreman of the Manson jury to clear up some questionable issues that came up concerning the jurors. Clearly, I was in no condition to hold a press conference, but this was international news, it could not wait. And so reluctantly I agreed.

The morning of the press conference was exceptionally beautiful; I remember the day so well. It was very warm and sunny and with no smog in sight, as if the good Lord wanted to warm up my weary spirits. My wife went along also to lend me some moral support. In the Ambassador cafe we met Mr. Farr and Mr. Stephen Kay; both men were from the District Attorney's Office. After we had a brief discussion over a cup of coffee it was decided that I would speak directly to the news reporters and not use a written questionnaire.

We walked out into the bright sunlight and into the back of the Ambassador and entered a lovely enclosed garden. There, the sight of all of the reporters, and the multitude of cameras all set up and waiting was enough to unnerve anyone. As I walked up and took my place on the platform, Mr. Farr stood near me and assured me of his assistance if needed.

He then addressed the audience and said this would be a short 10-minute interview. Minutes later, as the cameras were set into focus Mr. Kay observing my uneasiness smiled and told my wife to stand beside me for moral support. The news media sensed my uncomfortable anxiety and noticed my frayed nerves as my hands began to tremble slightly. However, the reporters were most considerate, they questioned me at a slow pace and the interview only related to the major issues of the Manson case.

Some of the important answers given;

The jurors had little difficulty convicting Charles Manson and his three "girls" or deciding that they should be executed for the Tate La Bianca murders.

Several jurors were undecided in the guilt or innocence of Leslie Van Houten but had not offered prolonged or stubborn resistance before finding her guilty.

In addition, the jurors never disagreed over whether death was the proper verdict for the four defendants, only whether death should be decreed for each of the 27 counts of first-degree murder and conspiracy to commit murder.

The jury members never thought nor had any doubts, that the three women defendants were mentally ill or that they did what they did because of chronic use of LSD.

There were no doubts in the minds of the jurors that Manson was the leader of the "family" group, despite his "girls" insistence that the 36-year old defendant was just another member of the Manson "family"

The jurors made their final decisions of guilt and penalty for the defendants strictly on the evidence that they heard from the courtroom witnesses.

In the case of the State's key witness Linda Kasabian, I and the rest of the jury members believed her story, however we didn't consider her testimony until all the testimony from the other witnesses was heard.

A question was asked about the proposed "package deal" for the juror's story, but as I had confirmed before, the subject was disclosed by one of the jurors after we had delivered the death penalty verdicts, and the majority of the panelists turned it down.

As to the question attributed to one juror, that some of the jurors (William Zamora) had been "promiscuous" during the long sequestration, I said that no "hanky-panky" went on that I was aware of. And in my opinion the juror that made such a rash insinuation without any evidence was indeed a small man. Our "frustrated juror" could have let off steam in other ways rather than denouncing the jury panel. We can be grateful though, that the intelligence of our news media is still among us and in a short time after further questioning and confrontation of the "perturbed juror" on television interviews, his true motive came to light.

I said I believed the long sequestration was necessary in the face of such a sensational murder trial, to guard the jurors against news reports and outside influence and I can attest that all efforts relating to the safe-guarding of the panel was effective and successful.

[EDITOR'S NOTE: Here is the transcript of the Ambassador Hotel Press Conference April 1, 1971.

From the UCLA Film and Television Archive Media; these are questions from reporters with the answers given by Jury Foreman Herman Tubick. The Press conference was arranged to clear up matters relating to this murder trial.

The UCLA video is broken up in many segments, it's a "raw type video"; sometimes it is difficult to hear the reporter's questions and so many times only an answer from Jury Foreman Herman Tubick is audible. There were certainly questions and answers that were not included in this raw video. There were many cutouts and breakups in the video. The video is 9 minutes long. Here is what Jury Foreman Herman Tubick said: (UCLA Film Archive)

QUESTION: About defendants;

HERMAN TUBICK: Well, I figured they were just flamboyant about the whole thing, they didn't seem like they cared one bit about anything. They ridiculed the Judge, the court and the laws in court and I didn't think it was proper for them to act this way.

QUESTION: Was that an influence on the jury's decision?

HERMAN TUBICK: No, not necessarily, our influence was mainly from the testimony on the witness stand. The jurors never disagreed over whether death was a proper verdict, only whether death should be decreed for each of the 27 counts of first-degree murder and conspiracy to murder. The jurors thought that the three women defendants were lying when they said Manson had nothing to do with the murders. We had no problems reaching a decision.

QUESTION: There was a question about financial deals.

HERMAN TUBICK: I'm not making any deals with anybody. But yes, I have heard of the proposed deal.

QUESTION: Did Larry Sheely ask the jury or say if we stayed together money could be made?

HERMAN TUBICK: Yes, and it was mentioned after the penalty phase of the trial ended, after it was all over. Well he mentioned something about if we all stuck together, that we could be making a package deal and we would capitalize on it (the trial.) He (Sheely) mentioned $200.000 selling the story to Life Magazine.

QUESTION: What was your reaction to that?

HERMAN TUBICK: My reaction; I was shocked. I didn't think it was right.

QUESTION: Why?

HERMAN TUBICK: I believe that I was rewarded that I was there, by doing God's will; it was God's will that I was performing a service, and this was my civic duty to Society and that justice was served.

QUESTION: Has Mr. Sheely continued in his efforts to bring you all together?

HERMAN TUBICK: No, I haven't' spoken to any jurors and I haven't spoken to anybody you folks here right now, this is the first time I've spoken with anybody at all.

QUESTION: About the deal, why is this objectionable?

HERMAN TUBICK: No, I looked at it this way; my purpose has been served to society and it was my civic duty and I figured it this way, it's all over with now and I just want to forget it.

QUESTION: Are you under any restraint about making a deal now for yourself or putting together a package for the jurors to sell?

HERMAN TUBICK: (smiles) I'm not making a deal at all; I am rewarded that I served society and I served my civic duty and saw that justice was brought about.

QUESTION: Do you have any...

HERMAN TUBICK: I am not making any deals with anybody as far as me capitalizing on this or anything like that.

QUESTION: Do you have any objections to doing that if somebody approached you properly?

HERMAN TUBICK: I don't see any sense in it. I'm serving God. I'm serving society and that's the way I look at it. I'm not looking for any finances or rewards. My reward is that I have already done my duty.

QUESTION: About reaching a decision.

HERMAN TUBICK: No, we had no hardships in reaching a decision, there were discussions, there were problems that came up.

QUESTION: What problems?

HERMAN TUBICK: Well we had a lot of the facts kept away from us, so we had to just go by what was coming off the witness stand.

QUESTION: About the "transcript."

HERMAN TUBICK: We didn't know anything about the transcript, I'm speaking for myself, I never knew there was even a transcript related to the Grand Jury.

QUESTION: Do you feel any threat at all, or have you been threatened?

HERMAN TUBICK: no.

QUESTION: Any phone calls, notes or anything else?

HERMAN TUBICK: No.

QUESTION: Any contact from the Manson family or anybody that might be associated with it?

HERMAN TUBICK: No sir.

QUESTION: Would you do it all over again?

HERMAN TUBICK: Would I do it all over again? If it was God's will, yes, I would. (Meaning would he serve again on a 9 ½ month trial)

QUESTION: One of the juror's has gone on record on television accusing some jurors of promiscuity;

HERMAN TUBICK: (smiles again); Well I don't know which way you mean that, we've had our associations, we had out inside jokes and we've played around, I mean we had to in order to amuse ourselves but if anybody was having any Hanky Panky or anything like that I really don't know (meaning he knew of no sexual activity going on among the jurors). If anyone brought that up it was very small of him. (Herman's brow furrowed, and his fists clenched) (William Zamora was anxious to be elected the jury foreman himself and had been unpopular with the other jurors because he was very impatient). We had our disagreements; I couldn't see eye to eye with him (Zamora) on everything but in the jury room we did see eye to eye.

QUESTION: but you have no regrets, almost a year of your life taken away from your family.

HERMAN TUBICK: It was worth it, and I'd do it all over again if I had to, I really mean it.

QUESTION: Do you feel it was proper to have the jury sequestered for this long a time and do you think it served its purpose?

HERMAN TUBICK: Yes, it has, and I have no objections to be sequestered all over again if I had to be.

QUESTION: Do you think it was necessary?

HERMAN TUBICK: I think it's necessary

QUESTION: Why?

HERMAN TUBICK: It could change any individuals outlook on giving the proper verdict.

QUESTION: Do you think they could have been swayed by publicity;

HERMAN TUBICK: Yes, I think so; I believe that's true of any case.

QUESTION: Question about the missing attorney Ronald Hughes.

HERMAN TUBICK: Well it held it up (the trial). And then I think Mr. Keith did a good job, he helped Leslie Van Houten. One juror had been impressed with defense attorney Keith's argument in the guilt or innocence phase of the trial but didn't offer prolonged resistance before finding her guilty.

QUESTION: Did the jury have any idea that Mr. Hughes might have fell a victim of foul play?

HERMAN TUBICK: No, we thought maybe Ronald Hughes just took off, maybe went on a vacation delaying the case, of course it upset us. We couldn't see why anybody should be taking a vacation while we were being sequestered.

QUESTION: Did you ever think he (Mr. Hughes) was dead?

HERMAN TUBICK: There was speculation on that, yes.

QUESTION: On possibility of parole.

HERMAN TUBICK: Well he (Manson) was the leader. I can't see him or anyone getting out on an appeal.

HERMAN TUBICK: Answer to a question; "well justice was done"

QUESTION: In other words, there was retribution for what they did?

HERMAN TUBICK: Yes.

QUESTION: That would be the only point of their execution?

HERMAN TUBICK: What else could I go on?]

❖   ❖   ❖

Finally, the press conference was over, and my wife and I headed for home. We wanted to forget the whole thing and tried to relax with a feeling of great relief. We were anticipating a return to normal life once again. But no sooner than we entered the apartment the phone started ringing. A news reporter said that he had missed the press conference at the Ambassador and wanted to know if I would grant a personal interview. Offering my regrets, I told the man that there would be no more interviews. Several more calls came from television press commentators; they asked if I would consider appearing on a newscast.

On the following day I reported for work at Rose Hills Memorial Park.

My supervisor called me into his office, he looked at me and said, "Herman, you need a vacation to rest up, we'll give you three weeks, and I'd advise you to leave town for a while until this thing blows over. Reporters have been calling and asking for you."

With grateful relief I thanked my supervisor and went on home and did exactly as I was advised. I bought two plane tickets and my wife, and I flew to Hawaii. I can't remember when I felt so much in need of a vacation, and just the thought of leaving all cares behind boosted my spirits.

The Tate La Bianca murder trial was a challenging experience for all of us and it demanded a great deal of patience. Despite the many hardships and problems and Court delays the Tate La Bianca jurors stood their ground in sheer determination.

I looked upon the jury panel with admiration, for despite all of the obstacles the jurors considered their civic duty a responsibility and an obligation. During the marathon trial the jurors griped, and they complained, but I believe under the trying circumstances and the stress, they had every right to do that.

The long confinement was difficult for all of us, more for some than others. It is difficult to describe the kind of frustration we had to go through during the dragged-out testimony in the courtroom. The nine and one-half month trial resulted in at least 20,000 pages of transcript. Those pages represented innumerable hours spent either in the courtroom listening, or having the lawyers having private discussions with the Judge about interpretations of the law. Those 20,000 pages of transcript do not reflect the hours spent over the evenings and weekends when we, as sequestered jurors were away from our daily lives, our families, and home cooked meals.

The toughest thing was the hotel confinement, it's something one has to experience to really know what it is like; a disruption of one's entire personal life. Freedom, it's an aspect of American heritage we take for granted. Until we are denied it, then it's takes on great importance. It felt at times like we were in prison for crimes we did not commit. But then we would override this negative thinking by a reassessment of the importance of our role in the workings of the legal system.

Many people have asked me this underlying question, "How could the Tate La Bianca jurors endure this long ordeal?" And in our story, I wanted to point out, not so much the extraordinary achievement of the Tate La Bianca jury, but rather, through the grace of God, the extraordinary endurance and harmony of the 12 selected panelists prevailed into the very end.

I believe it boils down to one solid question we should always be asking ourselves. What kind of citizen am I? It might sound corny and it can get maudlin, but we should be willing to get involved.

Our court laws can be changed for the betterment of our system and our Country. I have great confidence in the jury system as arbiter of life or death sentences.

I firmly believe in the death penalty for specific crimes; for premeditated murder, violent killings, for the slayings of law enforcement personnel, killings as a result of sky jacking, kidnapping and bombings.

After the Manson case and before my wife and I put together this manuscript as a historic accounting of my experience on February 18, 1972 the California Supreme Court declared the death penalty to be unconstitutional. Charles Manson, Susan Atkins, Patricia Krenwinkel and Leslie Van Houten all had their death sentences commuted to life in prison. A few months later, capital punishment was reinstated by the voters in California, but this did not have an impact on these cases. Although Manson and his followers escaped their punishment, I honestly believe it was a wise decision to reinstate the death penalty law.

In exercising and using our entire God given talents to bring about improvement and strict enforcement in our courts of law, will we continue to grow and expand as a leading Nation. And only then will the power and the future of our Country flourish and be preserved.

In conclusion, I want to add that serving jury duty on the Tate La Bianca murder trial was a challenging and unforgettable experience for me, and I am certain that it was for my fellow jurors as well.

CHAPTER THIRTY

POST-TRIAL JUROR'S COMMENTS ON SEQUESTRATION

The Jurors were often referred to in newspaper articles during the trial but could not give direct comments until the trial was complete. Here are some statements attributed to the various jurors as found in newspapers of the time.

Helen Tubick: "All the jurors and their families have suffered," said Helen Tubick, wife of the jury foreman, undertaker Herman Tubick. "It was like he was in prison." (Pittsburg Post-Gazette February 19, 1971)

Thelma S. McKenzie, juror number 1, from a December 22, 1970 Valley News newspaper, it reads; "Mrs. Thelma McKenzie looked at the bloody body of Miss Tate, eight months pregnant when she was killed. (from a color photograph shown by Prosecutor Bugliosi) and then stared at Manson."

Mrs. McKenzie took advantage of the long sequestration and lost 20 pounds. In 1995 Thelma commented on the OJ Simpson trial and the jurors who were sequestered for a record 265 days. She said about the Manson trial; "I have no regrets about the experience. It helped me grow, and it will help these people grow."

When the Manson trial ended Thelma S. McKenzie dashed past newsmen to say only that the jurors "tried desperately to find some reason why the women's lives should be spared." (Independent, Long Beach, CA, March 30, 1971)

Shirley B. Evans, juror number 2, in a newspaper from August 5, 1970; was asked by Judge Older what she thought of the Manson Guilty Headline newspaper from Nixon. She said her first thought was that it was ridiculous because she didn't think President Nixon would think such a thing.

She said she thought he had more important things to deal with.

William Thomas McBride III, juror number 3 remembered Shirley Evans as a very sweet little older lady. She knitted some pull-on wool slippers for all the jurors for Christmas 1970. -Bill McBride went on to court reporting after the trial ended and started his own business McBride and Associates in Northern California in 1987. He is now retired.

Bill McBride wrote to Rick Ortenburger; "I did receive a little homemade trophy for being the paddle tennis champ over Bill Zamora. It was a salad dressing bottle with a tennis ball on top. Ha-ha! I always took part in the field trips and dining outside of the Ambassador, because it got us out of the hotel. Yeah, we knew the Ambassador cafe well. Too well! We thought alike on most everything concerning the case. (Referring to Herman Tubick and William McBride)

William McBride at the end of the trial, "I felt sympathy for the women." But he said: "Sympathy can't interfere with justice. What they did deserved the death penalty." (www.nytimes.com) "He said there have been squabbles since the trial ended among the jurors who talked publicly and those who didn't. Some felt that if all kept quiet, they would be able to market "exclusive" stories at a higher price." But McBride said he felt jurors shouldn't try to make money from their experience and that he'd given interviews without payment. "I just don't care about it," he said. (Press Telegram, Long Beach, CA, April 1, 1971)

Alva King Dawson, juror number 4 was the oldest member on the jury. In the early years he lived in Los Angeles. He was a Deputy Sheriff.

Alva K. Dawson at the end of the trial; "I would certainly hope this will teach all those other young people not to make trouble, not to go out and kill people." (Los Angeles Herald-Examiner, March 30, 1971)

Jean Kathryn Roseland (Burton), juror number 5, commented during the trial, "well today's my day with Charlie. He had those eyes of his on me all morning. He just sat there staring at me. I wasn't ever able to stare him down. I always turned my eyes away from him first.

Some of the other jurors said they got him to look away once or twice, but I never managed it. I still don't know why I couldn't."

"You had to become a computer to keep your sanity. I did everything in my power to show absolutely no emotion. I just sat there day after day storing up all this horrible information in my computer banks for retrieval at a later date. "God, I don't think I'll ever get those sights out of my mind. They were in color you know." "Everything I start to talk about reminds me of something that happened either in that courtroom or in the hotel, and the pictures of the victims." "I swear to God, living like we did was a real hell. It was like being in a glass walled room.

Every time you looked out, the world you saw was like a motion picture with no sound." (The American Star, Tuesday, April 13, 1971 / New York, Associated Press)

Anlee Lorin Sisto, juror number 6, was genuinely enthralled by the enforced camaraderie of the jurors. As he put it later: "I miss the friendship. I always felt like I could go knock on someone's door and talk any time of the day or night, just like when I was in the Navy."

William Maurice Zamora, juror number 7 made a comment on his book (May 25, 2018) "Trial by Your Peers" on the www.cielodrive.com website about the accuracy and mistakes he made in his book and the hurried printing (in India) by the Publisher. He had one acting job on the *Fall Guy* (Three for the Road) TV Series appearing as a Waiter / Bartender in 1982.

William Zamora at the end of the trial said he was saving his comments for a book he was writing about the case. (Independent, Long Beach, CA, March 30, 1971) "I told them I was going to write this book. Watch yourselves." (Star-News, Pasadena, CA, April 1, 1971)

Marie Mildred Mesmer, juror number 8 stated at the end of the trial; "There's no doubt that he was the leader. He was the instigator. He's a dangerous influence on society." (Referring to Charles Manson) (www.nytimes.com)

I think I can go home with peace of mind now knowing I have protected society." (Idaho Free Press & Caldwell New-Times Tribune, March 31, 1971) "We made our decision early, but we agreed on all points so everyone would have a say-so." (The Daily Intelligencer, Doylestown, PA, 30 March 1971)

"Without Charlie none of this would have happened." (Daily Review, Hayward, CA, April 16, 1971)

Evelyn J. Hines (Davis), juror number 10. Towards the end of the trial there was a "flap" when Defense attorney Irving Kanarek made a motion for an evidentiary hearing in late January 1971. The motion was to determine if Mrs. Hines had taken up "drinking" after the juror's had been allowed to have a cocktail at dinner and that perhaps she was not capable of rendering a decision. Affidavits filed by the Bailiff's showed that no juror had been allowed to drink liquor any day until dinner time and then some had one or perhaps two drinks. In February 1971, James Hines said that his wife Evelyn became emotionally upset by the long absence from home and frequently declared tearfully "Oh my God I wish this was over!"

Evelyn J. Hines at the end of the trial; "I have no reservations. They knew what they were doing." (After voting for the death penalty) (www.nytimes. com) "I didn't think the girls were insane" (Los Angeles Herald-Examiner, March 30, 1971)

Larry D. Sheely, juror number 11, lived in Paramount, California during the trial and was picked to replace Walter Vitzelio about 14 days after the 1970 trial began. Larry Sheely is best known for trying to put together a "deal" with Life Magazine for the juror's exclusive story on what went on at the trial. That never materialized.

From ABC News in August 2009; Larry Sheely remembered riding the bus from the hotel to the courthouse with the windows blocked so he and other jurors wouldn't be able to read the headlines on the papers at the newsstands. Sheely was the youngest member of the Manson jury, age 23. He told ABC News that he believes the public fascination stems from the horror of Manson's crimes. He was also excused as a juror on February 16, 1971 near the end of the trial but was quickly reinstated at his replacement, Mrs. Kampman, fainted from being picked to replace him and didn't even make it to the jury seat.

Larry Sheely at the end of the trial said he was also saving his story to give it "exclusively" to a national magazine that had already contacted all jurors. (Independent, Long Beach, CA, March 30, 1971)

From the book "Witness to Evil," page 416 written by George Bishop, year 1972. "It should come as no surprise to followers of the Tate/La Bianca Trial that the jury, in their first official action, elected as their Foreman, Juror Herman C. Tubick."

From the book "Helter Skelter," page 410, written by Vincent Bugliosi & Curt Gentry year 1974. "Alva Dawson, the ex-Deputy Sheriff, and Herman Tubick, the Mortician, had tied. A coin was tossed, and Tubick was made Foreman. A deeply religious man, who began and ended each day of deliberations with silent prayer, Tubick had been a stabilizing influence during the long sequestration."

In this book my Uncle Herman Tubick referred to another juror as "that juror," "the agitated juror," "the discontented juror," "the disgruntled juror," "the loner," "the frustrated juror," etc. In the year 2019; let it be known 48 years after the trial ended (year 1971) that the jurors name was William Zamora.

From the Vincent Bugliosi and Curt Gentry book, "Helter Skelter." "One juror let it be known that he intended to write a book about his experiences, and some of the other jurors were apprehensive about how they might be portrayed. The same juror wanted to be elected Foreman and when he wasn't even in the running, was so piqued that for a day or two he wouldn't eat with the others." (That juror was William Zamora)

"One temperamental male juror slapped Bailiff Ann Orr one night when, against his wishes, she changed channels on the commercial TV. (Vincent Bugliosi and Curt Gentry book, "Helter Skelter").

"It's just havoc. Your whole life is disarranged." said Wanda Sisto, wife of juror Anlee Sisto. She said friends and neighbors were "very thoughtful and considerate but it was still difficult." She said sequestration was probably needed to guard jurors from exposure to trial publicity, but "I'm not happy about is because of my husband being away from home." She said that Anlee had resumed smoking two weeks after being locked up and that he had been off of tobacco for a year and a half. She said he also dropped 25 pounds. (Pittsburg Post-Gazette February 19, 1971)

From Rick Ortenburger

The quote at the beginning of this book "But from their graves...... they cry out for justice" was taken from the prosecutor's closing argument. It had a tremendous influence on all the jurors and especially my uncle.

I was so excited when my cousin entrusted this book to me to see that it is made available to the public. This case is sensationalized with the focus on the crimes themselves and the mystery of Charles Manson. However, by following the trial as it was experienced by the jurors, it is apparent the evidence to convict Charles Manson, Susan Atkins, Patricia Krenwinkel and Leslie Van Houten was overwhelming. There are many things to be learned about this time in our history and about the inside workings of our legal system by examining what this sequestered jury went through to meet the demands of their civic duty. I knew my Uncle and I know that he took his job very seriously. This jury examined every piece of evidence before making a determination.

This trial produced 20,000 pages of transcript. It would be impossible for most people to follow the case from beginning to end. This book shows what my uncle considered important in the testimony of the various witnesses, as the jurors were encouraged to take notes.

Deborah Herman, as co-author of this book, excerpted some of the testimony from the original trial transcripts as there were many motions and arguments outside of the presence of the jury which we felt would provide readers the advantage of a broader perspective. This information would have helped my Uncle Herman better understand the tensions that surrounded his experience as a juror, especially one in sequestration. We were very glad the jurors were asked to keep copious notes of the important facts as gleaned from the various witnesses. These quickly written shorter version notes were used later in the discussions during deliberation to determine guilt or innocence and whether punishment for these crimes was life in prison or death. My uncle's two notebooks of notes formed the basis of his original manuscript in the year 1973. We, as editors, were very glad that my Aunt Helen and Uncle Herman were able to create a narrative picture of his experience and such a complete guide to the testimony. Even though Uncle Herman expressed some frustrations with the defense attorney's methods and particularly attorney Kanarek's "obstructionist" ways, we believe the book shows he and the fellow jurors truly listened to the evidence and considered all aspects of the case before rendering what they emphatically believed was a just decision.

The jury was uninamous in deciding on the penalty of death and in spite of being deeply religious, I know my uncle felt it was the right decision based upon the law of the time and the brutality of the crimes for which the defendants were found guilty. The death sentence was decided on March 29, 1971, the same day attorney Ron Hughe's remains were discovered in the Sespe Springs area. In February of 1972 the California Supreme Court declared the death penalty unconstitutional and commuted the sentences of all four defendants to life in prison. Although the California death penalty was reinstated in 1977 this has no effect on the outcome of this case. I am confident my uncle would have felt this outcome was the will of God and would have felt justice was carried out by a much higher authority. He would not have questioned the purpose of having these defendants remain in the public eye as living reminders of these senseless crimes. I believe he would have felt God had a plan. Perhaps this book is still a part of this plan to remind people what can happen in a world where people can look to human beings, false prophets, as a way to find God.

My uncle was devoutly Catholic, but he would never have told anyone how to worship God. However, I am sure he would caution them to always reach upward in humility and faith. I know when he writes, "there was sorrow in my heart for all four defendants, especially for the women. There were moments in the courtroom, as I reflected on the wasted lives of these young girls, the thought crossed my mind; by the grace of God they could be my daughters," he truly meant this. I think many people felt this way then and still do to this day.

Perhaps this is the cautionary tale God does not want people to forget.

Deborah Herman

This book was the second opportunity I was given to deeply explore this case. I use the term "was given," because that is how it felt. I had been researching the subject for years in utter fascination as I am sure many people have. But my renewed interest in the summer of 2016 took on almost cosmic proportions. I had read Jeff Guinn's well-researched book simply titled *Manson* and said out loud to no one in particular, if I ever want to write a Manson book, this man has done an excellent job of research. I could start there. Then as if driven by an invisible force, I began re-watching movies and binge watching videos until my husband asked me why I was taking a journey into darkness. I had to explain that the case had everything to warrant attention especially for someone interested in cults, law and true crime. I decided to ignore his concerns and return to my deep dive.

One week later my husband sheepishly handed me an email received by our literary agency which said the following:

I am Dianne Lake, formerly known as Snake of the Manson family girls. I have an incredible story that I would like to share with the world. I have written my experiences with the Manson family and how I came to live with them at the age of 14- 16 and the consequences of that life. Now at 63, I am finally able to share this story of coming of age in the throes of drugs, sex, rock and roll and murder. I have been incredibly blessed, protected, and loved during my life then and now through what I can only attribute to be God's grace. I have achieved a successful happy life as a wife, mother, grandmother, daughter, sis-

*ter, aunt, niece, cousin and friend, as well as a special education specialist with
a masters degree. I have managed to live in So. California my whole life with
only a few people finding me, another example of God's grace.*
*I chose you from your 2015 guide book primarily because I loved what Debo-
rah wrote about the Writer's Journey and the Path of the Spiritual Messenger.*

Dianne had written to only one other agency. What was even more interesting is the article to which she was referring has been reprinted without
change in Jeff's yearly and now bi-annual tome *Jeff Herman's Guide to Book
Publishers, Editors and Literary Agents* for at least ten years. Only certain
people even notice it is in the book and when they do they typically write to
us about how it resonated with them.

I immediately called Dianne, we met and decided to collaborate on her
memoir about her experience as the youngest member of the Manson family. We were given an offer for the book which we completed by August, 2017
and the book was published October 24, 2017. Charles Manson died on
November 19, 2017.

Getting to know Dianne and learning firsthand what I had always suspected, there but for the grace of God go any of us. We can all look back at
Charles Manson and say, "oh, I never would have been caught up in something so crazy." No one ever says they want to grow up to join a cult. Cults
follow patterns that are not discernible until for many, it is too late. Dianne
thanks God every day that she was not part of the horrific crimes and in
some way was able to bring justice for the victims. Telling her story was a
way to exorcise her own demons and the hope was to put the story to rest for
others who for fifty years had seen Manson as the face of evil.

When we finished the book I know the journey felt complete for Dianne.
However, I felt there was still more for me to explore. As a former trial lawyer, I had become fascinated by what Manson was able to maneuver behind
the scenes during his trial. Dianne's book could only touch upon the trial
and focused the part she played. I had read a good part of the 20,000 page
transcript thanks to the digitizing by cielodrive.com and other sources and
felt there was so much more to tell. Manson showed so much of the true
story in his behavior and behind the scenes court arguments that I felt it was
an important part of the picture.

I was overjoyed when Rick Ortenburger gave me another chance at a
deep dive into the case as not only the publisher, but as a co-author. Now I
could take this historic document left by the Tubick's for posterity and fill
in the pieces to show the true picture of Manson. As much as possible I

was able to align the dates of testimony with the transcript to see what led up to Manson's outbursts and behaviors that to the outsider merely looked bizarre.

After once again seeing the case in context, I couldn't help but feel sad about the entire story. There were so many casualties, the first, of course being the victims. The crimes were so brutal as to be inhuman.

I am also struck by the fact that some of the followers were also victims. I know Dianne Lake was a victim and I feel blessed that in some way I might have played a part in her healing. It is difficult to imagine how a 16-year-old could have the courage to face Manson in court after being threatened the he was going to "skin her alive." She knew this was not an idle threat. She was familiar with how this man she saw as the epitome of love turned everything into brutality.

I also suspect by rereading the transcript that a few of the women who testified on behalf of Manson during the penalty phase might have been intimidated beyond what we will ever know. Manson made it a point to try to remove the screen in the jail when he would be interviewing potential witnesses. Even with that protective screen it is likely he terrified witnesses like Catherine Share who may or may not have been a true follower.

Manson showed his level of intimidation in the courtroom by his gestures to Linda Kasabian in front of the jury.

When I reread the transcript I could see tremendous native intelligence in Manson. No one fully understands the mind of a psychopath, but if there had been some way for his 'genius" to have been otherwise channeled perhaps ... We can certainly read Jeff Guinn's *Manson* if we want to find causes of Manson's rage and ultimate descent into madness. However, no one knows the answers to the question of nature vs nurture or we would be much further ahead in stopping violent crimes.

We do know more about cults and the patterns of programming. I contend that the leader may not always be aware that a cult is being created. There is a turning point where what is good turns dark. The fun turns to madness and the madness turns to horror.

There is much to be learned by studying the trial and contrast between what the jury perceived and what was happening behind the scenes. I think law students interested in trial law should study this case. As mad as he likely was, Manson used his survival skills to creatively maneuver the court to his own benefit. Thank goodness, the law prevailed. Manson was unable to undermine the process and justice was served.

This may be the final chapter in my work with analyzing and writing about Charles Manson, the "family" and a period of time like no other. Or perhaps it is still just the beginning. For whatever reason, I am becoming a defacto Manson and cult expert and know I have only scratched the surface. Manson was not the first false prophet and he will not be the last. As long as people need something outside of themselves to fill the void that can only be filled by real love and in my opinion, faith in God, we will have cults. As long as we have disintegration of families and disenfranchisement we will have gangs and domestic violence, which is akin to a family cult.

I believe the only way to combat cults, domestic violence and gangs is to help people feel connected, worthy and safe. That is what these false "families" provide. It is my prayer that we put our energy as a society into this solution. Perhaps this is the message we are to take away from this.

POSTSCRIPT

BY JEFF ORTENBURGER

The jury was sequestered 225 days, longer than any jury before it. Here is a brief "whatever became of," those people connected to the trial.

This list is in no particular order and is not comprehensive.

There were two deaths in families of the jurors' during the 9 ½ month trial; the father of alternate juror John Ellis and the brother of jury foreman Herman Tubick both died during the trial.

Rudolph Altobelli, the owner of the Cielo Drive residence, moved back into the house two weeks after the murders and lived there for 20 years. He sold the properly in 1989 for 1.6 million dollars. The house was eventually demolished, and the street address was changed. Rudy Altobelli died on March 26, 2011.

There were six victims murdered on the night of August 9; the unborn son, Paul Richard Polanski, was murdered also. We typically see a collage picture of the five victims on the first night of murder. We shouldn't forget the unborn 8-month-old son of Sharon Tate and Roman Polansky.

Herman Chester Tubick, juror number 12, was elected as the Jury Foreman on January 15, 1971. Herman Tubick died 24 December 1985 in Monterey Park, CA, his wife Helen died March 4, 2002 in Sylmar, CA. They are buried in Calvary Cemetery in Los Angeles, CA.

Herman Tubick (Jury Foreman) at the end of the trial; "We were unanimous, society has been served." (Los Angeles Herald-Examiner, March 30, 1971) "The trial has been very difficult. I pray to God that the verdict will be good for the youth of the Country." (Independent, Long Beach, CA, March 30, 1971) "We've had our inside jokes and playing around, but if anybody was having hanky panky, I don't know about it. If anybody brought that up, it's very small of him." "He may know something I don't know." Tubick stated that Zamora had "personality clashes" with other jurors during the sequestration. (News-Palladium, Benton Harbor, MI, April 2, 1971)

"He said if all the jurors stuck together, we could make some money, he mentioned $200,000." "I was shocked by the suggestion." "I felt I was doing God's will and my duty to society." (Referring to juror Larry Sheely putting together a package deal to sell to a magazine) (Raleigh Register, Berkley, West Virginia, April 2, 1971)

"Mr. Tubick's years as a funeral director in Whittier stood him in good stead as he faced down 40 reporters and five mobile camera crews assembled in one of the Ambassador's mimosa scented gardens. He had a professional flair for solemnity, an undertaker's practical eye for the working of God's hand. He could see divine will being done in his own selection to the panel, in prayerful and orderly deliberations, in the unaccustomed eloquence that touched his voice, as he argued in favor of death. But for Zamora's indiscretions, Tubick could only express dismay." (Life Magazine, April 16, 1971)

Helen Tubick (Ortenburger) died March 4, 2002 in Sylmar, California. She is buried at Calgary cemetery in Alhambra, California.

Paul J. Tate, a former Army intelligence officer, whose daughter was murdered by the followers of Charles Manson, died on May 18, 2005 in Coupeville, Washington of congestive heart failure. He was 82. (The Los Angeles Times, May 24, 2005)

Doris Gwendolyn Tate, the mother of Sharon Tate died July 10, 1992 in Palos Verdes Estates, Los Angeles County from a brain tumor. (The Los Angeles Times, July 11, 1992)

Patricia Gay Tate, the sister of Sharon Tate died June 3, 2000 of breast cancer in Rancho Palos Verdes, Los Angeles County. She was 42 years old. She became a victims' rights advocate after Sharon was murdered by the Manson Family in 1969 and attended the parole hearings of Susan Atkins and Patricia Krenwinkel in order to help prevent their release. She also represented heiress Abigail Folger at her killers' parole hearings.

Debra Tate, the sister of Sharon Tate has attended the parole hearings of every member of the Manson family currently imprisoned for the Tate La Bianca murders. She actively campaigns against the release of any of the Manson family convicted of murder.

Jane Louise Edwards (Van Houten), the mother of Leslie Van Houten passed peacefully in her sleep on March 17, 2005 at age 85, survived by her brother Jim and sister Margaret, her children, Paul, Leslie, Elizabeth and

David and seven grandchildren. (Los Angeles Times, October 29, 2005)

Charles Herman Older, the Judge who presided at the Manson Trial, died June 17, 2006. The cause was complications of a fall at his home in West Los Angeles, said Edward Cazier, a friend and former law partner. He was 88 years old. (Los Angeles Times, June 20, 2006)

Charles Manson, 83, died on Sunday, November 19, 2017, at a Kern County hospital." (The New York Times, November 20, 2017)

"Charles Manson was cremated, and his ashes scattered following a brief, private funeral. The Porterville Recorder newspaper reported the attendees included Manson follower Sandra Good along with Afton Elaine Burton, a woman Manson took out a license to marry in 2014 when he was 80 and she was 26. The couple never wed. (New York Post March 19, 2018)

Susan Atkins, convicted murderer, died September 24, 2009, at the Central California Women's Facility, Chowchilla, California of a brain tumor. (The Los Angeles Time, September 26, 2009)

Witness number 52, Juan Flynn; born November 9, 1943, died January 4, 2013 in Pahrump, Nevada.

Prosecutor Vincent Bugliosi died June 6, 2015 of cancer in Los Angeles. (The Los Angeles Time, June 10, 2015)

Aaron Stovitz died January 25, 2010 after a long battle with leukemia. He was 85 years old. He was the original assistant prosecutor on the Tate La Bianca murder trial but was removed in September 1970. (The Los Angeles Times, January 26, 2010)

Maxwell S. Keith, who became the Defense Attorney for Leslie Van Houten after the lawyer Ronald Hughes disappeared under mysterious circumstances, died on Tuesday March 6, 2012 in Templeton, Calif. He was 87. (The Los Angeles Times, March 8, 2012)

Witness #63 Ronni Howard died 3 October 1979. On September 21, 1979, she was kidnapped from a bus terminal by a person claiming to be a taxi driver. This happened at 11:30pm. She had just arrived back to LA from Vegas, with her husband Rudy and his brother. As Rudy and the brother-in-law returned to the bus station for the luggage, the cabbie took off with Ronnie. She was then driven to 60th and Western where she was robbed and beaten. She lost consciousness and woke up in the gutter. For several days after this incident, she had suffered from nausea, dizziness, and headaches and was becoming increasingly lethargic. On September 25, she was taken to Queen of Angels hospital, treated and released. Ten days later, on October 1st, she was at home and could not be roused from bed. They found that she had been incontinent. She was taken to Cedars Sinai. When they checked her in, they reported she had, "doll's eyes" that were "absent." She died at 12:30 pm on the 3rd of October 1979. (Scott Michaels, Dearly Departed Tours, Los Angeles, CA)

Witness # 69 Harold True died 16 May 2013.

Witness # 78 Paul Allan Watkins died August 3, 1990.

Witness # 50 Barbara Hoyt died December 3, 2017. Hoyt was a former family member and prosecution witness (# 53) in District Attorney Vincent Bugliosi's prosecution of Manson and his followers for the Tate La Bianca murders. The family tried to kill her in Hawaii so that she wouldn't testify.

Witness # 4 William Garretson, the sole survivor of the Tate La Bianca murders, passed away on August 16, 2016. He was 66. Garretson lived in the guesthouse at 10050 Cielo Drive in 1969 and was the property caretaker for house owner Rudy Altobelli. One of the victims, 18-year old Steven Parent, had been visiting Garretson that night. (lhs60.net) Although it was not in his testimony, resources indicate William Garretson had seen and heard things that were happening the night of the murders. Patricia Krenwinkel had tried to open the door of the guesthouse where he was living. According to Garretson's high school alumni page, Garretson passed away of cancer on August 16, 2016, one week and day before his birthday. (lhs60.net)

Ronald Hughes was the defense attorney for Leslie Van Houten and went "missing" on a November 10, 1970 Ventura County, California weekend camping trip during the trial. His body was found on March 29, 1971. Vincent Bugliosi, openly expressed suspicion about Hughes' death when he published "Helter Skelter." In 1976, Bugliosi himself received an anonymous phone call from someone claiming to be a former member of the Manson Family who told him that Hughes had been murdered. However, no evidence was ever found to implicate anyone in Hughes' death, which officially remains unsolved. ("Helter Skelter" and The Los Angeles Times, March 31, 1971)

Dianne Elizabeth Lake, witness number 81 and former "family" member has lived a completely normal and productive life and overcame the trauma of living under the influence of drugs and Charles Manson except for keeping it a secret. She was married for 32 years to a wonderful man until his passing and they had 3 beautiful children, all grown and out on their own. Dianne Lake wrote a book which was published in 2017 titled *Member of The Family: My Story of Charles Manson, Life Inside his Cult, and the Darkness that Ended the Sixties* (William Morrow) with co-author Deborah Herman.

Witness # 44 Ruby Pearl Molinaro, witness number 84, the Stable Manager at Spahn Ranch died on May 29, 2010 in Grants Pass, Oregon.

Witness # 28 (Penalty Phase) Catherine Irene Gillies died June 28, 2018 in Cave Junction, Oregon. (Find A Grave)

Linda Kasabian, the main prosecution witness lives in the Pacific Northwest under an assumed name. She has 4 children. She has said "I could never accept the fact that I was not punished for my involvement. I felt then what I feel now, always and forever, that it was a waste of life that had no reason, no rhyme." She has given two interviews since the murders, one with Larry King and Vincent Bugliosi in the year 2009 where she was disguised on camera. She told Larry King that she thought about the murders every day, that she didn't receive psychological help after the trial. She said she received help about twelve years ago. She told King she was trying to live a normal live, but it was hard to do. (YouTube.com) (www.bustle.com)

Joe Sage; (1970) Joe Sage was a Monk at a Buddhist retreat in Taos, New Mexico. In August 1970 Linda Kasabian came to the "retreat" to get away from Charles Manson after looking for her husband.

Linda Kasabian, after being there for about two days, told Joe Sage about the Manson murders. Joe eventually believed her story.

Joe said he realized that Linda had to tell her story to keep from going batty and that the horror was too much to keep to herself. Neither Sage nor his director reported Kasabian's story to the Police because of their roles as Priests and also because Manson's family still had Linda's daughter. If he had done so he thought Manson would certainly come after Linda.

Since Linda confided in Joe he was sought after by Los Angeles detectives and then by Manson family members for revenge after Linda turned State's evidence. He kept getting death threats, so he was on the move for years. He ran for President on the Environmental ticket after leaving the monastery. He was at the University of Arizona when Los Angeles police detectives contacted him for questioning. He realized that if detectives could find him so could Manson's family. It was at the time that he was getting weird phone calls from girls asking if he had turned Manson and his family in. He went to Eugene, Oregon on his campaign and got threatening calls there also, so he dropped his campaign.

He began traveling in his bus making and selling jewelry, but he was constantly on the run. He changed the color of his bus every six months and used the name of Jack Nolan. He was afraid of getting killed by one of Manson's followers.

He eventually bought a Cafe in San Francisco but after a few years he received more calls, from women and left again. Some of the women said "He was our friend, you turned him in."

At this time in an interview in 1978 he stated he was still not settled and said that he could move on within an hour's time. He keeps a low profile and said he has lost eight years of his life. He said he could have kept the Good Karma Café and settled down with a woman, played music on the national scene, but now he has nothing. (From the Berkeley Barb, December 30, 1977 – January 5, 1978; the title of this article reads "Still Haunted by Charles Manson" "8 Years on The Run")

Patricia Krenwinkel and Leslie Van Houten convicted of murder, are still in prison. Leslie Van Houten was approved for parole in the year 2017 but that was reversed by California Governor Jerry Brown.

October 5, 1970 was the day that Charles Manson leaped at the Judge with a pencil in hand. Deputies Bill Murray and Digby Rowe tackled Manson before he got to the Judge. One of the ironies is Attorney Kanarek and Charles Manson argued vehemently that Manson was being denied his rights by having his privileges of pencils and paper taken away during a time he was in "lock up" or "solitary confinement" for some infraction during the course of the trial. The ensuing fall was violent enough to break Digby's patella and tibia so severely that he was unable to return to work. His time spent serving in a "challenging and honorable profession" had come to an end, but his optimism remained. "Being a deputy sheriff proved to be a very productive and satisfying time for me." (Los Angeles County Professional Peace Officers Association, January 16, 2018)

The Spahn Ranch burned to the ground on September 26, 1970 during the murder trial. George Spahn was blind for five years, from about 1965 and died on September 22, 1974, and is buried in Eternal Valley Memorial Park in nearby Newhall.

The Barker Ranch where Manson and the girls were arrested burned in a fire in May 2009.

The Ambassador Hotel was demolished starting in late year 2005 and finished in early January 2006)

Defense attorney Daye Shinn was sentenced by Superior Judge Charles H. Older to three nights in jail for contempt of court after the lawyer admitted bringing into the courtroom the newspaper that Charles Manson showed to the jury. (The Los Angeles Times, August 6, 1970)

Addendum

This is the law that was given to the twelve jurors including Herman Tubick indicating how they were to apply the facts of the case during their deliberations. They were to determine the credibility of witnesses when deciding on the facts, but the law was very clear. Here are the exact words of Judge Older:

Ladies and Gentlemen of the jury: It is my duty to instruct you in the law that applies to this case and you must follow the law as I state it to you. 'As jurors it is your exclusive duty to decide all questions of facts submitted to you and for that "purpose to determine the effect and value of the evidence. In performing this duty you must not be influenced by pity for a defendant or by passion or prejudice against them.

You must not be biased against a defendant because he has been arrested for this offense or because a charge has been filed against him, or because, he has been brought to trial. None of these facts is evidence of his guilt and you must not infer or speculate from, any or all of them that he is more likely to be guilty than innocent.

In determining whether the defendant is guilty or not guilty you must be governed solely by the evidence received in this trial and the law as stated to you by the Court. You must not be governed by mere sentiment, conjecture, sympathy, passion, prejudice, public opinion, or public feeling. Both the People and the defendant have a right to expect that you will conscientiously consider and weigh the evidence and apply the law of the case, and that you will reach a just verdict regardless of what the consequences of such a verdict may be.

If the court has repeated any rule, direction or idea, or stated the same in varying, ways, no emphasis was intended, and you must not draw any inference therefrom. You are not to single out any certain sentence or any individual point or instruction and ignore the others. You are to consider all the instructions as a whole and are to regard each in the light of all the others.

The order in which the instructions are given has no significance as to their relative importance. You must not consider as evidence any statement counsel made during the trial; however, if counsel for the parties have stipulated to any fact, or any fact has been admitted by counsel, you will regard that fact as being conclusively proved as to the party or parties making the stipulation or admission. A "stipulation" is an agreement between attorneys as to matters relating to the trial.

As to any question to which an objection was sustained, you must not speculate as to what the answer might have been or as to the reason for the objection. You must never speculate to be true any, insinuation suggested by a question asked a witness. A question is not evidence and may be considered only as it supplies meaning to the answer.

You must not consider for any purpose any offer; of evidence that was rejected, or any evidence that was stricken out by the Court; such matter is to be treated as though you had never heard of it.

The masculine form as used in these instructions applies equally to a female person.

The word "defendant" as used in these instructions: applies equally to each defendant in this case except as you may be otherwise instructed.

The testimony of a witness, a writing, a material object, or anything presented to the senses offered to prove the existence or nonexistence of a fact is either direct or circumstantial evidence. Direct evidence means evidence that directly proves a fact, without an inference, and which in itself, if true, conclusively establishes that fact.

Circumstantial evidence means evidence that proves a fact from which an inference of the existence of another fact may be drawn. An inference is a deduction of fact that may logically and reasonably be drawn from another fact or group of facts established by the evidence. It is not necessary that facts be proved by direct evidence. They may be proved also by circumstantial evidence or by a combination of direct evidence and circumstantial evidence. Both direct evidence and circumstantial evidence are acceptable as a means of proof. Neither is entitled to any greater weight than the other.

You are not permitted to find a defendant guilty of any crime charged against him based on circumstantial evidence unless the proved circumstances are not only consistent with the theory that the defendant is guilty of the crime, but cannot be reconciled with any other rational conclusion, and each fact which is essential to complete a set of circumstances necessary to establish that defendant's guilt has been proved beyond a reasonable doubt. Also, if the evidence as to any particular count is susceptible of two reasonable interpretations, one of which points to a defendant's guilt and the other to his innocence it is your duty to adopt that interpretation which points to his innocence and reject the other which points to his guilt.

You will notice that the second paragraph of this instruction applies only when both of the interpretations appear to you, to be reasonable. If on the other hand, one of the interpretations appears to you to be reasonable and the other to be unreasonable, it would be our duty to adopt the reasonable interpretation t=and to reject the unreasonable interpretation.

Evidence that a defendant attempted to suppress evidence against himself in any manner), such as by the intimidation of a witness, may be considered by you as a circumstance tending to show a consciousness of guilt. However, such evidence is not sufficient in itself to prove guilt and its weight and significance, if any, are matters for your consideration.

It is permissible to prove that the defendant Patricia Krenwinkel was ordered by, the Court to make certain handwriting exemplars during the trial and that she failed to make such exemplars. Defendant Patricia Krenwinkel stated to the Court that her refusal to make such exemplars was based upon the advice of her attorney. The Court advised her in open court outside the jury's presence that she had no legal right to refuse, that she had an absolute right to make such exemplars notwithstanding her attorney advice to the contrary, and that her failure to make such exemplars might be the subject of argument to the jury by the prosecution and an instruction to the jury by the Court. The fact that she failed to comply with the order to make such exemplars is not sufficient standing alone and by itself to establish the guilt of Patricia Krenwinkel, but is a fact which if proven may be considered by you in the light of all other proven facts in deciding the question of guilt or innocence in accordance with all of the Court's instructions to you. Whether or not such conduct shows a consciousness of guilt and the significance to be attached to such a circumstance are matters for your determination.

You are not to consider such circumstance in connection with any defendant other than Patricia Krenwinkel.

Evidence has been admitted as against one or more of the defendants but denied admission as against the others.

At the time this evidence was admitted you were admonished that it could not be considered by you as against' the other defendants.

You are again instructed that you must not consider such evidence as against the other defendants. Your verdict as to each defendant must be rendered as if he were being tried separately.

Certain evidence was admitted for a limited purpose. At the time this evidence was admitted you were admonished that it could not be considered by you for any purpose other than the limited purpose for which it was admitted. You are again instructed that you must not consider such evidence for any purpose except the limited purpose for which it was admitted.

The Court has previously admonished you to consider the tape-recorded statement of Juan Flynn, introduced through the testimony of Officer Dave Steuber, for a limited purpose only. You are now instructed to disregard that previous instruction.

Juan Flynn, a witness in this ease, has testified about an incident that allegedly took place prior to his testifying here in court in which he received two notes. Note No. 1 began, "how many changes does it take to make one big change, or does it take ten little changes to make one big change..." And Note No. 2 began, "this is an indictment on your life because it is coming down, and when in the course of human events..."

At the time this alleged incident was testified to, you-were admonished that it was to be considered by you only in determining the state of hind of the witness Juan 'Flynn if you determined that such an incident took place. You are instructed that you may not consider this evidence for any other purpose.

Linda Kasabian, a witness in, this case,' has testified to a statement allegedly Made by "Gypsy," also known as Catherine Share, about the character and personality of Charles Manson as well as life in the. Family.

You and hereby instructed that you may consider such evidence only in determining the state of mind of Linda. Kasabian at the time "Gypsy" allegedly made such statement and for no other purpose.

Linda Kasabian, a witness in this case, has testified to statements-made by her to two young hitch-hikers on or about August 12 to August 15, 1969. This evidence has been received for the sole purpose, of determining, if necessary, the state of mind of witness Linda Kasabian at the time the statements were made.

Neither side is required to call as witnesses all persons who may have been present at any of the events disclosed by the evidence or who may appear to have some knowledge of these events, or to produce all objects or documents mentioned or suggested by the evidence.

Every person who testified under oath is a witness. You are the sole and exclusive judges of the credibility of the witnesses who have testified in this case. In determining the credibility of a witness, you may consider any matter that has a tendency in reason to prove or disprove the truthfulness of his testimony, including but not limited to the following:

His demeanor while testifying and the manner in which he testified;

The character of his testimony;

The extent of his capacity to perceive, to recollect, or to communicate any matter about which he testified;

The extent of his opportunity to perceive any matter about which he testified;

His character for honesty or veracity or their opposites;

The existence or non-existence of a bias, interest, or other motive;

A statement previously made by him that is consistent with his testimony;

A Statement made by him that is inconsistent with any part of his testimony:

The existence or non-existence of any facts testified to by him;

His attitude toward the action in which he testified or towards the giving of testimony:

His admission of untruthfulness:

His prior conviction of a felony.

A witness willfully false in one material part of his testimony is to be distrusted in others. You may reject the whole testimony of a witness who willfully has testified falsely as to a material point, unless from all the evidence you shall believe the probability of truth favors his testimony in other particulars.

However, discrepancies in a witness' testimony or between his testimony and that of others, if there were any, do not necessarily mean that the witness should be discredited. Failure of recollection is a common experience; and innocent mis recollection is not uncommon. It is a fact, also, that two persons witnessing an incident, or a transaction often will see or hear it differently. Whether a discrepancy pertains to a fact of importance or only to a trivial detail should be considered in weighing its significance.

You are not bound to decide in conformity with the testimony of a number of witnesses, which does not produce conviction in your mind, as against the testimony of a lesser number or other evidence, which appeals to your mind with more convincing force.

This does not mean that you are at liberty to disregard the testimony of the greater number of witnesses from caprice or prejudice, or from a desire to; favor one side as against the other. It does mean that you are not to decide an issue by the simple process of counting the number of witnesses who have testified on the opposing sides. It means that the final test is not in the relative number of witnesses, but in the relative convincing force of the evidence.

The fact that a witness had been convicted of a felony, if such be a fact, may be considered by you only for the purpose of determining the credibility of that witness. The fact of such a conviction does not necessarily destroy or impair the witnesses' credibility. It is one of the circumstances that you may take into consideration in weighing the testimony of such a witness.

Motive is not an element of the crime charged and need not be shown. However, you may consider motive or lack of motive as a circumstance in this case. Presence of motive may tend to establish guilt. Absence of motive may tend to establish innocence. You will therefore give its presence or absence, as the case may be, the weight to which you, find it to be entitled.

A Statement by a defendant other than at his trial may be either an admission or a confession.

An admission is a statement by a defendant, which by itself is not sufficient to warrant an inference of guilt, but which tends to prove guilt when considered with the rest of the evidence.

A confession is a statement by a defendant which discloses his intentional participation in the criminal act for which he is on trial and which discloses his guilt of that crime.

You are the exclusive judges as to whether an admission or a confession was made by any defendant and if the statement is true in whole or in part. If you should find that such statement is entirely untrue, you must reject it. If you find it is true in part, you may consider that part which you find to be true.

Evidence of an oral admission or an oral confession of a defendant ought to be viewed with caution.

No person may be convicted of a criminal offense unless there is some proof of each element of the crime independent of any confession or admission made by him outside of this trial.

The Identity of the person who is alleged to have committed a crime is not an element of the crime. Such identity may be established by an admission or a confession.

A person is qualified to testify as an expert, if he has special knowledge, skill, experiences training, or education sufficient to qualify him as an expert on the subject to which his testimony relates.

Duly qualified experts may give their opinions on questions in controversy at a trial.

To assist you in deciding such questions, you may consider the opinion with the reasons given for it, if any, by the expert who gives the opinion.

You may also consider the qualifications and the credibility of the expert.

In resolving any conflict that may exist in the testimony of expert witnesses, you should weigh the opinion of one expert against that of another. In doing this, you should consider the relative qualifications and credibility of the expert witnesses, as well as the reasons for each opinion and the facts and other matters upon which it was based.

You are not bound to accept an expert opinion as conclusive but should give to it the weight to which you find it to be entitled. You may disregard any such opinion if you find it to be unreasonable.

In determining the weight to be given to an opinion expressed by any witness who did not testify as an expert witness, you should consider his credibility, the extent of his opportunity to perceive the matters upon which his opinion is based and the reasons, if any, given for it. You are not required to accept such an opinion but should give it the weight, if any, to which you find it entitled.

In examining an expert witness, counsel may propound to him a type of question known in the law as a hypothetical question. By such a question the witness is asked to assume to be true a hypothetical state of facts, and to give an opinion based on that assumption.

In permitting such a question, the Court does not rule, and does not necessarily find that all the assumed facts have been proved. It only determines that those assumed facts are within the probable or possible range of the evidence. It is for you, the jury to find from all the evidence whether or not the facts assumed in a hypothetical question have been proved, and if you should find that any assumption in such a question has not been proved, you are to determine the effect of that failure of proof on the value and weight of the expert opinion based on the assumption.

A defendant in a criminal action is presumed to be innocent until the contrary is proved, and in case of a reasonable doubt whether his guilt is satisfactorily shown, he is entitled to an acquittal. This presumption places upon the State the burden of proving him guilty beyond a reasonable doubt.

Reasonable doubt is defined as follows; it is not a mere possible doubt, because everything relating to human affairs, and depending on moral evidence, is open to some possible or imaginary doubt. It is that state of the case which, after the entire comparison and consideration of all the evidence, leaves the minds of the jurors in that condition that they cannot say they feel an abiding conviction, to a moral certainty, of the truth of the charge.

Evidence that on some former occasion a witness made a statement or statements that were consistent or inconsistent with his testimony in this trial may be considered-by you as evidence of the truth of the facts as Stated by the witness on such former occasion. However, you are not bound to accept such statement or statements to be truthful in whole or in part, but you should give to them the weight to which you find them to be entitled.

It is a constitutional right of a defendant in a criminal trial that he may not be compelled to testify. Thus, the decision as to whether he should testify is left to the defendant, acting with the advice and the assistance of his attorney. You must not draw any inference of guilt from the fact that he does not testify, nor should this fact be discussed by you or enter into your deliberations in any way.

In deciding whether or not to testify, the defendant may choose to rely on the state of the evidence and upon the failure, if any, of the People to prove every essential element of the charge against him, and no lack of testimony on defendant's, part will supply a failure of proof by the People so as to support by itself a finding against him on any such essential element.

All persons concerned in the commission of a crime who either directly and actively commit the act constituting the offense or who knowingly and with criminal intent aid and abet in its commission or, whether present or not, who advise and encourage its commission, are regarded by the law as principals in the crime thus committed and are equally guilty thereof.

A person aids and abets the commission of a crime if he knowingly and with criminal intent aids, promotes, encourages or instigates by act or advice, or by act and advice, the commission of such crime.

A conviction cannot be had upon the testimony of an accomplice unless it is corroborated by such other evidence as shall tend to connect the defendant with the commission of the offense. Corroborative evidence is evidence of some act or fact related to the offense which, if believed, by itself and without any aid, interpretation or direction from the testimony of the accomplice, tends to connect the defendant with the commission of the offense charged.

However, it is not necessary that the corroborative evidence be sufficient in Itself to establish every element of the offense charged or that it corroborates every fact to which the accomplice testified. The evidence required to corroborate the testimony of an accomplice is sufficient if it tends to connect the defendant with the commission of the crime in such a way as may reasonably satisfy the jury that the witness who must be corroborated is telling the truth.

It is not necessary that the evidence used to corroborate the testimony of an accomplice prove independently that the defendant is guilty of the offense.

Evidence corroborating the testimony of an accomplice need not connect the defendant with the commission of the offence beyond a reasonable doubt. In determining whether an accomplice has been corroborated, you must first assume the testimony of the accomplice has been removed from the case. You must then determine whether there is any remaining evidence standing by itself or in conjunction with any other remaining evidence which tends to connect the defendant with the commission of the offense. If there is not such independent evidence which tends to connect defendant with the commission of the offence, the testimony of the accomplice is not corroborated.

If there is such independent evidence which you believe, then the testimony of the accomplice is corroborated.

If the crimes of murder or conspiracy to commit murder, the commission of which is charged against the defendants, were committed by anyone, the witness Linda Kasabian was an accomplice as a matter of law and her testimony is subject to the rule requiring corroboration.

The testimony of an accomplice ought to be viewed with distrust. This does not mean that you may arbitrarily disregard such testimony, but you should give to it the weight to which you find it to be entitled after examining it with care and caution and in the light of all the evidence in the case.

You are instructed that evidence sufficient to corroborate the testimony of an accomplice may be slight and entitled to little consideration when standing alone. The evidence is sufficient even though slight if it tends to connect the defendant with the commission of the crime.

You are instructed that the evidence required to corroborate the testimony of an accomplice may be either circumstantial or direct.

Murder is the unlawful killing of a human being with malice aforethought.

"Malice" may be either express or implied.

Malice is express when there is manifested an intention unlawfully to kill a, human being. Malice is implied when the killing results from an act involving a high degree of probability that it will result in death, which act is done for a base antisocial purpose and with a wanton disregard for human life or when the killing is a direct causal result of the perpetration or the attempt to perpetrate a felony inherently dangerous to human life.

The mental state constituting malice aforethought does not necessarily require any ill will or hatred of the person killed.

"Aforethought," does not imply deliberation or the lapse of considerable time. It only means that the required mental state must precede rather than follow the act.

All murder which is perpetrated by any kind of willful, deliberate and premeditated killing with malice aforethought is murder of the first degree.

The word "deliberate" means formed or arrived at or determined upon as a result of careful thought and weighing of considerations for and against the proposed course of action. The word "premeditated" means considered beforehand.

If you find that the killing was preceded and accompanied by a clear, deliberate intent on the part of the defendant to kill, which was the result of deliberation and premeditation, so that it must have been formed upon pre-existing reflection and not under sudden heat of passion or other condition precluding the idea of deliberation, it is murder of the first degree.

The law does not undertake to measure in units of time the length of the period during which the thought must be pondered before it can ripen into an intent to kill which is truly deliberate and premeditated. The time will vary with different individuals; and under varying circumstances. The true test is not the duration of time, but rather the extent of the reflection. A cold, calculated judgment and decision may be arrived at in a short period of time, but a mere unconsidered and rash impulse, even though it includes an intent to kill is not such deliberation and premeditation as will fix an unlawful killing as murder of the first degree.

To constitute a deliberate and premeditated killing, the slayer must weigh and consider the question of killing and the reasons for and against such a choice and, having in mind the consequences, he decides to and does kill.

The unlawful killing of, a human being, whether intentional, unintentional or accidental, which occurs as the result of the commission or attempt to commit the crime of burglary or robbery and where there was in the mind of the perpetrator the specific intent to commit such crime or crimes, is murder of the first degree.

The specific intent to commit burglary or robbery and the commission or attempt to commit such crime or crimes must be proved beyond a reasonable doubt.

Every person who enters any house with the specific intent to steal take and carry away the personal property of another of any value with the specific intent to deprive the owner permanently of his property is guilty of burglary. The essence of burglary is entering such a place with such specific intent, and the crime of burglary is complete as soon as the entry is made, regardless of whether the intent thereafter is carried out.

Robbery is the taking of personal property of any value in the possession of another, from his person or immediate presence, and against his will, accomplished by means of force or fear and with the specific intent permanently to deprive the owner or his property.

It a human being is killed by any one of several persons engaged in the perpetration of, or attempt to perpetrate, the crime of burglary or robbery, all persons who either directly and actively commit the act constituting such crime or who knowingly and with criminal intent aid and abet in its commission, or, whether present or not, who advise and encourage its commission,. are guilty of murder of the first degree, whether the killing is intentional unintentional, or accidental.

Under the Court's instructions to you a finding that any defendant is guilty of murder in the first degree as to Counts I through VII, inclusive, must be based upon either, a willful, deliberate and premeditated killing with malice aforethought, or a killing which occurred as the result of the commission or attempt to commit the crime of burglary or robbery, as these types of murder are defined elsewhere in these instructions. The jury must be unanimous as to the degree of murder if you find any defendant guilty of murder. The jury need not be unanimous as to which of those two types of murder a finding of murder in the first degree is based upon.

Murder of the second degree is the unlawful killing of a human being with malice aforethought when there is manifested an intention unlawfully to kill a human being, but the evidence is insufficient to establish deliberation and premeditation.

In the crimes charged in Counts I through VII, inclusive of the indictment, there must exist a union or joint operation of act or conduct and a certain specific intent. In the crime of murder, there must exist in the mind of' the perpetrator the requisite specific intent for each type of murder as set forth in the definitions of those offenses elsewhere in these instructions, and unless such intent so exists that crime is not committed.

The specific intent with which an act is done may be manifested by the circumstances surrounding its commission. But you may not find a defendant guilty of a willful, deliberate, premeditated murder of the first degree unless the proved circumstances not only are consistent with the hypothesis that he had the specific intent to kill a human being with malice aforethought which was the result of deliberation and premeditation as those terms are defined elsewhere in these instructions but are irreconcilable with any other rational conclusion.

Also, if the evidence as to such specific intent is susceptible of two reasonable interpretations, one of which points to the existence thereof and the other to the absence thereof, you must adopt that interpretation which points to its absence. If, on the other hand, one interpretation of the evidence as to such specific intent appears to you to be reasonable and the other interpretation to be unreasonable, it would be your duty to accept the reasonable interpretation and to reject the unreasonable.

The specific intent with which an act is done may be manifested by the circumstances surrounding its commission. But you may not find any defendant guilty of any of the offenses charged in Counts I through VII, based upon the unlawful killing of a human being occurring as a result of the commission or attempt to commit the crime of burglary or robbery, as distinguished from willful, deliberate and premeditated murder of the first degree or unpremeditated murder of the second degree, as those types of murder are defined elsewhere in these instructions, unless the proved circumstances not only are consistent with the hypothesis that he had the specific intent to steal, take and carry away the personal property of another of any value with the specific intent to deprive the owner permanently of his property, but are irreconcilable with any other rational conclusion.

Also, if the evidence as to such specific intent is susceptible of two reasonable interpretations, one of which points to the existence thereof and the other to the absence thereof, you must adopt that interpretation which points to its absence. If, on the other hand, the interpretation of the evidence as to such specific intent appears to you to be reasonable and the other interpretation to be unreasonable, it would be your duty to accept the reasonable interpretation and to reject the unreasonable.

The specific intent with which an act is done may be manifested by the circumstances surrounding its commission. But you may not find a defendant guilty murder in the second degree unless the proof circumstances not only are consistent with the hypothesis that he had the specific intent to kill a human being with malice aforethought but are irreconcilable with any other rational conclusion.

Also, if the evidence as to such specific intent is susceptible of two reasonable interpretations, one of which points to the existence thereof and the other to the absence thereof, you must adopt that interpretation which points to its absence. If, on the other hand, one interpretation of the evidence as to such specific intent appears to you to be reasonable and the other interpretation to be unreasonable, it would be your duty to accept the reasonable interpretation and to reject the unreasonable.

 Murder is classified into two degrees, and if you should find any defendant guilty of murder, it will be your duty to determine and state in your verdict whether you find the murder to be of the first or second degree.

If you are convinced beyond a reasonable doubt that the crime of murder has been committed by a defendant, but you have a reasonable doubt whether such murder was of the first or the second degree; you must give to such defendant the benefit of that doubt and return a verdict fixing the murder as of the second degree.

Before you may return a verdict in' this case, you 'must agree unanimously not only as to whether a defendant is guilty or not guilty, but also, if you should find him guilty of an unlawful killing you must agree unanimously as to whether he is guilty of murder of the first degree or murder of the second degree.

The intent with which an act is done is shown by the circumstances attending the act, the manner in which it is done, the means used and the soundness of mind and discretion of the person committing the act.

For the purposes of the case on trial you must assume that each of the defendants was of sound mind at the time of his alleged conduct which, it is charged, constituted the crimes described in the indictment.

A conspiracy is an agreement between two or more persons to commit any crime, and with the specific intent to commit such crime, followed by an overt act committed in this state by one or more of the parties for the purpose of accomplishing the object of the agreement. Conspiracy is a crime.

In order to find a defendant guilty of conspiracy in addition to proof of the unlawful agreement, there must be proof of the commission of at least one of the overt acts alleged in the indictments. It is not necessary to the guilt of any particular defendant that he himself committed the overt act, if he was one of the conspirators when such act was committed.

The term "overt act" means any step taken or act committed by one or more of the conspirators which goes beyond mere planning or agreement to commit a public offense and which step or act is done in furtherance of the accomplishment of the object of the conspiracy.

Each member of a conspiracy is liable for each act and bound by each declaration of every other member of the conspiracy if said act or said declaration is in furtherance of the object of the conspiracy.

The act of one conspirator pursuant to or in furtherance of the common design of the conspiracy is the act of all conspirators. Every conspirator is legally responsible for an act of a co-, conspirator that follows as one of the probable and natural consequences of the object of the conspiracy even though it was not intended as a part of the original plan and even though, he was not present at the time of the commission of such act.

To be an overt act, the step taken, or act committed need not, in and of itself constitute the crime or even an intent to commit the crime which is the ultimate object of the conspiracy. Nor is it required that such step or act, in and of itself, be a criminal or an unlawful act.

It is not necessary in proving a conspiracy to show a meeting of the alleged conspirators or the making of an express or formal agreement. The formation and existence of a conspiracy may be inferred from all circumstances tending to show the common intent and may be proved in the same way as any other fact may be proved, either by direct testimony of the fact or by circumstantial evidence, or by both direct and circumstantial evidence.

Evidence that a person was in the company of or associated with one or more other persons alleged or proved to have been members of a conspiracy is not, in itself, sufficient to prove that such person was a member of the alleged conspiracy.

No act or declaration of a conspirator that is an independent product of his own mind and is outside the common design and not a furtherance of that design, is binding upon his co-conspirators, and they are not criminally liable for any such act where a conspirator commits an act which is neither in furtherance of the object of the conspiracy nor to natural and probable consequence of an attempt to attain that object, he alone is responsible for and is bound by that act, and no responsibility therefor attaches to any of his confederates.

The act or declaration of a person who is not a member of a conspiracy is not binding upon the members of the conspiracy, if any, even though it is an act which tended to promote the object of the alleged conspiracy.

Evidence of the commission of an act which furthered the purpose of an alleged conspiracy is not in itself, sufficient to prove that the person committing the act was a member of such conspiracy.

Every person who joins a criminal conspiracy after its formation and who adopts its purposes and objects, is liable for and bound by the acts and declarations of other members of the conspiracy done and made during the time that he is a member and in pursuance of furtherance of the conspiracy.

A person who joins a conspiracy after its formation is not liable or bound by the acts of the co-conspirators or for any crime committed by the co-conspirators before such person joins and becomes a member of the conspiracy.

Evidence of any acts or declarations of other conspirators prior to the time such person becomes a member of the conspiracy may be considered by you in determining the nature, objectives and purposes of the conspiracy, but for no other purpose.

Any member of a conspiracy may withdraw from and cease to be a party to the conspiracy, but his liability for the acts of his co-conspirators continues until he effectively withdraws from the conspiracy. In order to effectively withdraw from a conspiracy, there must be an affirmative and bona fide rejection or repudiation of the conspiracy which must be communicated to the other conspirators of whom he has knowledge. If a member of a conspiracy has effectively withdrawn from the conspiracy, he is not thereafter liable for any act of the co-conspirators committed subsequent to his withdrawal from the conspiracy, but he is not relieved of responsibility for the acts of his co-conspirators committed while he was a member.

In Count VIII the defendants are Charged with conspiracy to commit murder in Violation of Sections 182.l and 187, Penal Code of California, a felony, as follows: That on or about the 8th through the 10th day August 1969, at and in the County of Los Angeles, State of California, Charles Manson, Charles Watson, Patricia

Krenwinkel, Susan Atkins, Linda Kasabian, and Leslie Sangston (whose true name is Leslie Van Houten), the said defendants, did willfully, unlawfully, feloniously and knowingly conspire, combine, confederate and agree together to commit the crime of murder, a violation of Section 187 Penal Code of California, a felony.

It is alleged that the following were overt acts which were committed in this state by one or more of the defendants for the purpose of furthering the object of the conspiracy:

OVERT ACT NO. 1

That on or about August 8, 1969, the said defendants, Charles Watson, Patricia Krenwinkel, Susan Atkins and Linda Kasabian did travel to the vicinity of 10050 Cielo Drive in the City and County of Los Angeles.

OVERT ACT NO. II

That on or about August 8, 1969, the defendants, Charles Watson, Patricia Krenwinkel and Susan Atkins did enter the residence at10050 Cielo Drive, City and County of Los Angeles.

OVERT ACT NO. III

That on or about August 10, 1969, the defendants, Charles Manson, Charles Watson, Patricia Krenwinkel, Susan Atkins, Linda Kasabian and Leslie Sangston (whose true tame is Leslie Van Houten) did travel to the vicinity of 3301 Waverly Drive, City and County of Los Angeles.

OVERT ACT NO. IV

That on or about August 10, 1969, the defendants, Charles Manson, Charles Watson, Patricia Krenwinkel and Leslie Sangston (whose true name is Leslie Van. Houten) did enter the residence at. 3301 Waverly Drive, City and. County of Los Angeles.

The defendants are also charged with the commission of the following public offenses:

COUNT I

That on or about the 9th day of August 1969, at and in the County of Los Angeles, State of California, the said defendants, Charles Manson, Charles Watson, Patricia Krenwinkel., Susan Atkins, and Linda Kasabian did willfully, unlawfully, feloniously and with malice aforethought murder Abigail Anne Folger, a human being.

COUNT II

On or about the 9th day of August 1969, at and in the County of Los Angeles, State of California, the said defendants, Charles Manson, Charles Watson, Patricia Krenwinkel, Susan Atkins and Linda Kasabian did willfully, unlawfully, feloniously and with malice aforethought murder Wojciech Frykowski, a human being.

COUNT III

That on or about the 9th day of August 1969, at and in the County of Los Angeles, State of California, the said defendants, Charles Manson, Charles Watson; Patricia Krenwinkel, Susan Atkins and Linda Kasabian did willfully; unlawfully, feloniously and with malice aforethought murder Steven Earl Parent, a human being.

COUNT IV

That on or about the 9th day of August 1969, at and in the County of Los Angeles, State of California, the said defendants, Charles Manson, Charles Watson, Patricia Krenwinkel, Susan Atkins and Linda Kasabian, did willfully, unlawfully, feloniously and with malice aforethought murder Sharon Marie Polanski, a human being.

COUNT V

That on or about the 9th day of August 1969, at and in the County of Los Angeles, State of California, the said defendants, Charles Manson, Charles Watson, Patricia 'Krenwinkel, Susan Atkins and Linda Kasabian did willfully unlawfully, feloniously and with malice aforethought murder Thomas John Sebring; a human, being.

COUNT VI

That on or about the 10th day of August, 1969, at and in the County of Los Angeles, State of California, the said defendants, Charles Manson, Charles Watson, Patricia Krenwinkel, Leslie Sangston (whose true name is Leslie Van Houten), Linda Kasabian and Susan Atkins did willfully, unlawfully, feloniously and with malice aforethought murder Leno A. La Bianca, a human being.

COUNT VII

That on or about the 10th day of August 1969, at and in the County of Los Angeles, State of California, the said defendants, Charles Manson, Charles Watson, Patricia, Krenwinkel, Leslie Sangston (whose true name is. Leslie Van Houten), Linda Kasabian and Susan Atkins did willfully, unlawfully, feloniously and with malice aforethought murder Rosemary La Bianca, a human being.

In the crime charged in Count VIII of the indictment, there must exist a union or joint operation of acts or conduct and a certain specific intent. In the crime of conspiring to commit murder there must exist in the mind of the perpetrator the specific intent to commit murder of the first degree by means of willful, deliberate and premeditated killing with malice aforethought, as that type of murder is defined elsewhere in these instructions, and unless such intent so exists that crime is not committed.

The specific intent with Which an act is done may be manifested by the circumstances surrounding its commission. But you may not find any defendant guilty of the offense of conspiracy to commit murder charged in Count VIII unless the proved circumstances not only are consistent with the hypothesis that he had the specific intent to commit murder of the first degree by means of a willful, deliberate and premeditated killing with malice aforethought, as that type of murder is defined elsewhere in these instructions, but are irreconcilable with any other rational conclusion.

Also, if the evidence as to such specific intent is susceptible of two reasonable interpretations, one of which points to the existence thereof and the other to the absence thereof, you must adopt that interpretation which points to its absence.

If, on the other hand, one interpretation of the evidence as to such specific intent appears to you to be reasonable and the other interpretation to be unreasonable, it would be your duty to accept the reasonable interpretation and to reject the unreasonable.

The intent with which an act is done is shown by the circumstances attending the act, the manner in which it is done, the means used, and the soundness of mind and discretion of the person committing the act.

For the purposes of the case on trial, you must assume that each defendant was of sound mind at the time of his alleged conduct which, it is charged, constituted the crime described in the indictment.

In this case, you must decide separately whether each of the several defendants is guilty or not guilty of each of the offenses charged against him. If you cannot agree upon verdicts as to all the defendants but do agree upon a verdict as to one or more of them, you must render a verdict as to the one or more upon which you agree.

Each count charges a separate and distinct offense. You must decide each count separately on the evidence and the law applicable to it, uninfluenced by your decision as to any other count. Each defendant may be convicted or acquitted on any or all of the offenses charged against him.

Your finding as to each defendant charged on each count must be stated in a separate verdict.

As to Count VIII of the indictment each defendant in this case is individually entitled to and must receive your determination whether he was a member or the alleged conspiracy. As to each defendant you must determine whether he was a conspirator by deciding whether he willfully, intentionally and knowingly joined with any other or others in the alleged conspiracy.

I have not intended by anything I have said or done, or by any-questions that I may have asked, to intimate or suggest what you should find to be the facts on any questions submitted to you, or that I believe or disbelieve any witness.

If anything, I have done or said has seemed to so indicate, you will disregard it and form your own opinion.

You have been instructed as to all the rules of law that may be necessary, for you to reach a verdict. Whether some of the instructions will apply will depend upon your determination of the facts. You will disregard an instruction, which applies to a state of facts which you determine does not exist. You must not conclude from the fact that an instruction has been given that the Court is expressing any opinion as to the facts.

Both the People and the defendant are entitled to the individual opinion of each juror.

It is the duty of each of you to consider the evidence for the purpose of arriving at a verdict if you can do so. Each of you must decide the case for yourself but should do so only after a discussion of the evidence and instructions with the other jurors. You should not hesitate to change an opinion if you are convinced it is erroneous. However, you should not be influenced to decide any question in a particular way because a majority of the jurors, or any of them, favor such a decision.

The attitude and conduct of jurors at the beginning of their deliberations are matters of considerable importance. It is rarely productive or good for a juror at the outset to make an emphatic expression of his opinion on the case or to state how he intends to vote. When one does that at the beginning, his sense of pride may be arouse and he may hesitate to change his position even if shown that it is wrong. Remember that you are not partisans or advocates in this matter but are judges.

In your deliberations the subject of penalty or punishment is not to be discussed or considered by you. If you return a verdict of guilty of murder in the first degree as to any particular count or verdict of guilty of conspiracy to commit murder as alleged in Count VIII, then the matter of punishment as to those counts will be considered and determined in a separate proceeding. If you return a verdict of guilty of murder in the Second degree as to any count, the matter of penalty or punishment as to that count will be determined in the manner provided by law.

You shall now retire and select one of your number to act as foreman who will preside over your deliberations.

In order to reach a verdict, all 12 jurors must agree to the decision. As soon as all of you have agreed upon a verdict, you shall have it dated and signed by your foreman and then shall return with it to this room.

.

Herman and Helen Tubick circa 1940s